THE UNIVERSITY OF
WINCHESTER

The German
...tion of Race

SUNY series, Philosophy and Race

Robert Bernasconi and T. Denean Sharpley-Whiting, editors

The German Invention of Race

Sara Eigen and Mark Larrimore, editors

State University of New York Press

Published by
State University of New York Press, Albany

© 2006 State University of New York

For information, address the State University of New York Press,
194 Washington Avenue, Suite 305, Albany, NY 12210-2384

Production by Kelli Williams
Marketing by Susan Petrie

Library of Congress Cataloging-in-Publication Data

The German invention of race / edited by Sara Eigen and Mark Larrimore.
    p. cm. — (SUNY series, philosophy and race)
  Includes bibliographical references and index.
  ISBN-13: 978-0-7914-6677-3 (hardcover : alk. paper)
  ISBN-10: 0-7914-6677-9 (hardcover : alk. paper)
  ISBN-13: 978-0-7914-6678-0 (pbk. : alk. paper)
  ISBN-10: 0-7914-6678-7 (pbk. : alk. paper)
    1. Race—Philosophy. 2. Philosophy, German—History. I. Larrimore,
Mark J. (Mark Joseph), 1966–   . III. Eigen, Sara. III. Series.

HT1521.E42 2006
305.8'001—dc22   2005021342

10 9 8 7 6 5 4 3 2 1

Contents

Acknowledgments

This book is the product of much hard work, institutional support, and a liberal dose of serendipity. The editors would like to thank the Herzog August Bibliothek in Wolfenbuttel, where we met over afternoon coffee; the German Department at Harvard University, which hosted the 2000 conference whose papers laid the foundations for the present book; and the Max Kade Foundation, which provided major funding for the conference. We are grateful to Robert Bernasconi for his steady support of this project, and to our research assistants Michael Macomber, Steven M. Press, Sara Szmodis, and Joseph Tinguely for their painstaking efforts in preparing the manuscript for press. As a final note, we would like to thank our editors at SUNY Press, who were all a pleasure to work with.

Introduction

The German Invention of Race

Sara Eigen and Mark Larrimore

Within four decades straddling the close of the eighteenth century, the word "race" was adopted in remarkably similar forms across Europe as a scientific term denoting a historically evolved, quite possibly permanent, and essentially real subcategory of the more inclusive grouping of living beings constituting a single species. The emergence of a *scientific* theory of race was the product of often fierce debate among scientists and philosophers, many of whom were clustered at universities in German-speaking lands. The figures most often cited include Immanuel Kant, Johann Gottfried Herder, Johann Friedrich Blumenbach, Samuel Thomas Sömmerring, Georg Forster, and Christian Meiners.

The complex and high-stakes philosophical and scientific debates, however, were not conducted in isolation. They were influenced, irritated, and accompanied by lively discussions and discoveries in theoretical and practical medicine, geology, geography, aesthetic theory, theology, and philology, to name just a few fields. As might be expected from such a multiplicity of discourses, theories regarding the "nature" and the usefulness of the race category varied widely. Subsequent histories of the idea of race have focused upon the details of late-nineteenth- and early-twentieth-century racial science, and have tended to oversimplify eighteenth-century positions. In the process, they have significantly underestimated the conflicted legacy of the Enlightenment. The variety of race concepts has not received the thoughtful attention that scholars have devoted to the theories and practices of later periods. Nor has the variety of alternatives to these concepts been considered.

There have been and continue to be important investigations that look further back into the history of human cultures in order to identify and compare attempts at ascertaining patterns of human difference, many of which come later to be identified as "racial." Prominent genres train their focus upon the era of New World conquest and genocide, the Spanish expulsion of the Jews, and the development of the slave trade. Such studies are vital for a developed understanding of the relationship between economic policies of exploitation, religious ideals and ideologies, and quasi-racial accounts of human difference. In their focus on those defenses of racial hierarchy and oppression which lead directly to the more infamous nineteenth-century "race scientific" positions, however, these works tend to oversimplify the rich and contradictory positions held by those eighteenth-century thinkers who made race a relatively stable concept.

Another genre of studies investigating the history of racial thinking comes primarily out of American, African-American, and cultural studies programs in the United States. These works, concerned predominantly with racist ideas and practices in the Americas, draw fairly exclusively upon Anglo-American source material. This is due, no doubt, to the geographic and political focus of the works as well as to the fact that crucial primary source materials in languages other than English have not been widely available. Many have never been translated.

A sea change is in sight. Within recent years, continuing interest in the history of the race idea has produced something much needed: namely, several volumes of primary sources republished or translated into English, with more to come. These open a door vital to theorists of race, philosophers, anthropologists, and historians of life science.

As the eleven essays in this book show, however, it is not enough to study works explicitly focused on the theory of race. Further, it is misleading to suppose that there was a single great debate—one uninflected by the local concerns and categories of writers in significantly different disciplines and societies—giving rise to modern racism and antiracism. The studies in this book seek to illuminate the particularities of works from German-speaking lands, and show how questions as different as those of hygiene, aesthetics, comparative linguistics, Jewish emancipation, and the status of science and philosophy shaped and were shaped by emerging discourses of race. Our title is intended as a multiple provocation. In the late-eighteenth- and early-nineteenth-century period that is our focus, "race," "invention" and—not least—"German" need to be interrogated. As the essays gathered here demonstrate, they need to be interrogated together.

I MODES OF DIFFERENCE: RACE, COLOR, CULTURE

This book opens with two essays that trace attempts made during the eighteenth century to make sense of, or write the significance of, human diversity as marked by skin color and by cultural practices. These essays each address a critical moment in the developing tendency to translate visible and cultural differences (which traditionally had multiple and fluid significance) into a static and hierarchical system that conflates and reifies biology, history, and culture.

Gottfried Wilhelm Leibniz has been thought a forerunner of the theory of race ever since Johann Friedrich Blumenbach identified him as such in his genealogy of racial typologies of 1795. In "What 'Progresses' Has Race-Theory Made Since the Times of Leibniz and Wolff?" Peter Fenves discusses Leibniz' (few) references to "race," and finds that Leibniz' metaphysics is altogether incompatible with the later biological concept of race. The views of humanity compatible with his metaphysics acknowledge patterns of similarity and variation without attributing to such patterns or groupings any qualitative, let alone essential, differences. Indeed, every individual is a species in itself. Decisive is only the distinction between creatures endowed with reason—here, synonymous with language—and those who lack it. Leibniz' position on the problem of diversity, according to Fenves, is that the problem should be understood through linguistic, not physiological difference.

More than language had to fall away before skin color could become the key marker of "racial" identity. In "*Laocoön* and the Hottentots," Michel Chaouli examines the "metaphoric exchange of racial and aesthetic terms" in Gotthold Ephraim Lessing's 1766 *Laocoön*. Chaouli fixes attention on the curious mirroring that occurs in the book between discussions of the famous statue of *Laocoön* (a man entangled with his sons by snakes, considered for centuries by art historians to be the apogee of aesthetic representation), and Lessing's account of the "disgusting deformations" of the Hottentots (the Khoi Khoin), who adorned themselves by darkening their skin and entangling themselves in entrails. Chaouli argues that nascent aesthetics required the beautiful human body be covered by a skin which bespoke a seamless and colorless—that is, a white—surface.

II Race in Philosophy: the Problem of Kant

Our second section turns to an issue that has received considerable attention in recent years. Robert Bernasconi has argued that it is Immanuel Kant who should be credited with having "invented" the concept of race, since it is Kant "who gave the concept sufficient definition for subsequent users to believe that they were addressing something whose scientific status could at least be debated."[1] Moving beyond both too quick a vindication of the emancipatory potential of the critical project and too quick a denunciation of Kant as mouthpiece of a racist Enlightenment, the next four essays offer new and more detailed perspectives from which to approach and analyze Kant's relationship and contribution to the emerging understanding of race.

In "Policing Polygeneticism in Germany, 1775: (Kames,) Kant and Blumenbach," John H. Zammito investigates what Kant and Blumenbach had in mind as they wrote what have come to be seen as the pioneering essays addressing the far-from-established concept or fact of "race" in 1775. Zammito's microhistory shows the contingency of the particular themes that Kant and Blumenbach chose to take up in these works, and highlights the tentativeness of these essays, as well as the broad differences between Kant's philosophical understanding of science and Blumenbach's more empirical view. Kant and Blumenbach critiqued the polygenetic views which were becoming fashionable, but for remarkably different reasons.

In "Kant's Concept of a Human Race," Susan M. Shell takes on the important question of why Kant, whose moral philosophy might seem to have cleared the way (if not indeed forced the way) to antiracism, should have been so taken by ideas that we now unhesitatingly identify as racist. Shell argues that Kant's interest in race must be understood in terms of his peculiar reinvention of teleology, and his understanding of the uneasy relation between reason and the experience of those embodied creatures who possess it (or at least the means to pursue it). Kant's fascination with race, which in the case of what he called the "idle races" meant the de facto inability to achieve reason or freedom, had less to do with the peoples he was ostensibly describing than with the tension-riddled status of embodied reason.

Kant's view of race might never have affected anyone had it not made a convert of Blumenbach. This conversion, as Robert Bernasconi shows in "Kant and Blumenbach's Polyps: A Neglected Chapter in the History of the Concept of Race," was far from assured. Blumenbach knew too much to accept Kant's view that skin color was a reliable marker of physiological difference, let alone sufficient on its own as such a marker. Nonetheless, Bernasconi argues that through discussions in Kant's *Critique of Judgment* not generally read as being concerned with the question of "race" at all, Blumenbach was gradually seduced, fatefully combining the very different authorities of nascent physical anthropology and philosophical teleology.

One interference pattern generated by the linkage of Blumenbach's and Kant's views of human diversity is explored in Mark Larrimore's "Race, Freedom and the Fall in Steffens and Kant." Through a reading of its appropriation by *Naturphilosoph* Henrich Steffens in Steffens' 1822 *Anthropologie*, Larrimore suggests that Kant's idea of race was understood by contemporaries in terms of theological narratives. Steffens claimed Kant's authority in presenting race as the consequence of the Fall, something which only redemption through Christ can overcome. Larrimore argues that Steffens' appropriation misunderstood the elusively "pragmatic" aim of Kant's, separation of the theory of "race" from any empirical account of the "races" or their relationship but so do most contemporary readings.

III RACE IN THE SCIENCES OF CULTURE

The ascent of race-theory in German lands was neither quick nor uncontested. The essays in the next section trace some of the other disciplines on the rise at this time. The sciences of culture were in some cases in their very origins explicitly opposed to those physical anthropological explorations which would congeal around the concept of race. By the early nineteenth century, however, they had blended with racial theories in unexpected, troubling ways. When Steffens' friend Friedrich Wilhelm Joseph von Schelling gave race a virtually metaphysical significance in his lectures on the "Philosophy of Mythology," delivered from 1821 until his death in 1854, his position closely paralleled emerging theories in comparative linguistics. Race is seen as a religious stigma, the consequence of a Fall which only white Europeans had (or could) overcome.

The earliest ethnology, based in the University of Göttingen, understood itself as antiracist. As Han F. Vermeulen recounts in "The German Invention of *Völkerkunde*: Ethnological Discourse in Europe and Asia, 1740–1798," the concepts and categories of the study of culture were as uncertain and contested as their counterparts in physical anthropology. No less than *Volk* and *Rasse*, the nature and possibilities of a human *Wissenschaft* were at stake. The contributions of particular thinkers, such as Johann Gottfried von Herder, to debates on race need to be understood against the backdrop of this shifting landscape of efforts to understand human diversity in non-physiologically reductive ways.

In "Gods, Titans, and Monsters: Philhellenism, Race, and Religion in Early Nineteenth-Century Mythography," George S. Williamson revisits and complicates Martin Bernal's claim that racism played a decisive part in the development of modern classical and mythographical scholarship. Through an account of the controversy around Friedrich Creuzer's *Symbolik und Mythologie der Alten Völker* in the 1820s, Williamson shows that the Philhellenism of the romantic inventors of an autochthonous white Greece was not always allied with racism, nor were Philhellenism's proponents the only racists in view. Philhellenism had important affinities also with the aspirations of a liberal-republican middle class, while the evocation of an Oriental—whether Egyptian or Indian—origin for Greek and Christian culture was often explicitly linked to political reaction.

The Aryan myth, Germany's other baleful contribution to the history of racial thinking, emerged entirely outside the "sciences" of race. As Tuska Benes shows in "From Indo-Germans to Aryans: Philology and the Racialization of Salvationist National Rhetoric, 1806–30," the origins of the Aryan myth lie in the complicated history of the secularization and re-theologization of accounts of "Indogermanic" history anchored in the study of language. It was only a matter of time before the characteristics of "Indogermanic" languages were linked at once to physiological differences, to agility and creativity of thought, to moral progress—and to a tendency toward territorial expansion. The "salvationist" rhetoric was only strengthened over the course of these developments.

IV RACE IN THE POLITICAL SPHERE

The final section brings us back down to Earth, if for some writers it is the sacred earth of German nationalism. While it may have seemed to some a scientific category par exellence, "race" had its grip on reality because of emerging views and practices of breeding, as well as political and cultural questions concerning both the assimilation of Jews and Germany's historical destiny. The cultural-nationalist context of early-nineteenth-century discussions made these questions always more than theoretical. The "natural" and "human sciences," for their part, were intimately linked to nationalist concerns by scientific views of the relation of *Volk*, language, and territory.

In "Policing the *Menschen=Racen*" Sara Eigen identifies the role that "race" played in theories of human improvement that broached the possibility of selective, state-controlled breeding. Reading Johann Peter Frank's widely influential *System einer vollständigen medicinischen Policey* [*System for a Complete Medical Police*], initially published in 1779, Eigen finds a provocative manipulation of the terminology associated with the idea of race in Frank's prescriptions for building and maintaining a healthy, fertile population. "Race" is for Frank a polemical term, designating real hereditary boundaries that might, for the purposes of argument and of hygienic-policy implementation, be located at orders of population magnitude ranging from a family through a clan, a region, a nation, and what we now think of as a "race," to the collective "human race" or species. Frank argues, surprisingly, that the physical and spiritual well-being of individuals, communities, and humanity as a whole requires the dissolution of boundaries between such varying groups by means of migration and intermarriage.

The language of racial theories had immediate political implications. Jonathan M. Hess argues in "Jewish Emancipation and the Politics of Race" that the key concept of "degeneration," assimilated into racial thinking from Georges-Louis Leclerc Comte de Buffon may be compatible with the worst forms of racial prejudice, but is still committed to the unity of humanity. As advocates of Jewish emancipation argued, what degenerates is capable also of regeneration. As a monogenetic concept, race inevitably resonated with debates about the political, no less than the theological, status of German Jews.

The discourse of race that emerges from these many projects and controversies is distinct from, but deeply resonant with, the "scientific" discourse of race perfected in Anglo-American practice. It is our hope that the interdisciplinary studies which compose this book help us understand why, and how, the concept of race was able to exercise such extraordinary power in Western thought and practice in the ensuing years. As the study of the German invention of race shows, race science did not have to build bridges to the human sciences, philosophy, and philosophies of history: it was in large part constituted by them.

Notes

1. Robert Bernasconi, "Who Invented the Concept of Race? Kant's Role in the Enlightenment Construction of Race," in *Race,* ed. Robert Bernasconi (Malden, MA & Oxford: Blackwell, 2001), 11.

I

Modes of Difference

Race, Color, Culture

1

What "Progresses" Has Race-Theory Made Since the Times of Leibniz and Wolff?

Peter Fenves

In 1788 the Prussian Royal Academy posed a question for its prize contest: what "progresses" has metaphysics made in Germany since the time of Gottfried Wilhelm Leibniz and Christian Wolff?[1] A similar question could have been posed: what "progresses" has the race theory made since the times of Leibniz and Wolff? Just as, for the champions of Kantian critique, a fitting response to the first question is readily available (all one need do is read the *Critiques*), even if the precise answer is not; so, too, is there an immediate response to the second question, which would, however, take an immense amount of conceptual and philological labor to develop in a satisfactory manner. The response is: by 1788 the idea of race answers to the question into which, according to Immanuel Kant, all philosophical inquiry in its "cosmopolitan sense" issues: *was ist der Mensch*? It goes too far, of course, to say that the new "science" of race, founded on critical self-reflection, serves as a replacement for Leibnizian-Wolffian metaphysics; and yet, from a certain perspective, something like this takes place: one of the first principles of Leibnizian metaphysics—that every individual is a lowest species—means that in reality there are no such things as members of the same species, much less members of the same variety, subspecies, or race. With the demise of the metaphysical principles that determine each *res* as its own species, race can assume the function previously assigned to the individual: it may not be the "lowest species" (*species infima*), but it nevertheless represents the lowest *self-sustaining* species of animalia, the lowest species in the animal kingdom that maintains itself intact, in contrast to ever "lower" ones that appear and disappear more or less at random. The immortal monads of Leibnizian metaphysics thus give way to the persistent races proposed by racial anthropology. Nothing is perhaps more instructive in this regard than the case of Johann Gottfried von Herder: remaining loyal to a Leibnizian legacy inherited from the young Kant (among others), Herder recasts rigorous monadological principles into effusive proposals: the *vis representativa* of Leibniz and Wolff becomes "formative force," while monadic immortality turns into the organic palingenesis. Consistent with his loyalty to a heavily transformed version of classical German metaphysics, Herder emphatically rejects the term *race*.

Leibniz, however, did not. Nor, however, did he use the term *race* very often. Still less did it function as a technical term—and for good reason: in those few places where he speaks of race, to my knowledge, it is vitiated by certain ambiguities that make it unfit for the rigors of philosophical discourse. I emphasize here "to my knowledge." Leibniz' writings are so vast, his interests so wide, his thought so intricate, and his influence—on Wolff, for example—at once so pervasive and so shallow that everything I propose here must remain preliminary. There is as yet no complete edition of his works, and many of the texts that would have to be reviewed for an adequate account of his conception of race—in particular, his immense series of historical, chronological, and genealogical studies—are only available in rare volumes or still stored away in archives. And added to this is a further difficulty: responding to a question like "what happened to the idea of race from Leibniz' time?" demands an equally careful assessment of which Leibnizian texts became available at what time for whom. The overwhelming majority of his writings went unpublished in his lifetime, and much of the rest appeared only in haphazardly organized and poorly distributed collections. Louis Dutens' six-volume edition of Leibniz' *omnia opera*, which began to appear in 1768, serves as the principal vehicle of Leibniziana for over a hundred years, and yet it represents only a tiny fraction of his production.

So, with this proviso, I turn toward the one passage, to my knowledge, where Leibniz explicitly defines the term *race*. It appears in a collection of definitions composed sometime between the years 1677 and 1686 and is first published in 1999. In response to John Wilkins' *Essay Towards a Real Character and a Philosophical Language* (1668), Leibniz defines a wide range of words—from the most general terms in Latin (*aliquid, nihil,* and *res*) to specific grammatical connectives in English. Of particular prominence are fifty or so words for "mixed relations pertaining to discrete quantities." The last of the terms designating relations among things or phenomena (as opposed to relations among words or times) is *race*, for which Leibniz offers the following definition (in my translation, as throughout this paper): "*Race*, genus, *Geschlecht*, generational series. *Genealogy*," he then adds, "is the explication of this series."[2] Leibniz does not so much define as translate *race*—first into Latin, which does not suffice, since *genus* no longer corresponds to its previous, generic definition but, instead, now implies a genetic relation, which finds expression in the highly ambiguous German word *Geschlecht* (both "sex" and "race" in the sense of "human race"). Nowhere in the notes to Wilkins's treatise on philosophical language does Leibniz consider the relation between a generic genus and a generative series, for these are, after all, merely notes; nevertheless, a little earlier in the same set of reflections, Leibniz (perhaps for the first time) introduces a term through which his thought will become widely known—*species monadica*, which is to say, an individual that is the sole member of its class, or an individual in the strict sense of the term: "the absolute lowest species is an individual" (A, 6, 4: 31–32). Such an individual cannot enter into a generative series, for, strictly speaking, it is related solely to its creator, who, in any case, transcends seriality. Whatever can be consigned to the relational term *race* cannot therefore be a real thing but must be, at best, a well-founded phenomenon, which is to say, a phenomenon that corresponds to, or harmonizes with, the order of monadic reality. And this harmony is, to use the well-known phrase, pre-established: the mind and body share no real relation other than the one "established" by their creator in advance of creation according to the principle of the best. All of this—which amounts to the basic outlines of Leibniz' subsequent metaphysics—is implied in the parenthetical remarks of the notes on Wilkins, and I mention it here only as a reminder. Nevertheless, these notes offer a propitious perspective from which to launch an inquiry into Leibniz' treatment of race, for they are composed in order to make good on the promise of Wilkins' work: the promise, namely, of devising a "universal" or "philosophical" language. And it is in preparation for this project—developing a philosophical language by examining in detail nonphilosophical ones—that all of Leibniz' reflections on race, to my knowledge, are conducted.

For the purposes of economy, I will outline three moments in Leibniz' treatment of race: (1) an early text related to his diplomatic and political missions; (2) a letter from his middle years that concerns the nature of historical languages; and (3) a passage from a late treatise that takes into consideration one of the principal topics around which his debate with John Locke revolves—the general problem of classifying things according to their essences.

Leibniz' efforts to develop a philosophical language are rooted in a political imperative: the establishment of perpetual peace. By means of a language in which conflicts can be solved by transparently valid calculations, disputed questions like the one around the idea of transubstantiation can be solved to everyone's satisfaction and hostilities, such as the Thirty Years' War, can be avoided for good.[3] Nevertheless, as the example of transubstantiation indicates, the peace for which Leibniz works as jurist and diplomat is limited to the sphere of Christendom. To this end, in 1671, he offers Louis XIV his famous *Consilium Aegyptiacum* or "Egyptian plan," the primary purpose of which is to divert France's imperial aspirations away from Holland and direct them toward the Turkish "barbarians" (Leibniz' term), who control the "Queen of the East" (Egypt). The concluding section of the plan indicates how Leibniz proposes to resolve the contradiction between humanistic universalism and Christian particularism—by representing non-Christians as nonhuman: "The following saying of a wise man is right," Leibniz admonishes Louis, "that a powerful and wise monarch is like the guide of the whole human race [*generis humani*]: that he is not only *philhelena* [friend of the Greeks] nor *philoromaion* [friend of the Romans] but *philanthropon*. And his war is not against human beings but against beasts (that is, barbarians), and not for the purpose of massacre but to defend his interests" (A, 4, 1: 379). This doctrine of preemptive warfare against a Muslim foe who had not directly harmed France went unheeded, as the Sun King sent his troops against the Dutch.

Nevertheless, in a brief addendum to this plan, first published in 1931, Leibniz goes further and specifies the nature of those human beings who fall outside the *genus humani*. This addendum consists in an even more daring proposal than the "Egyptian plan," for it describes how the latter could be universalized. Its imposing title says as much: "A method to institute a new, invincible militia that can subjugate the entire earth, easily seize Egypt or establish American colonies" (A, 4, 1: 408).[4] Here is the method in brief: take possession of a distant island like Madagascar, expel its inhabitants, bring slaves from "barbarian" regions like Africa, Arabia, America, and New Guinea; keep only the young males around twelve years old, suppressing any independent will; make them into expert soldiers who blindly obey their European-Christian masters without concern for their own welfare and who, as a result, have the capacity to terrify all potential enemies of the new global imperium. Having listed the names of the nations from which this militia will be formed— from "Ethiopians" and "Negroes" to "Canadians" and "Hurons"—Leibniz exclaims: *Pulchrum concilium semibestiarum*, "what a fine bunch of semi-beasts" (A, 4, 1: 408). Much could be said of this monstrous plan, which has been almost entirely overlooked by Leibniz scholars. But I will limit myself here to three points: to my knowledge, the proposal for a new militia never reappears in any of Leibniz' subsequent writings; nevertheless, this proposal conforms to the general outlines of Leibniz' geopolitical imaginary, in which the peoples of Europe along with those of China enjoy a distinct advantage over all other nations; and as with much of Leibniz' work, this plan for world conquest is at the same time a reflection on the nature of language. For, as Leibniz explains, the militia is to be divided into "as many classes as nations, that is languages" (A, 4, 1: 408); otherwise, its members could not cooperate. Yet it is equally essential that the captives speak as little as possible, that they be forced into virtual silence; otherwise, as Leibniz indicates, rebellion will ensue: "Take care lest troops of diverse languages ever get used to one another and thereby understand one another. . . . The same things must be guarded against among men of the same language. Let a Pythagorean taciturnness be introduced among them; let them be permitted to say nothing among themselves except when necessary or when ordered" (A, 4, 1: 408). These "semi-beasts" are, in other words, not born into this condition but, rather, made so, and the process of creating such a link between inarticulate beings and articulate ones consists at bottom in denying those who can speak access to their own tongues. The irony of this program may not have escaped Leibniz either: as the original philosopher-mathematician, Pythagoras had no need for language, since he— and his sect—understood things "intuitively," without the detour of discourse. The same may be supposed of those whom Leibniz proposes to dominate.

And from the perspective of Leibniz's mature thought, which culminates in the "Monadology" (1714), this new method of global conquest appears even stranger. For the soldiers whom the twenty-five-year-old jurist envisages appear as the very models of monadic individuality: none can directly communicate with another; all communication is mediated by their masters, who have so arranged things that the least possible *direct* communication among them is required. This is to say, in monadological terms, almost all the "windows" have been closed. And yet both the totality of existing monads and the entirety of effective soldiers are so well coordinated with one another that they act in perfect harmony despite the absence of direct communication. The military monasticism Leibniz proposes, in other words, is monadic: none of the "semi-beasts" is affected by the sight of their enemies; such is the source of their strength. And none of them is affected by the thought of his own miserable plight; such is the significance of their isolation. Leibniz may have had only an inkling of the metaphysical principles that would give direction to his later work; but the addendum to the *Consilium Aegyptiacum* anticipates—in a perverse form, to be sure—the vision of the ultimate structure of reality that Leibniz would seek to capture. Just as every monad is an image of the world, monadological metaphysics captures an image of a world in which something like Leibniz's new method of global conquest could be envisaged.

Leibniz does not use the term "race" in this addendum to the Egyptian plan, which is hardly surprising, since it has no Latin equivalent. In the midst of his massive attempt to discover the origin of, and relation among, all the languages of the world, he does, however, find occasion to use race in its new sense—not simply as a name for the species as a whole or for certain generational series (such as "noble lineages"), but also as a technical term for large-scale, inherited divisions within a single physiologically defined species (or genus). Among the many correspondences devoted at least in part to linguistic topics that occupied Leibniz' attention during the 1690s and early 1700s, one concerned the nature of Slavic languages and dialects. The importance of this topic lies in the prospect of the Slavic-speaking lands, especially Russia under the forward-looking Peter the Great, becoming the as-yet unrealized link between the civilizations of Europe and China. Leibniz' interlocutor was the Swedish scholar Johan Gabriel Sparwenfeld, who was writing a massive Latin-Slavonic lexicon.[5] In the course of this correspondence, selections of which were published as early as 1718 in a volume of miscellany,[6] Leibniz speculates on the origin of the Slavic peoples and, more broadly, on the relation among all the nations of the Earth. On January 29, 1697 he writes the following to Sparwenfeld:

> If it is true that the Calmucs as well as the Moguls and the Tartars of China depend on the Grand Lama in matters of religion, it is possible that this says something about the relation among their languages and the origin of these peoples. It's only that the size and constitution of their body is so different among them. I remember reading somewhere (but I cannot recall where) that a certain voyager divided human beings into certain tribes, races, or classes [*tribus, races, ou classes*]. He assigned a particular race to the Lapps and Samoyeds, a certain to the Chinese and neighboring peoples; another to the Negroes, still another to the Cafres or Hottentots. In America there is a marvelous difference between the Galibis or Carribeans, for example, who have a great deal of value and just as much spirit, and those of Paraguay who seem to be children or youth all their lives. (A, 1, 13: 544–45)

To which Leibniz immediately adds: "This does not prevent all the human beings who inhabit the globe from being all of the same race [*tous d'une meme race*], which has been altered by the different climates, as we see animals and plants changing their nature and becoming better or degenerating." The text to which Leibniz refers is an essay of François Bernier anonymously published in the *Journal des Sçavants* in 1684, the title of which is "A New Division of the Earth, by the Different Species or Races of Man [*les differentes Especes ou Races d'homme*]."[7] A point is worth making about this brief reflection on "A New Division" by the author of "A New System of the Nature and Communication of Substances," which had also appeared in the *Journal des Sçavants* and which represents Leibniz' first public announcement of his philosophical ideas: Bernier's essay, often called the beginning of modern race theory, evidently made so little impression on Leibniz that he cannot remember where it was published or which species-terms it uses. Whereas Bernier speaks of four "species or races," Leibniz remembers four "tribes, races, or classes," all of which belong to *the* race, which is to say, the *genus humani*. As if to reiterate this point, Leibniz immediately follows his uncertain recollection of Bernier's essay with a recommendation that Sparwenfeld do what a certain Father Thomassin had recently failed to do, namely, "provide us [an account of] the harmony of languages, and by relating them all to Hebrew, demonstrate that the human genus [*le genre humain*] derives entirely from Adam" (A, 4, 1: 545). In short, Leibniz wants a well-respected scholar to do what an amateurish priest cannot—establish a scientific defense of monogenesis, on the one hand, and carry out the "grand and beautiful enterprise" of making the harmony of languages audible to experts, on the other. Demonstrating the harmoniously differentiated unity of human languages takes precedence over any supposed delineation of discrete divisions of the species based on corporeal criteria. In this sense, Leibniz can be said to have forgotten the new "science" of race immediately after he half-remembers its first expression. Therein lies a lesson for scholars—and Sparenwald can certainly be counted among the most assiduous: concentrate on concrete linguistic investigations rather than on physiological speculations.

And Leibniz's letter to Sparenwald has another lesson for scholars as well. This letter enjoys a certain renown among those who are interested in the history of race theory, for Johann Friedrich Blumenbach makes use of it in his *De generis humani varietate nativa*.[8] What better way to demonstrate the soundness of one's endeavor than to cite one of the most respected minds in all German-speaking lands? Blumenbach, however, does not set out the context of Leibniz's remarks on Bernier's essay (his correspondence with Sparenwald) and, accordingly, fails to indicate in what low esteem Leibniz considered the program of research it proposes. Instead of giving Bernier's speculations his assent, he mentions them only in passing, forgetting much of their content, and bidding his partner in dialogue enter into a completely different terrain of scholarship: the demonstration of the harmoniously differentiated unity of human languages.

Leibniz wrote only two major philosophical treatises and published but one, the *Essays in Theodicy*. The other major treatise, namely, the *New Essays on Human Understanding*, was not published until 1765, some sixty years after its composition. A rambling dialogue with Locke's *Essay on Human Understanding*, the *New Essays* responds to empiricism on its own terms, without explicitly developing a monadological metaphysics. Of particular importance for Leibniz in this regard is the refutation of Locke's conception of classification, according to which the "frequent Production of Monsters, in all Species of Animals, of Changelings, and other strange Issues of humane Birth"[9] is proof enough that there are no real essences but only nominal ones. According to Leibniz, such monstrosities only indicate in very general terms that the lowest species has not yet been determined. What we call gold, for example, may turn out one day to be in reality two substances, each of which deserves a different name. The difficulties of this problem cannot be discussed here, of course, but the implicit motivation for Leibniz' solution is nevertheless clear from the start: Locke's assault on real essences does damage to the definition of the human being as a rational animal.[10] This motivation—and, with it, the driving force of the *New Essays* as a whole—makes itself apparent when Leibniz proposes the following scenario, which reads as if it were the despicable addendum to the Egyptian plan in a vengeful reverse:

> There may some day come to be animals that have . . . everything we have so far observed in human beings but who have a different origin than us. It is as if imaginary Australians inundated our country: it is likely that some way would be found of distinguishing them from us; but if not, and if God had forbidden the mingling of these races [*le melange de ces races*], and if Jesus Christ had redeemed only our own, then we should have to try to introduce artificial marks to distinguish the races from one another. No doubt there would be an inner difference, but since we should be unable to detect it, we would have to rely solely on the "extrinsic denomination" of birth, and try to associate it with an indelible artificial mark that would provide an "intrinsic denomination" and a permanent way of telling our race apart from theirs. (A, 6, 6: 400–401)

To this remarkable specimen of metaphysical speculation, for which there is no corresponding passage in Locke's *Essay on Human Understanding*, Leibniz immediately adds a caveat: "These are all nothing but fictions, for we have no need to resort to this kind of differentiation, since we are the only rational animals on this globe," (A, 6, 6: 401).[11] "Australians" will not inundate "our countries," and if something like this invasion does come to pass, the invaders can be converted to Christianity and thus be integrated into "our race." Decades earlier, as he turns his gaze toward the inhabitants of Africa and the Americas as the basis for his new method of global conquest, Leibniz momentarily names "New Guinea" (A, 4, 1: 408) as one of the places from which a European prince might capture adolescent boys for incorporation into his invincible militia. In the scenario of the *Nouveaux Essais*, by contrast, Australia attains an incontestable prominence: it functions as a mirror image of European aggression—with one major difference: nowhere does Leibniz imagine that the Australians will use Europeans as captives for the purpose of further colonization. Instead of arriving on the shores of Europe as invaders, they seem to appear as migrants, perhaps even supplicants, who merely wish to live on the other side of the Earth—and can be allowed to do so, as long as they are capable of conversion to Christianity.[12]

Australians must be capable of conversion; otherwise, it is no longer possible to maintain that Christianity is in principle "catholic." Unless all those who appear human can *in principle* be saved—regardless of the forbidding principle of Christian doctrine which states that "the elect are only very few"[13]—there can be no *principles* of grace. And if grace is as unprincipled as the term generally suggests, then suspicions will likewise be cast on the universality of the principle of reason, with the disastrous results for both science and faith. The complete correspondence between the principle of reason and that of grace demands that the idea of intrahuman "races" be used solely as the principle of a wholly counterfactual world—not the real one, in which there are no "racial" distinctions that divide one collection of human beings from another. The fiction of an Australian invasion of Europe is in this sense fully warranted, for, as Leibniz proceeds to explain, philosophical reflection can make considerable use of counterfactual possibilities—in this case, the possibility of a world that resembles ours in every detail except that on the other side of the earth there lives an unredeemable "race" of human beings:

> These are all nothing but fictions. . . . Nevertheless, these fictions allow us to gain knowledge of the nature of ideas, of substances, and of general truths about them. But if the human being is not taken for the *lowest species*, nor as the species of rational animals of the race of Adam, and if, instead of all this, the word meant a genus common to several species—to which only a single known race now belonged but to which others could still belong, distinguishable either by birth or by other natural marks, as, for example, by the imaginary Australians [*feints Australiens*]—then, I say, there would be *reciprocal propositions* about this genus, and current definitions of the human being would not be *provisional*. (A, 6, 6: 401)

The fiction of Australians inundating the shores of Europe is of service to philosophical reflection insofar as it is a logical possibility that happens to be impossible for political-theological reasons: it would render Christianity into a local doctrine, applicable only to a segment of the rational animals on Earth. Logic and political theology part ways at the intersection of Europe and Australia, so to speak. Yet, as Leibniz recognizes at the conclusion of this reflection on "racial" counterfactuals, there is one further element of philosophical reflection that he has entirely ignored—the element of history. A consideration of historical change makes his entire discussion of provisional propositions itself provisional. With respect to the definition of gold, philosophers have little to worry about, for, unless alchemists some day discover successful formulae for the transubstantiation of base metals into higher ones, there is every reason to conclude that the most valuable material is immutable. But this is not true of race, as Leibniz uneasily concedes in the concluding sentence of his discussion—and with this inconclusive conclusion changes the topic: "I have been supposing up until now that the race does not degenerate or change; but if the same race were to develop into another species, one would be all the more obligated to take recourse to other marks and intrinsic or extrinsic denominations, without relying on the race [sans s'attacher à la race]" (A, 6, 6: 402).

This last phrase, which is uncharacteristically ambiguous, points in two diametrically opposed directions: on the one hand, toward a racial "science" in which corporeal marks (both natural and artificial) express special distinctions that can then serve as the basis for the schematization of human history and the control of large-scale populations; and on the other hand, toward the only satisfactory solution to the problem of classification, from Leibniz' perspective—namely, the metaphysical proposition that each individual is a lowest species. According to the "Discourse on Metaphysics," which first lays out the elements of his mature philosophical program, "It is not true that two substances can be exactly alike and differ only numerically, solo numero, and what St. Thomas says on this point regarding angels and intelligences (that among them every individual is a lowest species) is true of all substances" (G, 4: 433). In order to assure the ordered relation among these singular, "angelic" substances Leibniz happily appeals to the Christian idea of a divine kingdom in which everything enjoys its rightful place. Such is the nature of divine goodness, which does its best to combine diversity with order. The assault that Kant's Critique of Pure Reason launches on the principles of Leibnizian metaphysics leaves no room for the principle that each substance is a lowest species. And in the same stroke it makes room for a mode of anthropological classification in which races function as the lowest species— or more accurately, as the lowest self-sustaining generative series of the human organism. That the philosopher who destroyed classical German metaphysics champions the new division of the human race into various races is therefore scarcely surprising: this division is a transformation—and travesty—of the monadological vision: instead of the principle of reason, there is the principle of pure practical reason, which demands respect for the "humanity" in each and every person; and in place of the principle of grace, there emerges a tenuous principle of reflective judgment, which ratifies the doctrine that only one race is graced, whereas the rest are not.

NOTES

An expanded version of this essay appears under the title "Imagining an Inundation of Australians: Leibniz on the Principles of Race and Grace," in *Race and Modern Philosophy*, ed. Andrew Valls (Ithaca, NY: Cornell University Press, 2005).

1. For the background of this question, see Karl Rosenkranz, *Geschichte der Kant'schen Philosophie*, ed. Steffen Dietzsch (1840; repr. Berlin: Akademie, 1987), 350–54. As usual, the question was posed in French: "Quels sont les progrès réals de la Metaphysique en Allemagne depuis le temps de Leibnitz et de Wolff?"

2. Gottfried Wilhelm Leibniz, *Sämtliche Schriften und Briefe*, ed. Preußische [later, Deutsche] Akademie der Wissenschaften (Darmstadt and Leipzig: Reichl, 1923–), 6, 4: 34; hereafter, A. It is unclear whether *race* in these notes should be understood as an English or French word. Of course, Leibniz knew French much better than English, but in the seventh category of "Transcendental Relations of DISCONTINUED QUANTITY or Number" Wilkins offers the following set of terms: "SERIES, *Rank, Row, Class, Successive, Chain, Course, Race, Collateral, Concatenation, Alphabet.*" *An Essay Towards a Real Character and a Philosophical Language* (London: Gellibrand, 1668), 34.

3. The same can be said of Wilkins' project for a philosophical language, for it seeks to "contribute much to the clarity of some of our Modern differences in Religion, by unmasking many wild errors, that shelter themselves under the disguise of affected phrases" *(An Essay Towards a Real Character and a Philosophical Language*, sig. B1).

4. One of the very few analyses of this fragment can be found in Marcelo Dascal, "One Adam and Many Cultures: The Role of Political Pluralism in the Best of Possible Worlds," in *Leibniz and Adam*, eds. M. Dascal and E. Yakira (Tel Aviv: University Publishing Projects, 1993), esp. 390–91. Paul Ritter's brief description of the fragment in his introduction to the Akademie edition is of little help; he calls it a "Phantasie" and indicates that the Janissaries and Mamelukes (accounts of which Leibniz had studied) were at the forefront of Leibniz's mind (A, 4, 1: xxvi). Leibniz refers in the margins to "A Relation of Pico Teneriffe," in Thomas Sprat's *History of the Royal Society*, which describes the corporeal hardening of the Guanchen; see *History of the Royal Society of London* (1667; Saint Louis: Washington University Press, 1958), 200–213.

5. For an analysis of Sparwenfeld's lexicon and a brief account of his life, see Ulla Birgegård, *Johan Gabriel Sparwenfeld and the Lexicon Slavonicum: His Con-*

tribution to the 17th-century Slavonic Lexicography (Uppsala: Almqvist & Wiksell Tryckeri, 1985), esp. 85–96 (for a discussion of his correspondence with Leibniz).

6. See Leibniz, *Otium hanoveranum, sive, Miscellanea: ex ore & schedis illustris viri quondam notata & descripta, cum ipsi in colligendis & excerpendis rebus ad historiam brunsvicensem pertinentibus operam navaret*, ed. Joachim Friedrich Feller (Leipzig: Johann Martinus, 1718).

7. François Bernier, "Nouvelle division de la terre, par les différentes especes ou race d'hommes qui l'habitent, envoyée par un fameux Voyageurs à Monsieur*** à peu près en ces termes (24. 4. 1684)," *Journal des Sçavants* 12 (1685): 148; T. Bendyshe's translation of Bernier's essay (1863–64) has recently been republished in *The Idea of Race*, ed. Robert Bernasconi and Tommy Lott (Indianapolis: Hackett, 2000), 1–4. For the identification of the essay, see the editorial apparatus to the Akademie edition, A, 1, 13: 544–45, which relies on Leibniz' excerpts from the essay published in *Otium hanoveranum*, 158–59.

8. Johann Friedrich Blumenbach, *De generis humani varietate nativa* (Göttingen: Vandenhoek and Ruprecht, 1795), sec. 83. Commentators have followed Blumenbach in this regard; see Antje Sommer's entry "Rasse," in *Geschichtliche Grundbegriffe*, ed. Otto Brunner, Werner Conz, and Reinhard Koselleck (Stuttgart: Klett-Cotta, 1972–), 4: 142–43; see also the brief remarks of Robert Bernasconi in "Who Invented the Concept of Race? Kant's Role in the Enlightenment Construction of Race," in *Race*, ed. Robert Bernasconi (Oxford: Blackwell, 2001), 12–13.

9. John Locke, *Essay on Human Understanding*, ed. Peter Nidditch (Oxford: Oxford University Press, 1975), 418; III, iii, 17.

10. Nicholas Jolley emphasizes the degree to which Leibniz' motivation for refuting Locke's conception of essence lies in Leibniz' desire to secure the concept of the human being as rational animal; *Leibniz and Locke: A Study of the New Essays on Human Understanding* (Oxford: Clarendon Press, 1984), 144–45.

11. Every other time Leibniz uses the term race in the *New Essays*, that usage is preceded by the adjective "human."

12. It is not out of the question that, when writing of "Australians" in this context, Leibniz has in mind the Jews, about whose legal status he writes extensively in "Judenschaft zu Frankfurt" (A, 4, 3: 44–60). The Jews in Frankfurt, as Leibniz would doubtless have known, were forced to wear distinctive marks on their clothing, and it is by no means clear to everyone at the time that they were capable of redemption. Leibniz's complicated relation to Judaism, Jewish philosophy (especially Maimonides), Jewish mysticism, and to the Jews of his time, including Spinoza, would be the subject of another study.

13. Gottfried Wilhelm Leibniz, *Essais de Théodicée*, ed. J. Brunschwig (Paris: Garnier-Flammarion, 1969), 435; sect. 56.

2

Laocoön and the Hottentots

Michael Chaouli

There is, to my knowledge, no racial theory that does without aesthetic values and categories. Conversely, there are many examples of aesthetic theory, as it is developed in the eighteenth century, that find themselves invoking race at the seemingly oddest moments. My aim is to read this mutual attraction, and I propose to do so by starting at a well-known point of intersection: the appearance of the Hottentots in Gotthold Ephraim Lessing's *Laocoön* of 1766. What are they doing in a book devoted to the debate about the limits imposed by different media on different arts?

The passage about the Hottentots occurs late in *Laocoön*, in the midst of a discussion of disgust. Recall with what evident pleasure Lessing relates the story of a Hottentot wedding that he has picked up from the English magazine *The Connoisseur*:

> We know how dirty the Hottentots are and how many things are beautiful, comely, and sacred to them that awaken disgust and loathing in us. A flattened cartilage of a nose, flabby breasts which hang down to the navel, the whole body covered with a layer of goat's fat and soot and tanned by the sun, the hair dripping with grease, feet and arms wrapped in fresh entrails—think of all this in the object of a fiery, worshiping, tender love; hear this expressed in the noble language of sincerity and admiration, and try to keep from laughing.[1]

It will not, I think, come as a surprise that this passage has earned the rebuke of those scholars concerned with the image of non-Europeans in

German literary and intellectual history. Thus, Sander Gilman, in his book *On Blackness without Blacks*, one of the earliest such studies, writes that Lessing "chose the antithesis of the civilized concept of beauty in the stereotype of the Hottentot [. . .] His view of the Black was rooted in his evaluation of Blackness as inherently disgusting. . . . For Lessing the physiognomy of the Black is repellent; his practices are merely laughable."[2]

There is undoubtedly truth to this claim. The passage from *Laocoön* would seem to offer yet another instance of aesthetic theory seeking to ratify its insights by gesturing towards racial images assumed to be beyond dispute, just as racial theories in the eighteenth century—those of Georges-Louis Buffon, Johann Friedrich Blumenbach, Christoph Meiners, Georg Forster, and Immanuel Kant, to name just a few—at some point will rely on supposedly unimpeachable judgments of beauty and of ugliness to establish their racial rankings. Indeed, the two discourses are at times so tightly intertwined that one is hard-pressed to disentangle the racial from the aesthetic, as when Edmund Burke, in his *Enquiry* of 1757, tells the story of a blind boy who, after a cataract operation, gains his eyesight at the age of fourteen: "the first time the boy saw a black object, it gave him great uneasiness," Burke reports, continuing: "some time after, upon accidentally seeing a negro woman, he was struck with great horror at the sight."[3] Burke has an interesting explanation for this horror: "Black bodies, reflecting none, or but a few rays, with regard to sight, are but so many vacant spaces dispersed among the objects we view." If a black body is nothing more than empty space, if it is in effect the absence of a body, then it stands to reason that this vacuum will cause horror in the viewer.

Yet the Hottentot passage maintains an uneasy relationship with the diagnosis that European aesthetic theories of the eighteenth century disparage blackness. In part, this is because in eighteenth-century anthropology, Hottentots are not even considered black: they are described as olive brown, yellowish brown, or copper brown, which, far from being a classificatory caprice, maintains the widespread notion that race is above all an effect of the environment; for it confirms the view that the further one moves from the equator, the lighter one's skin color becomes.[4] Besides, in our passage, the Hottentots' skin color is not natural but cultural: their tanned bodies are covered, we are told, by a "layer of goat's fat and soot." The category of "blackness" is far too coarse to account for the variability of their skin color.

But arguments such as Gilman's need to be rethought for another, more important reason: they go both too far and not far enough. Not far enough because they fail to account for the argumentative context in which Lessing's Hottentots appear. For the "Ekel und Abscheu" that their practices purportedly evoke in us are not vague affective categories; one of them, namely, *Ekel*, has been conceptually circumscribed by Lessing with some care. Disgust, in fact, occupies a crucial position in *Laocoön* as the singular exception to the Aristotelian precept, announced in chapter 4 of the *Art of Poetry*, that even things painful to our senses can please us when represented accurately (Aristotle mentions crawling creatures and corpses). The very act of comparing nature with its mimetic representation, Aristotle claims, fills us with a pleasure that nature itself may deny us. Except, Lessing counters, in those instances when the representation evokes disgust. Here he seeks philosophical support from Moses Mendelssohn, who, like many other aesthetic theorists of the eighteenth century,[5] singles out disgust as an affect incompatible with representation:

> The mental images of fear, sadness, terror, sympathy, etc. can only cause displeasure in so far as we take the evil for real. These can be dissolved into pleasant sensations through the reminder that it is an artificial fraud. . . . The repulsive sensation of disgust, however, works by virtue of the law of the imagination on the mere mental image in the soul, no matter whether the object is taken as real or not. . . . The sensations of disgust are thus always nature, never imitation.[6]

The traditional distinction between the beautiful and the ugly is supplemented—indeed supplanted—by the distinction between the ugly and the disgusting, thereby pulling the ugly into the circle of aesthetically legitimate, even pleasant, sensations, but forcing us to draw the line at the one affect incapable of providing us with pleasure, even in representation. To be precise, what disgusts cannot even appear as a representation, for unlike fear and sadness and sympathy, which permit the imagination to play in the space provided by the difference between reality and fiction, disgust closes this space entirely. Thus, the sensations of disgust are always experienced as real, or—in what amounts to the same thing—they are always experienced as imaginary. The distinction between reality and fiction, between nature and imitation collapses, and with it any surplus of pleasure we may have derived from the distinction itself.

In this case, then, Lessing's Hottentots would not even qualify as Gilman's "antithesis of the civilized concept of beauty," for an antithesis implies a structurally equal, if antagonistic, relationship with the thesis; in aesthetic terms, it implies the continued operation of the beautiful-ugly distinction. But as objects evoking disgust, the Hottentots would be unrepresentable, aesthetically and politically; outside the bounds of thesis and antithesis, beauty and ugliness; neither subject nor object, but rather, following Julia Kristeva's terminology, abject. They would make up the formless remainder produced by the process of redrawing the boundaries of what is aesthetic.[7]

But there is an important way in which such a reading goes too far—even while it fails to go far enough by relying on dubiously stable oppositions such as beautiful and ugly, Hottentot and German, Black and White, thereby missing the complex ways aesthetic and racial lines of thought can intersect. For the Hottentots are meant to provoke not only our disgust, but also our laughter, as the passage I cited earlier emphasized: "hear this expressed in the noble language of sincerity and admiration, and try to keep from laughing." The disgust in the passage permits the mouth to do something other than gag or vomit, namely, laugh. Far from remaining the unassimilable, indigestible leftover, what evokes disgust turns out to be aesthetically highly productive in Lessing's account. Indeed, immediately after citing Mendelssohn's ban on the disgusting, *Laocoön* proceeds to produce example after example in which disgust can—indeed *must*—be used to achieve certain aesthetic effects: laughter, terror, and above all hunger.[8]

If the Hottentots are so disgusting that they do not even permit the distinction between nature and imitation otherwise granted to every object, yet at the same time so laughable that they become irresistible elements in an aesthetic construct; if—put differently—they occupy a place neither within the proper bounds of aesthetic representation nor without, then where do they belong? What, if any, space is properly theirs in this text? The strange space that is neither inside nor out, that is both inside and out, the strange space of the Hottentots that turns out also to be the space of *Laocoön* and much of aesthetic theory is the skin. Skin is the boundary separating the body—indeed any object—from the world, something that at the same time does not entirely belong to that body.[9]

What interests Lessing about the Hottentots is not primarily the natural color of their skin, which lies, as we have seen, beneath a thick layer of soot and grease and metaphor (the bride's face, *The Connoisseur* reports and Lessing quotes, "shone like the polished ebony"). What does interest him is precisely that layer, the makeup of and on their skin: "A piece of flattened cartilage for a nose, flabby breasts which hang down to the navel, the whole body covered with a layer of goat's fat and soot and tanned by the sun, the hair dripping with grease." It isn't blackness that disgusts him, but a skin failing to hug the body tautly enough for body and skin to become one, as it does in a classical statue, as we'll see in a moment. And if the makeup—the *Schminke*—of goat's fat and soot and grease were not troubling enough to a conception of the body that requires a skin so smooth as to be invisible, Lessing adds that the Hottentots' feet and arms were "entwined with fresh entrails," turning the body inside out: rather than holding and hiding the impossibly large entrails, the skin finds itself enveloped by them.

It is becoming clearer how the Hottentots may be related to the title character of Lessing's book, for are Laocoön and his sons not just three guys with entrails around their feet and arms? Is this not a sculpture of the Hottentots? In a way it is, but in an even more disturbing way than it might seem at first. For what is missing in Lessing's account of the Hottentots— what he pointedly omits, for it is available in his source—is a reference to the event that stands, dramatically and spatially, at the center of the sculpture: namely, the piercing of skin. The sculptors have altered Virgil's account so as to train our eyes on this point in space and time: in Book II of the *Aeneid* two serpents devour the two sons first, only then to kill Laocoön by strangling him. There is no word of a bite. Here, however, everything is concentrated on the single moment at which the skin is breached, as Goethe recognized more clearly than anyone:

> To explain the position of the father as a whole and in all its body parts, it seems to me most advantageous to refer to the momentary feeling of the wound as the main cause for the whole movement. The snake has not bitten, but it is biting, namely, the soft part of the body above and slightly behind the hip.[10]

Neither Lessing nor his supposed antagonist Johann Joachim Winckelmann so much as mentions the bite. And we suspect why: if they did, they would have to account for its effect, namely, the wound in Laocoön's side. Even Goethe goes out of his way to close the wound he has opened by insisting that what we see here must be the first bite Laocoon suffers. Why? Because had he been bitten earlier, the viewer would be confronted with wounds, and that, Goethe writes, would be disgusting, *ekelhaft*.[11] The open wound is plugged by the very fangs that made the incision in the first place. *Laocoön*, then, is a sculpture that represents a body that both has and does not have a wound. It offers us a structure of disavowal: like Winckelmann and Lessing, we know very well that there is a wound, but we can at the same time proceed as though there weren't one.

Even in this configuration, the wound has not disappeared; it has merely been displaced upwards, where it can be more readily acknowledged, into the mouth, around whose opening both Winckelmann and Lessing lovingly, obsessively circle.[12] Lessing would have us believe that the mouth is in fact the real source of their disagreement:

> The scream had to be softened to a sigh, not because screaming betrays an ignoble soul [as Winckelmann had argued], but because it distorts the features in a disgusting manner. Force Laocoön's mouth wide open, and then judge! ... From a form which inspired pity because it possessed beauty and pain at the same time, it has now become an ugly, repulsive figure from which we gladly turn away. ... The wide opening of the mouth ... becomes in painting a mere spot and in sculpture a cavity, with most repulsive effects.[13]

Under the right conditions, even the mouth, a supposedly natural opening into the body, can turn into a horrifying and disgusting wound. Thus, Lessing's reading of the sculpture does everything it can to preserve the ideal image of the body by closing as many of the wounds as possible.

In this regard, he is far closer to Winckelmann's ideal body image than he might wish to admit. And that image is quite explicitly articulated by Winckelmann in his *Gedanken über die Nachahmung der griechischen Werke* of 1755:

> We see in most figures by modern masters, in those parts of the body that are pushed together, small wrinkles that are too strongly articulated; by contrast, when just such wrinkles arise in equally pressed parts in Greek figures, one rises out of the other with a gentle motion. . . . These masterworks show us a skin that is not taut, but one that is gently stretched over healthy flesh. . . . Unlike in our bodies, the skin never produces small, particular folds separated from the flesh.

> Similarly the modern works are distinguished from the Greeks' by a multitude of small impressions and by far too many and far too sensuous dimples. . . .[14]

The skin then draws two different kinds of boundaries, both imaginary yet indispensable: first, it distinguishes between body and world, preventing the former from disintegrating into raw matter and mingling with its environment. And secondly, it distinguishes real bodies, with their creases, wrinkles, hollows and openings, from the ideal male bodies represented in classical sculptures, in which the skin's supple embrace of the body makes its beauty visible. The skin permits the appearance in real bodies of something unreal—of an ideal, a soul, a divinity—but to do that it must render itself invisible. The perfect skin is one that appears perfectly transparent, one that allows us to see right through it, into incorporeality, into transcendence. This, then, is the paradox of skin: it is needed in order to perform the distinction of real from unreal bodies, yet it must appear invisible if this distinction is to be maintained. Sometimes you may see a wrinkle separating the skin from the flesh, or you may see a mouth torn wide open, or a skin layered with grease and soot; in those moments, the invisible basis of the distinction between real and ideal bodies becomes visible; something that was imagined as a transparent boundary suddenly reveals itself to be corporeal, thick, fleshy; in that moment, the distinction and with it the ideal body collapse into a disgusting mess. There is something under that skin, you think, but it's not a Greek sculpture. "'The human being under the skin,'" Nietzsche writes in *The Gay Science* (1882), "is, for all lovers, a horror and an impossible thought"—more precisely, an un-thought, *ein Ungedanke*.[15]

The distinction between real and ideal bodies, and, hence, the peculiarly paradoxical role of the skin, holds not just for the classical body-ideal prevalent during the late eighteenth century; it holds, I think, for any body processed by representation. It certainly holds for the artworks of aesthetic theory, which present us with sensory surfaces through which we are meant to fathom a transcendent, incorporeal truth. That, at any rate, is G. W. F. Hegel's very definition of an artwork: like Argus, it has eyes at every point of its surface that allow us to gaze into its soul. If the main aesthetic function of skin is to render itself invisible so that the soul may shine through, then a preference for white skin follows almost by itself. The natural signs—blushing, for example—through which the body is thought to speak the truth (in contrast with the arbitrary and potentially false signs emanating from the mouth) are taken by many thinkers of the eighteenth century to be legible on white skin only. The color white alone is proper to humanity, writes Wilhelm von Humboldt, "not because it is more beautiful, for that is a matter of taste," but for another reason: "because its clarity and transparency allows the subtlest expression and because it permits mixtures and nuances, for in black all color ceases to be."[16]

Let me conclude by offering a speculative link between aesthetic and racial theories in the eighteenth century that I can only sketch here. Just as the artwork offers us nothing but surfaces that are supposed to provide information about its depth, the racial body finds itself in a similarly perplexing relationship of outside and inside: to make its distinctions, no racial theory can dispense with purely outward signs, usually skin color. But because cutaneous distinctions are also, literally speaking, superficial, race theories must also rely on a far less malleable *internal* distinction, usually called blood. How blood and skin relate to one another is solved, if it is solved at all, very differently by different theorists. But there is in most cases a strange indeterminacy: blood is considered to be the more consequential medium by virtue of its assumed role in carrying heritable traits from one generation to the next. Yet this imaginary blood only becomes theoretically necessary to account for differences on the surface; while in theory blood runs deeper than skin color, it is skin color that calls blood into being as the phantom substance that is its cause. Because it has nothing but surfaces to go on, race theory is obliged to manufacture another body under the skin that it calls "blood" and that it proceeds to regard as the real body. All of this may clothe itself in the garb of science, real or sham, but on its most basic level, it is an aesthetic operation, for aesthetics is the science that attempts to fathom depths from surfaces.

And yet if race theory works like aesthetic theory, if it is really just a species of aesthetics, then we must wonder why it is needed as a distinct theory at all. This is where the Hottentot passage can perhaps help us. For there are instances in which the skin *fails* to render itself invisible, calling attention to its own materiality, immobilizing us with disgust. In those cases, we need new ways of drawing new invisible lines. One of these we call "race."

NOTES

1. "Man weiß, wie schmutzig die Hottentotten sind; und wie vieles sie für schön und zierlich und heilig halten, was uns Ekel und Abscheu erwecket. Ein gequetschter Knorpel von Nase, schlappe bis auf den Nabel herabhangende Brüste, den ganzen Körper mit einer Schminke aus Ziegenfett und Ruß an der Sonne durchbeizet, die Haarlocken von Schmeer triefend, Füße und Arme mit frischem Gedärme umwunden: dies denke man sich an dem Gegenstande einer feurigen, ehrfurchtsvollen, zärtlichen Liebe; dies höre man in der edeln Sprache des Ernstes und der Bewunderung ausgedrückt, und enthalte sich des Lachens!" Lessing, *Laocoön: oder über die Grenzen der Malerei und Poesie. Werke und Briefe*, vol. 5, part 2, ed Wilfried Barner (Frankfurt a. M.: Deutscher Klassiker Verlag, 190), 9–206, 175–6/ *Laocoön: An Essay on the Limits of Painting and Poetry*, trans. by Edward Allen McCormick (Baltimore: Johns Hopkins University Press, 1984), 132–3 (translation modified).

2. Sander Gilman, *On Blackness without Blacks: Essays on the Image of the Black in Germany* (Boston: G. K. Hall & Co., 1982), 27–29.

3. Edmund Burke, *A Philosophical Enquiry into the Origin of our Ideas of the Sublime and the Beautiful*, ed. Adam Phillips (Oxford: Oxford University Press, 1990), 131 and 133.

4. This is a point also made by Andreas Mielke; see *Lessing und die Hottentotten, oder über die Grenzen von Reisebeschreibung und Satire* (Baden-Baden: Valentin Koerner, 1993).

5. For a thorough overview see chapter 1 of Winfried Menninghaus' *Ekel: Theorie und Geschichte einer starken Empfindung* (Frankfurt: Suhrkamp, 1999).

6. "Die Vorstellung der Furcht, der Traurigkeit, des Schreckens, des Mitleids usw. können nur Unlust erregen, insoweit wir das Übel für wirklich halten. Diese können also durch die Erinnerung, daß es ein künstlicher Betrug sei, in angenehme Empfindungen aufgelöst werden. Die widrige Empfindung des Ekels aber erfolgt, vermöge des Gesetzes der Einbildungskraft auf die bloße Vorstellung in der Seele, der Gegenstand mag für wirklich gehalten werden, oder nicht. . . . Die Empfindungen des Ekels sind also allezeit Natur, niemals Nachahmung," in *Briefe, die Neueste Litteratur betreffend*, parts I–V, eds. Moses Mendelssohn, G. E. Lessing, and Friedrich Nicolai, 1759–60 (Repr. Hildesheim: Georg Olms, 1974), I here cite part V: 102.

7. Cf. Susan Gustafson, "Beautiful Statues, Beautiful Men: The Abjection of Feminine Imagination in Lessing's *Laocoön*," *PMLA* 108 (1993): 1083–97.

8. This point is convincingly made by Carol Jacobs in "The Critical Performance of Lessing's *Laocoön*," *MLN* 102 (1987): 483–521.

9. For a rich cultural history of skin, see Claudia Benthien's *Haut: Literaturgeschichte, Körperbilder, Grenzdiskurse* (Reinbek: Rowohlt, 1999). See also her, *Skin: On the Cultural Border Between Self and the World*, trans. Thomas Dunlap (New York: Columbia University Press, 2002).

10. "Um die Stellung des Vaters sowohl im ganzen als nach allen Teilen des Körpers zu erklären, scheint es mir am vorteilhaftesten, das augenblickliche Gefühl der Wunde als die Hauptursache der ganzen Bewegung anzugeben. Die Schlange hat

nicht gebissen, sondern sie beißt, und zwar in den weichen Teil des Körpers, über und etwas hinter der Hüfte." Goethe, "Über Laocoön," *Sämtliche Werke: Briefe, Tagebücher und Gespräche*, ed. Friedmar Apel et al (Frankfurt: Deutscher Klassiker Verlag, 1985–), vol. 18, 493–94.

11. Ibid., *Sämtliche Werke*, 498.

12. For an illuminating reading of Laocoön's open mouth, see David Wellbery, "The Pathos of Theory: *Laocoön* Revisited," in *Intertextuality: German Literature and Visual Art from the Renaissance to the Twentieth Century*, eds. Ingeborg Hoesterey and Ulrich Weisstein (Columbia, SC: Camden House, 1993), 47–63.

13. "[Der Meister] mußte Schreien in Seufzen mildern; nicht weil das Schreien eine unedle Seele verrät, sondern weil es das Gesicht auf eine ekelhafte Weise verstellet. Denn man reiße dem Laocoön in Gedanken nur den Mund auf, und urteile. . . . Es war eine Bildung, die Mitleid einflößte, weil sie Schönheit und Schmerz zugleich zeigte; nun ist es eine häßliche, eine abscheuliche Bildung geworden, von der man gern sein Gesicht verwendet . . . Die bloße weite Öffnung des Mundes. . . . ist in der Malerei ein Fleck und in der Bildhauerei eine Vertiefung, welche die widrigste Wirkung von der Welt tut." *Laocoön*, 29 / 17, translation modified.

14 "In den meisten Figuren neuerer Meister siehet man an den Theilen des Cörpers, welche gedruckt sind, kleine gar zu sehr bezeichnete Falten der Haut; dahingegen, wo sich eben dieselben Falten in gleichgedruckten Theilen Griechischer Figuren legen, ein sanfter Schwung eine aus der andern wellenförmig erhebt. . . . Diese Meisterstücke zeigen uns eine Haut, die nicht angespannt, sondern sanft gezogen ist über ein gesundes Fleisch, welches dieselbe ohne schwülstige Ausdehnung füllet . . . Die Haut wirft niemahls, wie an unsern Cörpern, besondere und von dem Fleisch getrennete kleine Falten. Eben so unterscheiden sich die neuern Wercke von den Griechischen durch eine Menge kleiner Eindrücke, und durch gar zu viele und gar zu sinnlich gemachte Grübchen . . . " Winckelmann, *Gedancken über die Nachahmung Griechischer Wercke in der Mahlerey und Bildhauer-Kunst*, in Helmut Pfotenhauer et al., (eds). *Frühklassizismus: Position und Opposition: Winckelmann, Mengs, Heinse* eds. (Frankfurt: Deutscher Klassiker Verlag, 1995), 11-50, 22 [author's translation].

15. "'Der Mensch unter der Haut' ist allen Liebenden ein Greuel und Ungedanke. . . .'" Nietzsche, *Kritische Studienausgabe* vol. 3 (München: dtv, 1988), 423 [*The Gay Science*] Section 59, translation modified.

16. "Das aber lässt sich mit unumstösslicher Gewissheit behaupten, dass, wenn man den Menschen in seinen höchsten Beziehungen auf Intellectualität und Empfindung, Dichtung und Kunst nimmt, die weisse Farbe allein die seinem Geschlechte bestimmte seyn kann; nicht weil sie die schönste ist, denn dies ist Geschmackssache, aber weil ihre Klarheit und Durchsichtigkeit jeden leisesten Ausdruck erlaubt, und weil sie Mischungen und Nuancen zulässt, da das Schwarz vielmehr ein Aufhören aller Farbe ist." Wilhelm von Humboldt, "Über die Verschiedenheiten des menschlichen Sprachbaues," in *Werke in fünf Bänden*, eds. Andreas Flitner und Klaus Giel (Darmstadt: Wissenschaftliche Buchgesellschaft, 1963), vol. 3, 249–250.

II

Race in Philosophy

The Problem of Kant

3

Policing Polygeneticism in Germany, 1775 (Kames,) Kant, and Blumenbach

John H. Zammito

The title of this anthology, the "German Invention of Race," is, I trust, interrogative rather than assertive. I would very much hope that we not presuppose a "monogenetic" view of the origins of race theory. I suggest that the stress of the title should be on the "local creation" of a discourse of "race" in Germany, rather than on its singular epiphany there for all Europe. I would think, further, that "inflection" might well contest with "invention" as our proper category. And, of course, it must be of central concern to all of us just what "race" we mean in *our* title, and whether it is the same "race" they meant in the eighteenth century. This is not to dispute the fervidly presentist agenda of the inquiry, but rather to urge that it be given texture, precision, and substance by a complementary historicism.

I am interested in one striking historical fact, namely, that in Germany in 1775 two authors—independently, as I shall demonstrate—produced texts on human (racial) variety which from our present vantage appear to be decisive departures toward what Robert Bernasconi and others would term a "scientific theory of race."[1] (One doesn't know where or how many scare quotes they or we should insert in that entire phrase to indicate its multitude of provocations.) My project is to go back and investigate the local circumstances of the composition of these two texts. So I will ask, first, how did Immanuel Kant come to write and publish his first essay on race? Then I will ask how Johann Blumenbach came to publish his dissertation on human variety in that same year. Answering these questions will perhaps incite keen questions opening out onto the grander issues of our work.

THE BACKGROUND OF KANT'S "ESSAY ON RACE"

The 1770s are legendary among Kant scholars as the "silent decade," the era of Kant's painstaking composition of the *Critique of Pure Reason* (1781).[2] In that context, we must register Kant's eagerness to publish the essay on race in 1777 as a matter demanding some historical explanation. Indeed, even his motivation for the 1775 version is worthy of greater historical scrutiny than it has hitherto occasioned.[3] Two questions arise at once. First, how did the issue of racial variation feature in Kant's philosophical agenda? Second, what sort of "scientist"—*Naturforscher*, to use Erich Adickes's term—did Kant take himself to be in 1775? I would like to situate both these questions in a larger, and perhaps more provocative one: what were Kant's ambitions, in 1775, vis à vis the German public sphere, generally, and vis à vis the German "scientific community," more specifically? I mean to suggest that the essay on race was a highly strategic intervention on Kant's part, and to show what was at stake.

Let us start with the most immediate context. Kant published the 1775 essay on race as an advertisement for his course in physical geography offered summer semester 1775. First we have to consider what function such texts served at the University of Königsberg at this time, and how Kant had hitherto made use of this genre. These advertisements were the only vehicle (roughly up to 1770) that non-salaried faculty could use to make known to students what courses they would be offering and thus drum up enrollments and income, since these courses were not entered into the official catalog of the university. Kant had certainly published other such advertisements, but they were in the period when he was a *Magister*. He had even published an advertisement for his physical geography course before, precisely when he instituted the course and in order to explain its unique ambitions in the curriculum. That was some twenty years earlier.[4] But let us consider the situation of 1775. Kant was now an ordinary professor. His need to advertise his courses should significantly have altered in that light. Moreover, he was by 1775 something of a legendary teacher—certainly at Königsberg, and plausibly more widely throughout Germany.[5] To drum up enrollments, then, seems improbable as a sufficient motivation.

To press the matter still further, Kant had *other* courses in the offing that well might have warranted specific advertisement. There are *two* such courses that I would like to point to—the obvious one, his *anthropology* course, which he inaugurated in 1772 and revised dramatically at just about the moment under consideration; and *another* that has hitherto not received the attention it deserves, his course entitled "Philosophical Encyclopedia," which he inaugurated in 1767 and, after a hiatus of several years, was offering again in just this year of 1775. Why, in short, would Kant have chosen to advertise the physical geography course he had been offering for twenty years running, to significant acclaim in German academic circles, and not these newer and perhaps still not sufficiently understood courses? And, of course, on top of all these questions, why would Kant have highlighted "race" in the physical geography course?

I would like to propose some answers from the specific German context of the early 1770s. The opening wedge for my claims is a phrase I am profoundly grateful to Karl Fink for having coined: "Storm and Stress Anthropology."[6] I will ungratefully appropriate it for my own purposes, of course. Bluntly, Kant *hated* storm and stress. I have been trying to bring that element in his attitudinal structure into greater prominence in Kant interpretation for some time now, and I will persist in that endeavor here. I suggest that the early 1770s brought into currency in Germany a set of ideas and inquiries that Kant could not but find profoundly dangerous to German scholarly "rigor." He would with increasing vehemence endeavor to *police* these transgressive impulses in German public discourse, specifically in German "science," for the balance of his "critical" career. It will come as a surprise to no one who knows anything of my work that the main culprit Kant saw in all this was his former student, Johann Gottfried Herder. But Kant had other foes to counter as well. In the European frame, some key names are Voltaire, David Hume and Lord Kames, of course. In Germany, the names I wish to introduce here are Ernst Platner and Christoph Meiners.

In 1770 Kant finally became ordinary professor, after having languished as *Magister* for some fourteen years. Let me put that in our terms for a moment: Kant was an adjunct lecturer, without tenure, without even a regular salary, for fourteen years. The publication of his runner-up prize essay for the Berlin Academy in 1764 had brought him to the attention of prominent philosophers in Germany—Moses Mendelssohn and Johann Heinrich Lambert, particularly—but he was certainly better known for his belle-lettristic *Observations on the Feeling of the Beautiful and the Sublime* (1764) than for any philosophical achievements. His concern to establish his prominence in the latter field comes through in the claims he made in the letters he wrote about his *Inaugural Dissertation* of 1770, especially in the letter to Lambert.[7] In a word, Kant in the early 1770s was concerned for his status in the profession.

At the same time, 1770 is conventionally the time Kant scholarship assigns to the breakthrough to the "critical" philosophy, especially in light of the radical revision of the theory of space and time which Kant articulated in the *Inaugural Dissertation*.[8] In 1775 Kant was, as we noted at the outset, deeply immersed in working through the inordinate complexities of his *Critique of Pure Reason*. He anticipated that this work would have a revolutionary impact on philosophy and certainly elevate his place among the members of the German academic discipline. Indeed, so important did he take this labor to be that we must find it peculiar that he would devote time to what would seem a distraction from that task: the essay on race. Phillip Sloan has endeavored to discern in the reasoning in Kant's essay— and in the physical geography lecture notes we have retained from students of the era—explicit revisions in the conceptualization of geography and (natural) history attendant upon the "critical turn" in the *Inaugural Dissertation* regarding space and time.[9] That is one fruitful way of making sense of the essay.

But the whole field of philosophy in Germany was undergoing a metamorphosis in just these years, as powerful currents of *Popularphilosophie* came to challenge the entrenched Wolffian *Schulphilosophie* of the universities.[10] Central in this challenge were Johann Feder and Christoph Meiners, both called to Germany's premier university, Göttingen, in 1768 and 1772 respectively, to rejuvenate the program in philosophy.[11] Many of us know Feder and Meiners as Kant's despised foes of the 1780s.[12] What needs to be retrieved is a far more affirmative relation with Johann Feder in the very years we are considering. From 1768 onward, Kant taught a new course entitled "Philosophical Encyclopedia" for which he chose a textbook by Feder.[13] That is, Kant had enlisted in a significant measure in the revisionist program in philosophy. But when, in 1772, Christoph Meiners gave a much more explicit formulation of what this *Revision der Philosophie* betokened, I suggest, Kant may well have realized that he could not reconcile his own ambitions as metaphysician with the program of popular philosophy he had initially found congenial.[14] In a word, Feder and Meiners were engineering a revision of philosophy which would have eliminated metaphysics in favor of empirical psychology, and the new "critical" Kant could not abide this. The course of Kant's thinking from 1772 onward not only aimed privately toward the grounding of the critical philosophy, but also aimed publicly toward policing this waywardness of popular philosophy.

Ernst Platner represents an even more direct provocation.[15] (Incidentally, Platner explictly linked his project with that of Meiners in the introduction to his work.) Here we are in the thick of the genesis of Kant's course on anthropology, and even more, of its early and fundamental mutation.[16] In a very important letter to Marcus Herz, provoked by Herz's favorable review of Platner's *Anthropologie für Ärtze und Weltweise* (1772), Kant spelled out his quarrel with Platner and how his vision of anthropology departed from Platner's.

[M]y plan is entirely different [from Platner's]. The intention I have is to present through it the sources from all the sciences which [bear on] mores [*Sitten*], efficacy [*Geschicklichkeit*], socializing [*Umgang*], the method of cultivating and governing men, and in the process to open up everything practical. In this I am more interested in phenomena and their laws than I am in the first grounds of the possibility of the *modification* of human nature in general. Therefore the subtle and in my view eternally vain investigation of the manner in which the organs of the body enter into relation with thinking I leave entirely aside.[17]

The upshot of his claims would be the distinction of a *pragmatic* from a *physiological* anthropology, i.e., one which separates what man actively makes of himself (character/culture) from what nature makes of him (temperament/ physiology).[18] Kant became increasingly adamant not only about the priority of the former inquiry, but also about the impossibility of the latter. That is striking in two regards. First, Kant's discourse of "race" belongs squarely in the latter, which would make it epistemologically problematic for him to infer *at all* from physiology to culture in this domain. Second, we must ask in what measure Kant believed that man's active self-constitution could *overcome*, indeed, *annihilate* the merely native. If character could overcome temperament, could the categorical imperative annul "race" difference? That is, can we discern here a radical significance for the blatant disjunction between Kant's transcendental philosophy and his anthropology?[19]

How did the European discourse of "polygeneticism" (Voltaire and Kames) fit into this local constellation of issues? Both Erich Adickes and Phillip Sloan urge, against Johannes Unold's claims for Kant's awareness and rebuttal of Kames, that there is no explicit evidence that Kant read Kames's *Sketches* in 1775.[20] On the other hand, Kant's failure to mention an adversary by name is not at all unusual, and there is strong reason in terms of the general context in Germany to suppose that Kant would have been aware of the text. A German translation was immediately available and widely circulated in that year.[21] Blumenbach makes the point that polygeneticism was "much discussed in these days," and no other source of polygeneticism in Germany can be *immediately* connected with the year 1775.[22] It is true, of course, that the views of Voltaire and Hume were already circulating and provoking rebuttal in a European context, for example, by James Beattie and John Hunter.[23] Kant clearly knew the arguments of Voltaire and Hume, yet the likelihood that Kames—whose prominence for Kant on questions of aesthetics was already quite well-established— played a role in triggering the essay on race remains quite strong.

Kant saw polygeneticists as threats primarily to a religious-metaphysical set of commitments he entertained. Their race doctrine smacked to him of materialism and atheism ushered in by an all-too-beguiling literary flair—an aestheticization of science (*schöne Wissenschaft*) with lethal religious-moral consequences.[24] They were part of a dangerous project which sought somehow to naturalize the account of the human, to blur what were for Kant eminently to be guarded boundaries between the inorganic and the organic, as well as between the human and the animal.[25] "Scientists" should know better. That explains how Kant conceived his mission as a "natural scientist." His calling was to legislate the methodology of science and to clarify the concepts with which it proceeded.[26] He was confident he had a powerful warranting exemplar to offer his community in 1775: his treatment of the issue of "race."

Kant's original essay on race is hard to reconstruct, since in the *Akademie Ausgabe* we are given the 1777 version (slightly modified), and we must resort to the *Lesearten* in the notes to reconstruct how the original appeared. It has never yet been fully and accurately rendered into English, though we can perhaps hope for that from the forthcoming Cambridge edition. Working from a reconstructed version of the 1775 text, the first point to make is that the *audience* for the text was the students at the Albertina, *not* the general public. Kant invited them to a course designed as "useful entertainment rather than wearisome labor," more "play" than "inquiry."[27] He explained, at the close of the advertisement, that his physical geography course had a distinctive pedagogical mission, namely, to foster "knowledge of the world" (*Weltkenntnis*), that is, something *pragmatic*, not academic, aimed to equip students for their activities in the wider world. Accordingly, he would present things in a "cosmological" manner; that is, he would concentrate on "the relation of the whole [context] in which [particular matters] stand, within which every person will need to take a stance."[28] While these framing remarks are dropped from the 1777 version, the intention they express may well explain Kant's eagerness to place an expanded and revised form of the essay in J. J. Engel's series, *Der Philosoph für die Welt*. This was a hugely successful publication in the vein of *Popularphilosophie*.[29] Kant's active pursuit of inclusion in its second volume speaks to his effort both to situate himself in the public space of the movement and to rival others in that movement whose excesses he decried (albeit for the moment discreetly).[30]

As Adickes observed, "the picture [of race theory] that Kant found before him in 1775 was quite a colorful one [*ein recht buntes*]."[31] Puns aside, what Adickes meant is that when Kant took up the matter, there was nothing approaching unanimity regarding either the concept of species or the concept of racial classification in European discourse. Adickes identified three objectives in the essay: (1) to offer a conceptual clarification of the term "race" for natural history; (2) to offer a determinate categorization of human varieties on that basis; and (3) to offer a hypothesis regarding the causal genesis of racial variation. Essential to all three is Kant's self-conception as a *Naturforscher*, namely, as someone authorized to assert methodological principles and to clarify operating concepts. Thus, the essay opens with a strong distinction of natural speciation from logical classification, explicitly upholding Georges-Louis Leclerc Comte de Buffon against Linnaeus. The essay continues immediately, though without names, to uphold monogeneticism against polygeneticism on this basis. It is noteworthy that the original 1775 argument concludes with just this same assertion of monogeneticism, though that gets blurred by the new ending Kant adds in 1777. That is, policing polygeneticism is the methodological framework for Kant's whole endeavor. And this task Kant takes up quite earnestly: no gaming, here.

A return to the language of entertainment comes with the question of cataloguing human variety. "We take pleasure," he writes, "in becoming aware of how we can account for the origin of the different stock of human beings according to the variety of causes that account for these differences."[32] This is the "game" that Kant enjoys playing. In his letter to Johann Gottlieb Immanuel Breitkopf in 1778, Kant elaborates in a very revealing manner. While he expresses willingness to publish more extensively on race, he declines taking up a thorough natural historical inquiry because

> in that case my frame of reference would need to be widely expanded and I would need to take fully into consideration the place of races among animal and plant species, which would occupy me too much and carry me into extensive new reading which in a measure lies outside my field, because natural history is not my study but only my game [*Spiel*], and the most important intention I have with it is aimed at using it to correct and to extend the knowledge of man.[33]

Which and how many human "races" there might be—matters of extreme significance to us—are, for Kant, in substantial measure merely playful conjecture.

More important for us, of course, are the criteria Kant presented for the conceptual clarification of "race" in natural history. There were three. First, Kant upheld Buffon's definition of natural species. "Race" could only be defined in natural history as a real "degeneration" within a fixed, permanent species. Kant articulated two decisive conceptual determinations. First, a race's traits had to be unalterably sustained by succeeding generations *even under change of ecological setting for protracted periods of time.*[34] Second, and perhaps most exciting for Kant in 1775, when members of two distinct races reproduced, their offspring had always and without exception to produce hybrids demonstrating equal inheritances of both parents which were then perpetuated unaltered. This criterion of literal "half-breeding" *(Halbschlachtigkeit)* was what seems to have inspired Kant to believe he had a clear principle on the basis of which to distinguish "race."[35] Twenty years later, in a book whose importance in the history of German science is becoming increasingly apparent, Christoph Girtanner celebrated Kant for having codified this "natural law" of hybridity.[36] Kant, in the published version of his anthropology lectures in 1798, pointed to Girtanner's essay as having capsulated everything he had to say on the question of race.[37]

The misfortune for Kant, however, was that he had no sooner worked out this clever principle in 1775 than new evidence became available which threw the same principle into utter question. Between 1775 and 1777, Kant substantially revised his view, though the revision did not get carried through clearly in the text, resulting in significant confusion. Thus, at the outset, in the language of 1775 preserved unaltered in 1777, Kant writes of four races: "They are: (1) the white race; (2) the Negro race; (3) the Hun race (Mongol or Kalmuck); and (4) the Hindu or Hindustani race."[38] But at the end of section III of the 1777 version Kant presents the schema of his four races as follows: first, "noble blond (northern Europe)"; second, "copper red (America)"; third, "black (Senegambia)"; and fourth, "olive-yellow (Asian-Indians)."[39] Thus, the Mongolians are no longer one of his four races, but the American Indians, not a distinct race in 1775, are advanced to this status in 1777.

The microhistory of this shift deserves attention. Adickes ascribed it principally to the impact on Kant of reading Pallas's *Sammlungen historischer Nachrichten über die mongolischen Völkerschaften* (1776).[40] What struck Kant in Pallas's text was evidence that mixture of Russian and Mongolian peoples did not result uniformly in a consistent "half-breed." This put his whole construction of race in jeopardy, and his classification of races wavered accordingly. His struggle with the conception of the Mongols and of the Amerindians as full-fledged or only partially established races suggests both the tentativeness of his criteria and the consequent fluidity of his classes.[41]

Between 1775 and 1777—not least, I suggest, with a shift in intended audience—Kant shifted his tone. At the outset of the enumeration of racial types in 1775, for example, he had written with brisk professorial authority: "I believe that we can make do with four such races in order to derive all the inheritable and self-perpetuating differences among them." In 1777 he wrote: "I believe we need only *assume* four races in order to be able to derive all of the enduring differences within the human genus *that we can observe directly*" (italics mine).[42] Most famously, in 1775 Kant was confident that the white race remained very close to the original race, and that he could know this original race stemmed from central Asia, "between the 31st and 52nd parallels of the old world." But he attenuated this claim about the original race substantially in the 1777 version. He would still "want . . . to *assume* that this form is that of the lineal root genus," to "take all this as a *tentative* account of the origins of the real "races" (italics mine), but he now cautiously conceded "To be sure, we cannot hope now to find anywhere in the world an unchanged example of the original human form."[43] Kant, I suggest, recognized his wider audience and his lessened authority within the same, and considerably qualified his assertion. But I cannot agree with Phillip Sloan that "when he raised the issue of race in 1777, Kant had considered himself but a novice in anthropology and natural history."[44] Sloan takes Kant's remarks to Breitkopf too literally. He fails to register that there is a ferocious seriousness behind Kant's "playfulness." Moreover, as Adickes recognized, while Kant *should* have regarded himself as such a novice, he did not, but rather, despite how "completely hypothetical not only [his] assumptions but also his conclusions are," Kant "builds such castles of fantasy with every indication of pleasure and abandon."[45] This recklessness, however self-indulgent, cannot be written off to self-conscious dilettantism. Kant *meant* to be taken seriously, even if he had no intention of departing extensively from his project with the *Critique of Pure Reason*. That seriousness, especially about policing these sciences, became apparent in the disputes with Herder and Forster a decade later.

BLUMENBACH'S DISSERTATION OF 1775

In September 1775, a brilliant young natural scientist at the cutting edge University of Göttingen defended a dissertation entitled "On the Natural Variety of Mankind." Johann Friedrich Blumenbach was only twenty-three at the time. In sharp contrast to Kant, his career success came swiftly. In 1776 he was made extraordinary professor of medicine at Göttingen and in 1778 ordinary professor. He would go on to be the patriarch of what Timothy Lenoir has called the "Göttingen school" of the life sciences in the era 1790–1840.[46] Blumenbach and Kant would have a very important interaction in the 1790s, and the extent of their mutual impact is a matter that still needs considerable sorting out.[47] But Blumenbach only became *aware* of Kant by reading the essay of 1777 and only became *interested* in Kant in the wake of his controversy with J. G. Herder and Georg Forster in the late 1780s. He first contacted Kant in 1790, envoying a copy of the second edition of his *Über den Bildungstrieb* (1790), presumably in response to Kant's favorable mention of his work in the context of the dispute with Forster. Kant responded with a cordial letter and several additional references to Blumenbach in his published work (and in the draft for his article against Samuel Thomas von Soemmerring in the mid-1790s).[48] In 1775, accordingly, there was no reason for either to have had the least inkling that the other was taking up the question of human variety.

The source of their independent adoption of this project must be traced to the wider context. Blumenbach made explicit that, in addition to local circumstances which we will consider below, he was motivated directly by the challenge of polygeneticism. Certainly, Kames was a provocation for Blumenbach.[49] To ascertain how Kames figured in the actual genesis of Blumenbach's dissertation, we have to reconstruct the formation of Blumenbach's intellectual identity. In Jena, where Blumenbach commenced his university studies, he worked with J. E. I. Walch, one of the pioneers in German natural history (though he was a professor of rhetoric!). In 1772 he moved on to Göttingen to pursue medical studies, but he was drawn as well to C. C. Heyne, the great classical archaeologist, who took him under his wing. At Göttingen, the medical faculty was still deeply infused with the spirit and the thought of Albrecht von Haller, even though he had left the university to return to Switzerland some twenty years earlier. Heyne saw to it that Blumenbach entered into correspondence with Haller in 1775, and this correspondence Blumenbach acknowledged as seminal in his entire formation as a natural scientist.[50] Haller and Heyne became the lodestars of Blumenbach's education.

But Blumenbach draws our attention as well to a "whimsical but remarkable" professor, Christian Wilhelm Büttner, whose collections of natural history became the basis for the ethnographic museum of Göttingen which Blumenbach became instrumental in developing.[51] Blumenbach studied natural history with Büttner, and was drawn especially to Büttner's extensive "quantity of books of voyages and travels" as well as motivated by Büttner's insistence that humans should be a primary topic in natural history. Blumenbach sums up: "It was thus I was led to write as the dissertation for my doctorate, *On the natural variety of mankind . . .* "

Of so much we can be certain. If we go forward in time several decades, we know with equal certainty that Blumenbach engaged in explicit controversy with two figures over the question of blacks and racial equality. Those figures were Christoph Meiners and Samuel Thomas Soemmerring.[52] The issue I wish to raise is whether we can trace the conflict with Meiners, which broke out in public in 1790, to an earlier period, i.e., that surrounding Blumenbach's dissertation. It will be remembered that Meiners became a (short-lived) sensation in German philosophical circles with the publication of his *Revision der Philosophie* in 1772. It had earned him a calling to a professorship in philosophy at Göttingen in that same year. Three years later, i.e., exactly at the moment Blumenbach presented his dissertation, Meiners published, under the unrevealing title *Vermischte philosophische Schriften*, a collection of his essays which had been appearing in German journals since the late 1760s. In those essays Meiners already displayed his interest in ethnography and questions that verge on race theory. The historian of the later conflict, Frank Dougherty, makes a very telling observation, namely that Meiners "had been interested *just as long* as Blumenbach in questions of human history . . . , so that he felt qualified as a competent scholar to challenge Blumenbach publicly in the domain of anthropology" (italics mine). Blumenbach charged Meiners in 1790 with perpetrating "a kind of anthropological enthusiasm [*Schwärmerei*] in the tradition of Lavater's physiognomy," Dougherty adds.[53]

I suggest that Christoph Meiners—ironically, for widely different reasons—might have been the precipitator of both Blumenbach's and Kant's essays on race. In Kant's case, of course, this was not really about race at all, but a preliminary gesture in the grand campaign of "critical philosophy" against popular philosophy. In the case of Blumenbach, however, it might well have been a matter of a scientific anthropologist resisting an ill-informed and dangerous ideologue. Certainly in the 1780s and 1790s Blumenbach—and another intimate of the later circle, Georg Forster—firmly and clearly repudiated the racism towards Blacks and the implicit endorsement of slavery which were central to Meiners and to Soemmerring in their respective works on the black race.[54] It is possible that Meiners already provoked some of these sentiments in Blumenbach as early as 1775, not only through his writings, but also through his utterances, which pervaded the Göttingen scene in these years.

I would even like to pick up on the mention of Johann Casper Lavater here to extend my conjectures. The line I mean is well-drawn already. It leads from Johann Joachim Winckelmann's raptures over the Grecian profile through Lavater's physiognomy to Petrus Camper's theory of the "facial angle" as the key to racial classification.[55] What is here decisive is the intervention not only of cranial measurement, but also of ethnocentric aesthetic judgments, of which Stephen Jay Gould has had so much to say.[56]

Blumenbach's dissertation of 1775, as is the wont of its genre, supplies extensive evidence of its sources and its sponsors. The opening page cannot say enough of the "immortal labours of the great Haller," of his "profound sagacity."[57] Blumenbach sought immediately to ground his specific inquiry in Haller's theory of generation. His specific project was to investigate: "What is it which changes the course of generation, and now produces a worse and now a better progeny, at all events widely different from its original progenitors?"[58] The causes Blumenbach could find adumbrated in the literature were climate, nourishment, and mode of life in general. Because with Haller he subscribed to preformation, and because he further followed Haller in doubting Buffon's definition of species, Blumenbach thought it essential to address the question of the fertility of hybrids, that is, "the conjunction of animals of different species."

By 1775, as Kames had been ruthless in demonstrating, Buffon himself had thoroughly compromised his own thesis.[59] Thus Blumenbach could write: "There is no reason for doubting that hybrids have sprung from the union of the fox and the dog, and those too capable of generation . . ."[60] While Blumenbach agrees with Buffon that effective interspecies generation is *unlikely* and that infertile hybrids are so typical that enumerating instances is "tiresome," he will not adopt Buffon's principle as a necessary and sufficient criterion for species differentiation. For the specific issue of his dissertation, Blumenbach is none-theless confident to assert: "even if it be granted that lascivious male apes attack women [an idea that ran sensationally through the travel literature], any idea of progeny resulting cannot be entertained for a moment . . ."[61] Thus, the insinuation of simian origins of African populations, entertained by Voltaire and others, gets thrown out at once.

Blumenbach, like Buffon and Haller, believed that man should be cat-egorically distinguished from the other animals. While there were morpho-logical elements to this distinction, the essential difference for Blumenbach as for Buffon (and for Kant, incidentally) had to be "the endowments of the mind."[62] He elaborated: "man alone ought to be held to possess *speech*, or the voice of reason, and beasts only the language of the affections."[63] While the orangutan might be "like man in structure," Blumenbach asserted, it was incapable of speech.[64] While he noted that "Linnaeus could discover no [ana-tomical] point by which man could be distinguished from the ape," Blumenbach was convinced of the importance of some distinctions, in particular erect posture. While Kant welcomed Pietro Moscati's claims that erect posture caused physiological problems for man, Blumenbach disputed them as "not quite serious."[65] A crucial difference between Blumenbach and Kant is that the former was interested in (and actually performed) systematic anatomical dissections of various "animals which are most like man," in order to inves-tigate empirically what morphological relations obtained between them.[66] Drawing on all this work, Blumenbach disputed the assertion by Jean-Jacques Rousseau and by others (Lord Monboddo and Julien Offray de La Mettrie, in all likelihood) that orangutans were of the same species as man, making the point bluntly that such writers were "ill-instructed in natural history and anatomy."[67] Blumenbach, having carefully followed the research on apes, recognizes two distinct species—chimpanzee and orangutan.[68] He was al-ready aware that Petrus Camper had conducted dissections of the latter.[69]

Reaching, finally, the central issue of polygeneticism in human origins, Blumenbach ascribed the revival of this view ("much discussed in these days") to "ill-feeling, negligence, and the love of novelty," rather than to any scien-tific soundness. Bluntly, he charged, "it was much easier to pronounce [hu-mans] different species than to inquire into the structure of the human body, to consult the numerous anatomical authors and travellers, and carefully to weigh their good faith or carelessness, to compare parallel examples from the universal circuit of natural history, and then at last to come to an opinion, and investigate the causes of the variety."[70] He specifically identified Voltaire and Kames as guilty here. Clearly, it was on the basis of the alternative and appropriate method he accused them of neglecting that Blumenbach came to the opposite conclusion, namely, monogeneticism.

    The problem, then, was how to account for the variety among humans, especially since, "when the matter is thoroughly considered, you see that all do so run into one another, and that one variety of mankind does so sensibly pass into the other, that you cannot mark out the limits between them."[71] Blumenbach clearly saw any classification scheme as "very arbitrary indeed both in number and definition." He followed Linnaeus in settling upon four "varieties" (he eschewed the term "race" in the entire discussion), of which "the first and most important to us (which is also the primitive one) is that of Europe, Asia this side of the Ganges, and all the country situated to the north of the Amoor, together with that part of North America, which is nearest both in position and character of the inhabitants."[72] This is a striking congeries of peoples, one might observe. Blumenbach acknowledged this: "Though the men of these countries seem to differ very much amongst each other in form and colour, still when they are looked at as a whole they seem to agree in many things with ourselves."[73]

    In discriminating varieties, Blumenbach invoked "the whole bodily constitution, stature, and colour" first, then "the particular structure and proportion of individual parts."[74] The former group of traits he identified as "owing almost entirely to climate alone."[75] Like Kant, Blumenbach conceived a relation between heat and moisture: "That in hot countries bodies become drier and heavier; in cold and wet ones softer, more full of juice and spongy, is easily noticed."[76] While Kant left it at the level of generality, Blumenbach carefully adduced all the comparative anatomical research that had been done to establish the generalization. Stature, too, Blumenbach assigned to cold and heat: "the latter obstructs the increase of organic bodies, whilst the former adds to them and promotes their growth."[77] He brusquely dismissed Kames for having "presumed with the greatest confidence to think otherwise."[78]

    While Blumenbach conceded to the polygeneticists that differences among humans would seem to warrant considering them "as forming different species of mankind," he insisted nonetheless that this was misguided. "There is an almost insensible and indefinable transition from the pure white skin of the German lady through the yellow, the red, and the dark nations, to the Ethiopian of the very deepest black."[79] Variation *within* any population of humans was so rife that to leap to a species discrimination among humans, as Kames did, left Blumenbach "astonished."[80] Unlike Kant in his effort to determine a fixed rule for *Halbschlachtigkeit*, Blumenbach saw a continuous spectrum of changes in skin tints whereby "the most distinct and contrary colours so degenerate, that white men may sensibly pass and be changed into black, and the contrary."[81] His conclusion was unequivocal: "from all these cases, this is clearly proved, . . . that colour, whatever be its causes, be it bile, or the influence of the sun, the air, or the climate, is, at all events, an adventitious and easily changeable thing, and can never constitute a diversity of species."[82] While Kant in 1775 and especially in 1777 made skin color his decisive criterion for racial discrimination, Blumenbach found this trait so equivocal that he turned rather to the structure of the skull—a portentous turn in these matters for which Kant did not yet see the need.[83] Already Petrus Camper, following upon aesthetic value judgments of Winckelmann, had begun to conjecture about the ideal facial angle.[84] Blumenbach showed the influence of this aesthetic orientation: "J. B. Fischer has published a drawing of a Calmuck's skull, and it is ugly, . . . and in many ways testifies to barbarism."[85] But he quickly supplied counterevidence from Pallas, who "describes the Calmucks as men of a symmetrical, beautiful and even round appearance."[86] (One presumes the discourse is of skull shape.) Blumenbach found "the physiognomy and the peculiar lineaments of the whole countenance in different nations" a "very vast and agreeable field," but he believed that "almost all the diversity of the form of the head in different nations is to be attributed to the mode of life and to art," that is, that these were not matters of natural endowment.[87] He then went on to discuss at length the artificial interventions (including mutilations) of humans in their own appearance. It was to this that he believed the beardlessness of Amerindians might in all likelihood be ascribed.

What are we to make of this dissertation? If we juxtapose it to Kant's three aims in his essay, we must say that Blumenbach did not offer a clear conception of "variety" analogous to that which Kant sought for "race," and as a result his discrimination of varieties cannot be paralleled to Kant's discrimination of "races." It is clear that Blumenbach's approach was one of comparative morphology, involving the idea of the "total habitus" of the organism, as it had been taught to him by Haller and Heyne, and that thus he was involved in a Linnaean project of classification, rather than in any project of strict "natural history" such as Kant affirmed in Buffon. But because he had no clear criterion for variety, and indeed insisted repeatedly on the fluidity and arbitrariness of such classification schemes, Blumenbach's fourfold division of the human varieties seems even less motivated than that of Linnaeus. Blumenbach in 1775, then, appears to have derived monogeneticism from the indeterminacy of any categorial discrimination among varieties of human.

SOME TENTATIVE CONCLUSIONS

I have tried to suggest that the local German context proved crucial in inciting the publication of both texts of 1775 on race. Moreover, notwithstanding their historical prominence in the etiology of "scientific" race theories, I have stressed how tentative, exploratory, and even equivocal both texts appear upon careful scrutiny. Kant was changing his views between the two versions of his essay in not insignificant ways, and Blumenbach relativized his findings so substantially as to lead one to question whether he had a firm theory of "race" in 1775, even without the word. Finally, my reading rouses the suspicion that for these Germans already in 1775, polygeneticism was problematic not only for scientific reasons (metatheoretical in Kant's case; substantive-empirical in Blumenbach's) but also for moral-political ones. I must dissent from the widely shared view that Blumenbach expressed strong "racialist" bias in his early texts and only came later in his career, for instance, to the defense of Blacks. There is every reason to contend that he—and even Camper—in the 1770s stood sturdily against arguments, many of them polygeneticist in spirit, which would affirm the radical inferiority of other "races"—and particularly of Blacks.

NOTES

1. Robert Bernasconi, "Who Invented the Concept of Race? Kant's Role in the Enlightenment Construction of Race," in *Race,* ed. Robert Bernasconi, (Malden, MA and Oxford: Blackwell, 2001), 11–36.

2. Wolfgang Carl, *Der schweigende Kant* (Göttingen: Vandenhoeck & Ruprecht, 1989).

3. I wish to go into the microhistory of these publications both because they shed very important light on Kant and because they suggest something about the climate in which the peculiar "speciation" of race theory we are investigating emerged in Germany. There is good reason to maintain that the text of record for Kant should be the 1777 version of his essay on race, for this is the text that entered into the public discourse of anthropology in Germany. It was an object of disputation already in 1778 by Zimmermann, and there is some reason to suspect that Blumenbach may have read it in that form. (See Erich Adickes, *Kant als Naturforscher* (Berlin: de Gruyter, 1925), vol. 2:412n.) It was also on the basis of the 1777 publication that Breitkopf contacted Kant with the proposition that he produce a more extended work on this topic. (Editorial notes to Immanuel Kant, Gesammelte Schniften-Akademie Ausgabe (Berlin: Walter de Gruyter, 1905–), vol. 2, Textausgabe, 520. Hereafter referred to as AA. See Breitkopf to Kant, AA 10:211.)

4. Immanuel Kant, "Entwurf und Ankündigung eines Collegii der physischen Geographie nebst dem Anhange einer kurzen Betrachtung über die Frage: Ob die Westwinde in unsern Gegenden darum feucht seien, weil sie über ein großes Meer streichen," (1757), AA 2:1–12.

5. Werner Stark, "Kant als akademischer Lehrer," in *Königsberg und Riga*, ed. Heinz Ischreyt (Tübingen: Niemeyer, 1995 = Zentren der Aufklärung, 2), 51–68; "Die Formen von Kants akademischer Lehre," *Deutsche Zeitschrift für Philosophie* 40 (1992): 543–562.

6. Karl Fink, "Storm and Stress Anthropology," *History of the Human Sciences* 6 (1993): 51–71.

7. Kant to Johann Heinrich Lambert, 2 Sept., 1770, AA 10:92–95.

8. Giorgio Tonelli, "Die Umwälzung von 1769 bei Kant," *Kant-Studien* 54 (1963): 369–375; Lothar Kreimendahl, *Kant—Der Durchbruch von 1769* (Cologne: Dinter, 1990).

9. Phillip Sloan, "Buffon, German Biology, and the Historical Interpretation of Biological Species," *British Journal for the History of Science* 12 (1979): 109–153, esp. 126ff.

10. I treat Kant's relation to this movement extensively in *Kant, Herder and the Birth of Anthropology* (Chicago and London: University of Chicago Press, 2002).

11. Walther Zimmerli, "'Schwere Rüstung' des Dogmatismus und 'anwendbare Eklektik': J. G. H. Feder und die Göttinger Philosophie im ausgehenden 18. Jahrhundert," *Studia Leibnitiana* 15:1 (1983), 58-71.

12. Reinhard Brandt, "Feder und Kant," *Kant-Studien* 80 (1989): 249–264.

13. See Immanuel Kant, *Vorlesungen über Enzyklopädische Philosophie*, ed. Gerhard Lehmann (Berlin: Akademie, 1961). I treat this course in the new monograph mentioned above.

14. See Christoph Meiners, *Revision der Philosophie* (Göttingen & Gotha: Johann Christian Dieteriel, 1772).

15. Ernst Platner, *Anthropologie für Ärzte und Weltweise* (1772; repr., Hildesheim: Olms, 2000).

16. Reinhard Brandt, "Kants pragmatische Anthropologie: Die Vorlesung," *Allgemeine Zeitschrift für Philosophie* 19 (1994): 41–49; Brandt and Werner Stark, "Einleitung," *Kants Vorlesungen*: Bd. II: *Vorlesungen zur Anthropologie* (AA 25:1): vii–cli.

17. Kant to Herz, end of 1773, AA 10: 38–39.

18. This is stated most explicitly in the published *Anthropology* of 1798, but it is already the basis for a revised course in anthropology after 1773, the first evidence of which we still retain being student lecture notes from 1775.

19. This is the essential philosophical challenge concerning Kant and racism, in my view. I cannot agree with the contentions about the interfusion of Kant's race theory with his transcendental philosophy offered by Emmanuel Eze, "The Color of Reason: The Idea of 'Race' in Kant's Anthropology," in *Anthropology and the German Enlightenment: Perspectives on Humanity*, ed. Katherine Faull (Lewisburg: Bucknell University Press, 1995), 200–241. I think Mark Larrimore, "Sublime Waste: Kant on the Destiny of the 'Races,'" *Canadian Journal of Philosophy*, supplementary volume 25, 1999 [= *Civilization and Oppression*, ed. Catherine Wilson], 99–125), and Robert Bernasconi (see note 1) have been more careful here. Robert Louden, (*Kant's Impure Ethics* (NY: Oxford University Press, 2000), 93–106, and Thomas Hill and Bernard Boxill, "Kant and Race," in *Race and Racism*, ed. Bernard Boxill (NY: Oxford University Press, 2001), 448–471 have made proper criticisms of endeavors such as those of Eze. That still leaves us, of course, with a substantial racism in Kant that cannot be disputed.

20. Johannes Unold, *Die ethnologischen und anthropogeographischen Anschauungen bei I Kant und J. Rein[hard] Forster* (PhD diss. Leipzig, 1886); Adickes, *Kant als Naturforscher*, 449n; Sloan, "Buffon," 125.

21. Lord Kames, *Versuche über die Geschichte des Menschen*, 2 vols. (Leipzig: Johann Friedrich Junius, 1774–75).

22. Blumenbach, "On the natural variety of mankind [1775]," in *The Anthropological Treatises of Johann Friedrich Blumenbach*, trans., and ed. Thomas Bendyshe (London: Anthropological Society, 1865), 98.

23. Beattie's response, directed at Hume, is conveniently reproduced in Emmanuel Eze, ed., *The Idea of Race in the Enlightenment* (Oxford: Blackwell, 1997), 34–37; Hunter's dissertation of 1775 is reproduced in *The Anthropological Treatises of Johann Friedrich Blummerbach,* 357–394.

24. For Kant's concerns in this light, see especially the *Blomberg Logic* and certain *Reflexionen* from the very years under consideration.

25. John H. Zammito, "'Method' versus 'Manner'? Kant's Critique of Herder's *Ideen* in the Light of the Epoch of Science, 1790–1820," in *Herder Jahrbuch/Herder Yearbook*, 1998, ed. Hans Adler and Wulf Koepke (Stuttgart: Metzler, 1998), 1–26; Hans Adler, "Ästhetische und anästhetische" Wissenschaft: Kants Herder-Kritik als Dokument moderner Paradigmenkonkurrenz," *Deutsche Vierteljahrsschrift für Literaturwissenschaft und Geistesgeschichte* 68 (1994): 66–76.

26. Adickes, *Kant als Naturforscher*, 407.

27. Kant, "Von den verschiedenen Racen der Menschen," AA 2:429.

28. Ibid., AA 2: 443.

29. J. J. Engel, ed. *Der Philosoph für die Welt*, I (Leipzig: Dyckische Buchhandlung; 1775), II (Leipzig: Dykische Buchhandlung, 1777), III (Berlin: Myliussische Buchhandlung, 1800). One would do well to consult the contents of both volumes I and II to discern how radically different in genre Kant's contribution was from the preponderantly literary balance in each volume. Again, it must be striking that Kant should so actively have *sought* to be included in this series.

30. We can discern further indications of Kant's ambitions in his correspondence with Engel and with Feder in the late 1770s, AA 10:249–257.

31. Adickes, *Kant als Naturforscher*, 449.

32. Ibid., 431.

33. Kant to Breitkopf, 1 April, 1778, AA 10: 213. The text of this letter is not included in earlier editions of AA, but may be found at http://www.ikp.uni-bonn.de/dt/forsch/kant/briefe (letter 133).

34. Bernasconi (note 2) aptly discriminates this commitment to permanence in racial types in Kant from the view shared by Buffon, Camper and many others—including Blumenbach at this point, as we shall see—that racial characteristics were reversible by the same forces which induced them originally.

35. Adickes, *Kant als Naturforscher*, 420.

36. Christoph Girtanner, *Über das Kantische Prinzip für Naturgeschichte. Ein Versuch diese Wissenschaft philosophisch zu behandeln* (Göttingen: Vandenhoeck & Ruprecht, 1796).

37. Immanuel Kant, *Anthropology from a Pragmatic Point of View* (Carbondale and Edwardsville: Southern Illinois University Press, 1978), 236; AA 7: 320.

38. Kant, "Von den verschiedenen Racen der Menschen," AA 2:432.

39. E. Adickes, *Kant als Naturforscher*, 441.

40. Ibid., 408, 414.

41. There are several other distinct shifts from 1775 to 1777. In 1775, Kant considered three criteria in empirical discriminations among human races: skin color, facial features, and general physical structure. By 1777, the only one he felt confident in upholding was skin color, because it alone held prospect of sustaining his theory of hybridity. Additionally, in 1777, Kant elaborated considerably upon his "chemical"

theory of skin coloration, offering a more elaborate theory of the impact of climate upon the chemical composition of the subcutaneous layer. Finally, Kant inserted more material on the *cultural distinctions* among human races, both anecdotally and in terms of generalizations about "national character." While already in 1775 Kant allowed himself to parrot Buffon and Cornelius de Pauw on the inferiority of Amerindians, including a footnote quite callously connecting this with failure at slave labor. In 1777, Kant added a cultural twist to his characterization of black physiological difference. Where in 1775 he had written, "in short, the negro emerged, who was well adapted to his climate: strong, fleshy, supple, with blood warmed by agitation and sluggish from the limpness of the vessels." In 1777, he wrote: "in short, the negro emerged, well suited to his climate: that is, strong, fleshy, supple, but because he is so amply provided for by his motherland, also lazy, soft and dawdling." (Immanuel Kant, "Von den verschiedenen Racen der Menschen," *Lesarten* 520; AA 2:438.)

42. Kant, "Von den verschiedenen Racen der Menschen," *Lesarten* 520; AA 2:432.

43. Ibid., AA 2:440–441.

44. Sloan, "Buffon," 130.

45. Adickes, *Kant als Naturforscher*, 416.

46. Timothy Lenoir, "Kant, Blumenbach and Vital Materialism in Germany Biology," *Isis* 71 (1980): 77–108; "The Göttingen School and the Development of Transcendental Naturphilosophie in the Romantic Era," *Studies on History of Biology* 5 (Baltimore: Johns Hopkins University Press, 1981), 111–205; "Teleology without Regrets: The Transformation of Physiology in Germany," *Studies in the History and Philosophy of Science* 12 (1981): 293–354.

47. In a panel entitled *Epigenesis in Science and Literature from Buffon to Blumenbach* which I chaired at the ASECS national conference, New Orleans, April 2001, Robert Bernasconi and Phillip Sloan presented papers on these matters: Bernasconi, "Kant and Blumenbach on the Bildungstrieb"; Sloan, "Kant and Epigenetic Embryology: The Implications of his post–1790 Philosophy."

48. Kant to Blumenbach, 5 Aug, 1790, AA 11:176–7; Kant on Blumenbach: AA, 5:424; 7:89; 7:289; 8:180.

49. He refers to him repeatedly and heatedly in his notes (e.g., *On the Natural Variety of Mankind* [1775], 98n; 103n; 109n), always condemning his arbitrary judgments.

50. Blumenbach, On the Natural Variety of Mankind [1775], 69–70.

51. Hans Pflischke, *Die Ethnographische Sammlung der Universität Göttingen, ihre Geschichte und ihre Bedeutung* (Göttingen: Vandenhoeck & Ruprecht, 1931); Rudoph Wagner,"On the Anthropological Collection of the Physiological Institute of Göttingen," in *The Anthropological Treatises of Johann Friedrich Blummenbach*, 347–355.

52. Frank Dougherty, "Christoph Meiners und Johann Friedrich Blumenbach im Streit um den Begriff der Menschenrasse," in *Die Natur des Menschen: Probleme der Physischen Anthropologie und Rassenkunde (1750–1850)*, ed. Gunter Mann and Franz Dumont (Stuttgart/NY: Gustav Fischer, 1990 = *Soemmerring Forschungen* VI), 89–111; Frank Dougherty, "Johann Friedrich Blumenbach und Samuel Thomas

Soemmerring: Eine Auseinandersetzung in anthropologischer Hinsicht?" in *Samuel Thomas Soemmerring und die Gelehrten der Goethezeit*, ed. Gunter Mann and Franz Dumont (Stuttgart/NY: Gustav Fischer, 1985 = *Soemmerring Forschungen* I), 35–56; Uta Sadji, *Der Negermythos am Ende des 18. Jahrhunderts in Deutschland* (Frankfurt/Bern/Las Vegas: Peter Lang, 1979), 222–227.

53. Dougherty, "Christoph Meiners," 91.

54. Sadji, *Negermythos*, 50–53; 222–227.

55. Rober Paul WillemVisser, *The Zoological Work of Petrus Camper (1722–1789)* (Amsterdam: Rodopi, 1985), ch 4.: "Man's Place in Nature." Visser makes clear that while Camper had taken a clear stance against claims of the racial inferiority of Blacks in an inaugural oration of 1764, he was more notorious for his lectures at Groningen in 1770s developing his idea of the "facial angle." The published fruit of this conception came only posthumously, but the oral transmission was swift and potent, and Blumenbach notes at several points in the 1775 dissertation that he has learned key features of Camper's theories from mutual acquaintances. For the most recent and complete consideration of this matter see Miriam Meijer, *Race and Aesthetics in the Anthropology of Petrus Camper (1722–1789)* (Amsterdam: Rodopi, 1999).

56. See Stephen Jay Gould, "The Geometer of Race," in *The Concept of "Race" in Natural and Social Science*, ed. Nathaniel Gates (1994; repr., NY/London: Garland, 1997), 1–5.

57. Blumenbach, On the Natural Variety of Mankind [1775], 69.

58. Ibid., 71.

59. Kames, *Sketches of the History of Man* (Edinburgh: W. Creech; London: Strahan and Cadell, 1774), 6–10; Sloan, "Buffon," 124.

60. Blumenbach, On the Natural Variety of Mankind [1775], 73.

61. Ibid., 81.

62. Ibid.

63. Ibid., 83.

64. Ibid. Blumenbach believed at this time that there were no anatomical or physiological differences in apes to account for their failure at speech: "I have myself found the uvula in apes, and the other parts of the larynx exactly like those in man." (Ibid., 84n) Later, Petrus Camper would conduct a definitive dissection of an orangutan and demonstrate that in fact this organism *did* lack anatomical features in the larynx that made speech possible.

65. Ibid. "As to those who make out the erect position to be the fomenter of disorders, they must forget both veterinary practice and the diseases which we find afflict both wretched men and fierce quadrupeds." (Ibid., 88)

66. Ibid., 91.

67. Ibid., 95.

68. Ibid., 96.

69. Ibid., 97.

70. Blumenbach, *On the Natural Variety of Mankind*, 98.

71. Ibid., 98-9.

72. Ibid., 99.

73. Ibid.

74. Ibid., 100.

75. Blumenbach,*On the Natural Variety of Mankind*, 101.

76. Ibid.

77. Ibid., 103.

78. Ibid.

79. Ibid., 107.

80. Blumenbach,*On the Natural Variety of Mankind*, 109.

81. Ibid., 111.

82. Ibid., 113.

83. See Stephen Jay Gould, "The Geometer of Race," and more extensively, *The Mismeasure of Man* (NY: W. W. Norton, 1981).

84. See Meijer, *Race and Aesthetics,* (note 55 above).

85. Blumenbach, *On the Natural Variety of Mankind [1775],* 116–117.

86. Ibid., 117.

87. Ibid., 121.

4

Kant's Conception of a Human Race

Susan M. Shell

❧

What are we to make of Kant on race? No aspect of Kant's thought is as distressing to the contemporary reader as his seeming conviction as to the mental, and perhaps moral, inferiority of the nonwhite races. And yet few thinkers have more forcefully defended the equal rights of nonwhite peoples, or spoken out more emphatically against the predatory colonial practices of Europe. Consider, for example, the following passage from *Perpetual Peace* (1795):

> If we compare with [man's cosmopolitan] end the *inhospitable* con-
> duct of the civilized states of our continent, . . . the injustice that
> they display in *visiting* countries and peoples (which in their case is
> the same as *conquering* them) stretches to the point of horror. America,
> the Negro countries, . . . etc., etc., were looked upon at the time of
> their discovery as ownerless territories; for the native inhabitants
> were counted as nothing. . . . The worst (or from a moral point of
> view . . . the best) thing about all of this is that the [conquering]
> countries do not benefit from their violence. . . . And all this is the
> work of powers who make endless ado about their piety, and who
> wish to be considered as chosen ones while drinking in injustice like
> water. (AA 8: 358–9)

But consider, too, the following passage, from Kant's unpublished reflections:

(Whites:) contain all natural motive springs in affects and passions, all talents, all predispositions to culture and civilization and can obey as well as rule.

They are the only ones who constantly progress toward perfection. . . . Blacks can become disciplined and cultivated but never truly civilized. . . .

All races will become exterminated/uprooted [*ausgerottet*] (Americans and Blacks cannot govern themselves. They thus serve only as slaves) only not the Whites. The stubbornness of Indians in their usages is the reason why they do not melt down with the Whites into a single people. It is not good that they intermix. Spanish in Mexico.

On the race of Whites, who have brought about all revolutions in the world. Nomads have only brought about violent revolutions, not ones that sustain themselves. . . . Our (ancient) history of man reliably proceeds only from the white race. (AA 15: 878–9)

Equally disturbingly, Kant seems to single out a special, privileged role for German "blood" (at least in his unpublished notes): "German blood is engrafted onto all (other European families); Spirit (Roman) and discipline (German)" (AA 15: 880).

So, what is it to be? Is Kant the avatar of the UN Charter (as is generally believed) or of the ravings of Houston Stewart Chamberlain? To put the matter more succinctly and pertinently, is there a *necessary* link between the critical philosophy and Kant's notions about race? In what follows, I hope to provide some suggestions toward an answer.

This must be said on Kant's behalf. Kant's most unqualified published remarks on racial inferiority precede the appearance of the *Critique of Pure Reason* (1781). Such remarks precede, in other words, his considered, final view as to the ultimate radical independence of our intelligible character and its sensible, or physically conditioned embodiment. There is, in short, a pattern of diminishing public reliance on empirical conclusions as to the mental or spiritual inferiority of nonwhite races, following on Kant's discovery of the transcendental principle of autonomy, which imposes an unconditional moral duty on all human beings whatever their physical make up or temperament. In the face of that unconditionality, the inconclusive character of present knowledge about racial difference seems to strike Kant with new force; in his review of J. G. Herder's Ideas of 1785, for example, he admits that on the basis of the contradictory data available one may prove *"if one wishes,"* "that Americans and Blacks are races which have sunk below the level of other members of the species in terms of spiritual predispositions (*Geistesanlagen*)— or alternatively, *on the evidence of no less plausible accounts*, that they should be regarded as the equal, in respect to natural predisposition (*Naturanlage*), to all the other inhabitants of the world." (AA 8: 62; emphasis added) Finally, there is the simple fact that the published version of Kant's anthropology lectures, which appeared in 1798, contains almost no direct reference to race at all (though it includes a lengthy discussion of innate differences among the European nations).[1]

To be sure, Kant also notes in passing, in the same publication, the probable "unwholesomeness" (*Unzuträglichkeit*) for the human race (*Menschengeschlecht*)—all "so-called philanthropy not withstanding"— of a "mixture of stems (*Stämme*) (by extensive conquests)"—a mixture in which the stems' diverse characters would gradually be lost (AA 7: 320). (We are thus given a racially less-innocent reason for Kant's championing of the rights of non-European peoples against European conquest.)

In his review of Herder, Kant suggests that without the "preparatory labor" (*Vorarbeiten*) of a "critical-historical head" to put right the facts as to the question of racial difference, all efforts at a philosophic history of man must appear as the ruinous (*baufälliger*) hypotheses of systems erected on wavering foundations (*wankende Grundlage*). What makes Kant, whose *Idea for a Universal History from a Cosmopolitan Point of View* had appeared the previous year, sure of his own ability to separate the racist wheat from the falsely philanthropic chaff? To begin to answer that question, it is first necessary to turn to Kant's long-standing interest in the concept of race, which he claims to be the first to adequately define.

Kant's interest in physical and moral differences among men of different regions of the Earth is evident as early as 1763 in his essay *Observations on the Feeling of the Beautiful and the Sublime*, and in the *Announcement* of his course in 1765–66 on Physical Geography. The first elaboration of a precise concept of race, however, appears only in the 1770s—a decade in which Kant, absorbed in work on his incipient critical system, published little else. Kant's definition of the concept of race, from which he hardly wavered thereafter, combines an observable fact with a singular a priori principle. The fact is the phenomenon of hybridization, or the invariable inheritance by offspring of the differing characteristics of both parents. Such inheritance is to be distinguished from the equally normal case in which the characteristics of both parents are not invariably inherited. In the former case, the qualities of the parents are blended in the offspring (as with the child of a dark and a light-skinned parent). In the latter case, this blending does not occur (the child of a blue-eyed and a brown-eyed parent will have blue *or* brown eyes, not eyes that are invariably hazel).

The phenomenon of hybridization provides Kant with powerful evidence for his favored theory of epigenesis, which insists upon the contribution of both parents to the act of reproduction, as distinguished from competing theories of encapsulated "evolution." But this phenomenon also poses an apparent challenge to his understanding of organic form, and to the principle of constancy that underlies it. Organisms, according to Kant, are (or must at least be judged by us to be) closed systems of reciprocal causation, in which each element exists for the sake of every other. Mechanical causation, on the other hand, flows in only one direction. Hence, the only kind of cause we have on hand to render the possibility of an organic system thinkable is, on the analogy of our own practical rationality, that of a purposive artifact, arranged according to an idea (say the watchmaker's idea of a watch). To be sure, unlike an artifact, such a system is made up of elements that are themselves purposes (or must be thought of by us as purposes) for one another. (Hence, the best example, or analogy, for organicism may well be political—for example, the "complete transformation" (*Umbildung*) by which a people constitutes itself reciprocally, with a view to the idea of a republican government.)[2] And unlike an artifact, such a system can reproduce itself through the assimilation of foreign matter according to a determinate rule.

The key to this conception of organic form is a principle of germinal constancy, to which Kant clings (almost) unwaveringly, from his very early *Universal Natural History and Theory of the Heavens* (1755) onward:[3] nothing can affect the germ which constitutes an organism's original inheritance from the first propagator of its species. How, then, to reconcile this principle with the fact of hybridization? That fact suggests either that there are some invariably inherited characteristics that are not universal to the species, or that the parents of a hybrid descend from different original stems. Kant rejects the latter, polygenetic hypothesis on the grounds that the possibility of fertile interbreeding between different species is even more difficult to explain than the problem at issue. The only ready conclusion—a conclusion that constitutes the essential basis of his concept of race—is that the parents descend from common, original stock in which different, invariably inherited characteristics subsequently developed. (The concept of "race" is itself a "hybrid" of empirical observation and determinate, a priori principle.) Kant suspects that these differences arose as a response to the varying conditions (as revealed by geological research) that impinged on a dispersed humanity in the earliest epochs of the species. But unlike other thinkers, who posit a direct, mechanical modification of the human germ, Kant understands these environmental effects as merely occasioning the development of predispositions present in the species from the beginning. The original man and woman, so to speak, had the germinal potentiality to become white, black, yellow or red, depending on the demands of the environment in which they or their descendents subsequently found themselves. Once activated, these *predispositions* became permanent, preventing activation of the others or reversion to a pre-racialized germinal state (though Kant entertained the notion, early on, that a future merger of the races might bring back the original stock in a fully developed form—a pro-miscegenationist Utopia he later came to abandon).[4] Kant is thus able to explain the fitness of certain races for a specific region of the Earth, without calling upon a special providence at odds with science as he understands it.[5]

Kant's understanding of organic form is indebted to the Baconian critique of traditional (Aristotelian) taxonomic schemes based on visible similarities.[6] The charge of experimentally fruitless arbitrariness to which species classification is vulnerable, in Bacon's view, is met, for Kant, by Georges-Louis Leclerc Comte de Buffon's definition of a species: that is, the charge is met not by shared looks, but by a common capacity for fertile reproduction.[7] The criterion of fertility has the advantage of being open to an experimental-experiential touchstone.[8] It has the disadvantage, however, of allowing for a plasticity of species that is in principle unlimited: nothing intrinsic to that criterion precludes a walrus, say, from giving birth to fertile kittens, or suggests that the common specieshood of parents and offspring in such a case would be anything but normal. Kant's insistence on the teleological principle of an original and unchanging germ provides against such concerns by adding to Buffon's criterion of specieshood—shared capacity for fertile reproduction—the specification that reproduction take place according to a fixed or determinate rule.[9] Accordingly, species can be understood genetically (as with Buffon) without ceasing to be teleological in a way that identifies each species with a specific and determinate character.[10]

Kant's innovation not only assimilates genetic explanation and teleology; it also gives teleology a "historical" dimension (albeit one different from the non-teleological "history" of Buffon) that is absent from its Aristotelian counterpart; indeed, Kant's insistence that a genuinely scientific account of living beings must be "historical," rather than merely "descriptive," distinguishes his teleology from the traditional classification of living kinds on the basis of a specific "look."[11]

Where Aristotle distinguishes the efficient and the formal or final cause (the "out of which" and the "toward which" of a living being), Kant collapses those causes into a single principle (or generative "force"). For Aristotle there is nothing untoward about flies emerging out of rotting meat. For Kant, on the contrary, such a *generatio equivoca* is literally unthinkable. Kant's understanding of species in terms of genetically uniform descent from a common stem has the advantage of permitting an empirical test of specieshood (along Buffonian lines), while maintaining the relevance of species character.

There is still another way in which Kant's genetic teleology contrasts with the traditional teleology of Aristotle. For the latter, the "toward which" expressed by living beings is linked with a notion of their perfection (or specific "nature"), available (as with natural "kinds" in general) through our immediate awareness of the world in its heterogeneous complexity. For Kant there is no such immediate awareness of natural kinds. Instead, living beings present themselves (or are adjudged by us) as "organisms," i.e., as self-maintaining, self-replicating systems of mutually dependent tools (or "organs"). We understand living beings teleologically, on Kant's account, not because we have immediate access to their "natures," but because we cannot think the possibility of such a living system without presupposing a concept of what the organism is "to be" in the mind of some hypothetical, infinitely artful author.

Kant's teleological innovation replaces the old Aristotelian "perfections" with "marks," or empirical indications of the peculiar predispositions that equip a species for survival under conditions that may, in turn, vary over time. (Thus a certain species of bird has a double layer of feathers, to equip it for the changes of climate it may encounter over an extended period of time.) Such natural-historical changes are themselves subject to scientific study (e.g., geology). And, indeed, such study is necessary if one is to adequately judge the purposiveness of specific organic features. The price of Kant's approach, however, is a frank admission that the unchanging lineage the approach presumes posits an origin that is beyond the limits of experience. Natural history, or "the natural study of origins," is thus both necessary, if one is to properly understand the character of a particular species, and necessarily "fragmentary," inasmuch as the plan of its infinitely artful author is regulative for human understanding rather than constitutive.

Finally, Kant's non-Aristotelian teleology of nature separates our judgment as to the beauty of a living being (which falls for him under the rubric of the "aesthetic") from our objective appraisal of it as purposive—an appraisal that looks not (as with Aristotle) to what is "fine" but only to the survival of the individual and the reproduction of the species. What is beautiful or fine, for Kant, is "purposive *without* purpose"—or, alternatively (in the case of the sublime), only *negatively* purposive as an exhibition of the ascendancy of reason over nature. Kant's infinitely artful author of organic beings is, it seems, an artisan and not an artist.

As a consequence of such considerations, a definition of the human species—an answer to the question, "what is man?"—becomes newly problematic.[12] Man, like other living beings, must be judged to be naturally purposive; and yet, unlike nonrational organisms, man can have purposes of his own. An adequate Kantian definition of man would thus have to combine such purposiveness with the (rational) freedom to defy it. An adequate definition of man would require a "natural history" of reason—a history, in other words, that is literally inconceivable.[13] Reasons such as these eventually lead Kant to characterize our unmeetable need for such a history as itself humanly defining.[14]

We are finally in a position to better understand Kant's confident dismissal of Herder's approach, in his *Ideas*, to human history—a dismissal that proves to turn on the two parties' respective attitudes toward "race" as Kant defines it (AA 8:62). Herder, who had studied with Kant in the 1760s and 1770s, had some reason to think that his work would meet with Kant's approval, and he was deeply offended by the first installment of Kant's review. Herder responded with pointed criticisms of Kant in the later parts of the *Ideas*—criticisms that Kant, in turn, took up in the second and third installments of his review.

In doing so, Kant grants that he and Herder have much in common: each rightly rejects both the system of evolutionary preformation and a purely mechanical account of organic form. Moreover, Kant accepts Herder's alternative appeal to a vital principle (or "genetic force"), in explaining human variation, so long as it is understood as an expression of the development of germinal rudiments *(Keime)* and/or predispositions already present in the original stock from which the organism derives. Herder, on the contrary, grants to genitive force a seemingly limitless plasticity. Kant's vital principle is "purposive," in the sense of being guided from within, according to a plan mapped out in advance (by a hypothetical author), and is thus intrinsically self-limiting. Hence, Kant's reiterated complaint that Herder, despite his protestations of reliance on experience, wanders in a metaphysical wasteland.

Kant's insistence on the self-limiting character of natural production is nowhere clearer than in a passage in the *Critique of Judgment* in which he grants the sheer possibility of "generatio homonyma," or generation of one species out of another, and thus yields more to the claims of Herderian plasticity than he had been willing to do elsewhere. What is most interesting

about Kant's admission, for our purposes, is where it stops. Mother Earth may have given birth initially "to creatures of a less purposive form, with these then giving birth to others that became better adapted to their place of generation and to their relations to one another." And one species may even have arisen out of another (although such interspecies transformation is without experiential example). Eventually, however, nature's womb "rigidified, ossified, and confined itself to bearing definite species that would no longer degenerate, so that the diversity remained as it had turned out at the end of operation of that fertile formative force" (AA 5: 419–20). The finite fecundity of nature, where the development of *species* is concerned, is a necessary corollary of the rational demand for knowledge of origins.[15] Without the assumption of such finitude, one could no longer presume to seek experiential traces of nature's purpose, and natural history, as the investigation of unknowable origins, would cease entirely to be reasonable. As he puts it in *The Definition of a Concept of a Human Race* (1785).

> If the magic force of imagination, or the artfulness of man is given to have a capacity in animal bodies to alter the generative force itself . . . one would no longer know from which original nature may have proceeded, or how much it might deviate from that original, and, since human imagination knows no boundaries, into what grotesque forms of genuses and species it might finally degenerate/run wild [*verwildern*]. . . . The limits of reason [thus] . . . broken through, illusions would penetrate through the gap by the thousands. (AA 8: 97)

But racial differentiation—or the permanent, invariable inheritance of certain climatically induced features not universal to the species as a whole—is, for Kant, the quintessential, observable example of such germinal self-limitation. Each racial germ is ready in advance, in the original human stock, for whatever circumstances might occasion its development. And complete emergence of each racial germ (unlike those destined to develop in the species as a whole) precludes emergence of the others. Kant thus sharply distinguishes between the fixed transformations that express potentialities limited to race, and the unlimited aptitude of humankind generally, as the species whose purpose-setting capacity gives purpose to nature as a whole.[16] The concept of race turns the phenomenon of hybridization—which would otherwise challenge the principle of germinal constancy—into the latter's natural-historical bulwark.

The teleological concept of race, applied to the empirical phenomenon of climatically related, hybridizing features, sets a standard for the more adequate approach to natural history that Kant will take up in *On the Use of Teleological Principles* (1788). Though the concept of race cannot by itself determine how far climatically related differences extend, it can focus empirical inquiry, e.g. by raising to preeminence the question whether a given feature is invariably and permanently inheritable. Natural history may never move beyond "wavering hypotheses"; still, it is science of a kind (AA 8: 162). And teleologically guided, empirical investigation of racial difference is Kant's readiest example of such natural-historical inquiry.

None of these considerations, each of which relates race to certain visible climatic adaptations (e.g., skin color), requires one to conclude that nonwhite races are inferior in their intellectual or moral capacities. What, then, so attracts Kant to that conclusion, which is not directly entailed by his concept of race as such?

Kant's views as to the inferiority of non-European peoples—a view that predates his articulated concept of race—receives its most emphatic expression in his early *Observations on the Feeling of the Beautiful and the Sublime* (1763). That essay links the particular superiority of European "spirit," not to any explicitly racial character, but, rather, to a unique aesthetic sense fostered through the courtly relations of the sexes—an unparalleled combination, if you will, of a feeling for the sublime (shared by Asiatics and by North American Indians) and a feeling for ideal female beauty (unknown on any other continent). To be sure, Kant's argument, in that essay, is beset by a too-often-neglected irony: the words of an African whom Kant notoriously cites not only immediately belie the "cowardice" that Kant attributes to all Africans, but threaten to expose the tenuousness, in Kant's own mind, of a claim crucial to his thesis as a whole—namely, that European women deserve the reverence that is paid to them.[17]

The notion that reason is decisively affected by the conditions of its embodiment—a notion that reaches to the heart of Kant's *Critique of Pure Reason*—is already in play in Kant's earliest published essay: *On the True Estimation of Living Force* (1749), and it receives its most colorful expression in the appendix to *The Universal Natural History and Theory of the Heavens* (1755). There Kant postulates an interplanetary community of living beings, whose spiritual force varies in inverse proportion to the density of their matter and/or their distance from the sun. Toward the center Kant locates spiritual beings "sunk" in such a torpor of physical grossness "as to border on unreason." At the outer limits of the system he posits the existence of beings whose material "rarity" "lifts them up" to greater freedom of action and allows their thought to approach the instantaneousness of divine comprehension. Between these two extremes, earthbound man occupies a "dangerous" middle road.

Neither vaporously raised (like the Saturnians) to effortless generalizations, nor stuck (like the Mercurians) in guiltless inertia, man finds himself torn between "wisdom and unreason." He alone (or with the Martians) must not only struggle to achieve the perfection of which he is capable, but also accept the blame for his own failure (AA 1: 366). In some human beings, "the capacity to combine abstract concepts, and to master the inclination of the passions through free application of the understanding, comes late," if ever. And in all, the capacity to generalize:

> is rather weak, and serves the lower forces over which it ought to rule, and in whose government consists the excellence of man's nature. When one regards the nature of most men, man seems to be created as a plant, to draw sap and grow, to propagate his kind, and ... die. ... He would indeed be the most contemptible of all creatures, if hope of the future did not lift him up, if there were not a period of full development in store for the forces shut up in him. ... If one seeks the cause of the obstacles that keep human nature in such deep abasement, it will be found in the grossness of the matter in which his spiritual part is sunk. ... The nerves and fluids of his brain deliver only gross and unclear concepts. ... and ... he cannot counterbalance sufficiently powerful representations against the enticements of sensible perceptions. (AA 1: 356)

Rational clarification is thus:

> a fatiguing condition, in which the soul cannot set itself without opposition, and out of which the soul would, through the natural inclination of the bodily machine, soon fall back into a passive condition, in which sensory enticements govern and determine all its actions. (AA 1: 356)

Half a decade later, Jean Jacques Rousseau would teach Kant to give up his Saturn-envy. Post-Rousseau, Kant relinquishes his pride in theoretical achievement, and his contempt for ordinary people. Thereafter, he sets his store in human dignity and would regard himself as less useful than the common worker, were everything he did not calculated to establish the common rights of man (AA 20: 40).[18]

Given this new elevation of the republican idea, Kant does not so much abandon his earlier progressive coordination of mental and bodily refinement as transpose it onto an Earth-centered, or "geographic" plane. His 1765–66 *Announcement* includes a course on physical geography in which Kant hopes to provide a unified account of the physical and moral relations of the human species (AA 2: 312–13). The first, "physical" section of the geography contains the "real foundation of all history." A second, "moral" section "lay[s] before the eyes a great map of the [natural and moral differences within] the human species," without which one could "only with difficulty" make "general judgments about man." And a third, "political" section aims to describe the "condition of states and nations throughout the world," a condition that constitutes, as he puts it, "the reciprocal relation of those physical and moral forces" (AA 2: 313). Kant's incipient account of racial difference (he does not yet have the concept of race in hand) is thus part of a larger attempt to gain an overview of man's worldly relations in their totality. Kant's course on geography is both *for* the young and—as insofar as it supplies the unity without which "all our knowledge is nothing but a fragmentary patchwork"— a making-youthful (*Verjüngung*) of science itself.

His first published essay on race, *Of the Different Human Races* (1775), is an expanded version of part of another announcement of courses, which now include anthropology as a separate subject. Anthropology's purpose— earlier described, along with that of physical geography, as the maintenance of "social intercourse" (AA 2: 313)—is now said to be "pragmatic" knowledge of the world (AA 2: 443). But how is knowledge of specific advantages and of limitations of non-European peoples pragmatically useful to Kant's young audience? One can only guess (since these courses are accompanied by courses in ethics and metaphysics that stress the dignity of all men), that its main purpose is to prepare that audience for what Kant regards as conscientious and enlightened world-citizenship (cf. AA 7: 120). The intended effect is—evidently—not to encourage plunder of Europe's inferiors but to hearten youthful efforts at spiritual and moral self-conquest. Here, he seems to tell his youthful charges, are the superior tools and talents that nature has given you to achieve a common human goal. If you fail to use them well, you have only yourself to blame. Pragmatic anthropology, as he later puts it, is concerned, not with what men should do, or with what they will do, but with what they can and should make of themselves.

Kant's published *Anthropology from a pragmatic point of view* (1798) adds the precision that knowledge is properly "pragmatic" not when it is an extensive knowledge of things in the world—for example, the animals, plants and minerals of various lands and climates—but only when it is knowledge of man as a *"world citizen."* "Accordingly," he adds, "even knowledge of the races of men as produced by the play of nature is [only theoretical and] not yet . . . pragmatic" (AA 7:120). Such theoretical conclusions, it seems, have no direct implications for moral and political conduct. What the non-European may be able to make of himself is his own pragmatic concern, which it is up to him to assume, to the extent that he is able. (If he is unable to take on that concern, to him Kant reserves the prospect of another life—another role of the embodying dice—in which to develop his latent rational faculties.)[19] In the meantime, Kant's published anthropology has the advantage of providing to the reading public "exhaustive" headings around which useful and entertaining information can be collected. Anthropology is thus popular science in the deepest sense: each reader is invited to contribute his own insights under the appropriate division. In this way "the labors of the lovers of this study divide themselves of their own accord, and become united, through unity of plan, into a single whole" (*Anthropology* AA 7: 122). By its singular plan of organization (which in the published version includes, without filling in, the heading of "race"), Kant's *Anthropology* sets in motion a human machine, fueled by "delight," through which anthropology—a study that would otherwise remain merely fragmentary—can perfect itself "pragmatically."

The peculiar interplay between what we are accountable for, and what we are not, in our own moral development, finds remarkable expression in a note from Kant's last extended public treatment on race. After due disclaimers as to the present inconclusiveness of such reports, Kant cites the (not insignificant) views of one M. Spengel, who, in responding to Ramsey's effort to use black slaves as free labor, notes "that among the many thousands of freed blacks . . . encountered in England and America," not one "carried on a business that one could properly call work *(Arbeit)*." "Should one not conclude from this," Kant observes:

> that beyond the *capacity* to work, there exists an immediate drive toward activity, independent of all enticement [*Anlockung*] (and, especially, the maintaining of activity that is called perseverance [*Emsigkeit*])—a drive that is interwoven especially with certain natural predispositions; and that Indians as well as Blacks bring and pass on no more of this impulse [*Antrieb*] in other climes than was necessary for their maintenance in their old motherland; and that this inner predisposition as little disappears as those outwardly visible. For the much reduced needs in those lands, and the small effort [*Mühe*] needed to provide for them, required no great predisposition to activity (AA 8: 174n.).

Kant is here willing to venture a tentative conclusion (because the critical-historical *Vorarbeiten* are now further advanced?) from which his earlier review of Herder refrained: nonwhite races are inwardly inferior to the white race. At the same time, one is struck by Kant's equivocation on the crucial question whether those nonwhite races should be blamed for their lack of perseverance. Kant's formulation has it both ways: insofar as industry or *Emsigkeit* is called a "drive" *(Trieb)*, it is distinguished from "natural Anlagen," with which it is said merely to be "interwoven." Insofar as *Emsigkeit* is deemed an "impulse" *(Antrieb)*, on the other hand, it is itself identified as an "inner Anlage" (and, indeed, as one that is passed on invariably).[20] As with the spiritual hierarchy of the *Universal History and Theory of the Heavens*, composed over thirty years earlier, human virtue is a function of one's willingness to make an effort, a willingness the precise moral status of which remains obscure. This ambiguity is especially important, given Kant's late insistence (in *Religion within the Limits of Reason Alone*) that our willingness to make an effort is, in the last analysis, the *only* thing that is morally imputable to us.[21] The responsibility of the inferior races for their lack of development—their unwillingness, so to speak, to make an effort— is no less morally ambiguous.

The issue is all the more pointed, given the attention paid in Kant's essay *On the Use of Teleological Principles in Philosophy*, to the "work" of human reason as such. Torn between the dual requirements of mechanical and teleological explanation, reason keeps itself in bounds by using teleology, not to escape the "free" labor of empirical inquiry but to pursue it the more effectively and systematically.[22] Accordingly, Kant defends his earlier rejection of the derivation of all species from a common source on the grounds that such an hypothesis would be altogether fruitless:

> There is nothing here to make the investigator of nature recoil, as from a monster [a recoil of which Kant's reviewer had accused him][23] (for it is a game that many have entertained, but have given up because nothing came of it); the investigator would, however, be repelled, inasmuch as he strayed imperceptibly from the fruitful soil of natural investigation to the wasteland [*Wüste*]of metaphysics. Concerning this I know a not unmanly fear, namely, repulsion from all that unbends/releases [*abspannt*] reason from its first principles and permits it to wander in unbounded imaginings. . . . True metaphysics recognizes the boundaries of human reason, and, among others, this hereditary defect [*Erbfehler*] that it can never disavow [*verläugnen*]: namely, that it should not and cannot devise a priori fundamental forces (because it would in this case contrive merely empty concepts), but can go no further than to reduce to the smallest possible number those of which experience teaches (insofar as they are distinguished in appearance, though they may be fundamentally identical.). . . . But

of a fundamental force (which we know only through the relation
of cause and effect), we can give no other concept and find no
other appellation than that which is taken from the effect and which
expresses precisely this relation. (AA 8: 180)

Fundamental forces cannot be posited *ad libitem* (though it is our specific, "hereditary flaw" to wish to do so), but must be met with in the "fruitful
soil" of experience, where we know such forces only by their effects. Absent
this principle (as in Herder's metaphysical wasteland), one could explain
"everything one wished, the way one wished," and reason would not have to
make an effort (*Mühe*) (AA 8: 180–81).

Herder's implicit identification of force and substance destroys reason's
self-motivating purchase on the world—the "ambiguous standpoint" that arises
from reason's "contradictory demands" for knowledge (which, for us, is always merely "knowledge of effects") and for access to the source of those
effects. As "the natural investigation of origins," history (*Geschichte*) marks
the center of that ambiguous standpoint (AA 8: 163).

The tension between what reason seeks and what it is capable of
finding tempts it constantly, either to confuse its regulative ideas with
objects of knowledge (in which case, it succumbs to "dialectical illu-
sion"), or (as with Herder) to replace them with ideas of the imagination.
By signifying both what is to be *sought* in experience with a view to the
investigation of origins, *and* the limits to which such inquiry can be pushed,
Kant's concept of race helps reason meet, without collapse, the contradictory demands it makes upon itself. And yet, in extending the criteria of
racial difference, beyond skin color, to—above all—*Emsigkeit*, he also
betrays his uncertainty as to the ground of reason itself. If human reason
is self-generating, we must trim our hopes of nature favoring reason's
purposes, and with it, the strength of our conviction that the ideas of
reason are more than idle, and hence imaginary, wishes. If human reason
is not self-generating, but owes its origin to certain natural *Anlagen*, it is
difficult to see how humanity can, as Kant insists, take credit for itself.
(Herder, by way of contrast, is content to credit our development to foreign influence.)[24] Kant's tentative solution is to let us take credit, not for
the origin of our reason but for the effort we employ in cultivating it. And
yet, as the note from the essay *On the Use of Teleological Principles in
Philosophy* reveals, even this ability or willingness to make an effort may
(or may not) derive from qualities that are differentially inherited.[25] At the
very least, they may, as Kant puts it, be "interwoven" with such qualities.
The question as to the spiritual aptitude of nonwhite races—a question
that Kant seems never to have fully settled in his own mind—is insepa-
rable from the problem of human origins generally.

CONCLUSION

One is reminded, in conclusion, of Kant's punning linkage, at the beginning of *On the Use of Teleological Principles*, of "race" (*Rasse*) with "root" or "reason" (as in *radicaler*)—race's etymological source (AA 8: 163).[26] Since human reason is itself, according to Kant, a hybrid (*Bastart*), whose laudable efforts toward self-union run the constant risk of straying into unproductive wastelands,[27] it is no wonder that Kant was fascinated by the phenomenon of race as he perceived it, and that he was both attracted and—even more—repelled by the prospect of racial intermixture. As the literal inhabitants of unproductive wastelands, the idle races of Africa and of America are nature's way of guaranteeing human occupation of the world, while leaving it entirely to man to make that occupation fruitful. The idle races are as far as nature can go in signifying man's essential worldliness without sapping the "drive to activity" with which the cosmopolitan idea is necessarily associated. The idle races, in their very idleness, provide double assurance that cosmopolis is possible and hence no idle dream. They show, by their effortless existence, that nature, which thus fitted men for survival over the entire surface of the Earth, cooperates in such a cosmopolitan scheme; and they show, by the evident contrast between their idle ways and those of Europe, that the latter peoples are naturally suited for accomplishing that cosmopolitan scheme. In the absence of an *image* of cosmopolitan perfection—an absence on which the critical philosophy insists—the arrested development of the nonwhite races provides tangible evidence that European man, at least, is heading in the right direction.[28] The non-European peoples (especially those of Africa and of America) contribute to the achievement of man's moral destiny on Earth, less directly than in the manner of an inner wasteland, providing an historically emergent humanity with a means of gauging the distance it has traveled from its (otherwise unknowable) inner point of origin—that is, a means of measuring its progress. Racial theory is in this sense a direct, though necessarily muted, offshoot of Kant's efforts toward an a priori history of the human race.[29] Race is the natural-historical trace of man's mysteriously hybrid character.

NOTES

1. Instead, Kant refers the reader to C.G. Girtanner's *Ueber das kantische Prinzip für die Naturgeschichte* (Göttingen: bei Vandenhoek und Ruprecht, 1796), as "in keeping with my [Kant's] principles" [cf. Gesammelte Schriften=Akademie Ausgabe (Berlin: Walter de Gruyter, 1905–), 7: 320 hereafter referred to as AA. Girtanner's comments on the moral and intellectual differences among races largely repeat Kant's own views;

they are balanced by an insistence, with which Kant might be presumed to concur, on the importance of culture (in the sense of cultivation) for the full development of people of every race (see especially pp. 219–20). On Girtanner's relation to Kant and Johann Friedrich Blumenbach, see Robert Bernasconi, "Who Invented the Concept of Race?," in *Race*, ed. Robert Bernasconi (Oxford: Blackwell, 2001), 16–19.

2. Kant, *Critique of Judgment*, AA 5: 375n.

3. Kant, *Critique of Judgment*, AA 5: 420n.

4. See Kant, *Reflections on Anthropology*, AA 15: 635, 637, 650, and 781.

5. Compare Mark Larrimore's provocative suggestion that according to Kant's deeper view of the matter, the formation of distinct races is the "wasteful" consequence of a premature dispersal of human beings still lacking artful means to survive under extreme climatic conditions. See Larrimore, "Sublime Waste: Kant on the Destiny of the 'Races,' " *Canadian Journal of Philosophy* (1999): 99–125. Such a deeper (and unpublished) view would take nothing away from the usefulness of anthropological study of the sort described below. Human history is intrinsically, for Kant, both purposive and wasteful (or beautiful and sublime).

6. See, for example, Sir Francis Bacon, *Great Instauration* preface.

7. According to Buffon, a species is "a constant succession of similar individuals that can reproduce together." See Georges-Louis Leclerc Comte de Buffon *Histoire Naturelle* (Paris: de l'imprimerie royale, 1749), 4: 384–5; cited and discussed in Bernasconi, "Who Invented the Concept," p. 16.

8. At least in principle. In practice (ironically enough!) it condemned investigators (as Blumenbach was later to complain) to long and often fruitless efforts to get many animals from different regions of the world to copulate. See Johann Friedrich Blumenbach, *Uber die naturlichen Verschiedenheiten im Menschengeschlechte* (Leipzig: Breitkopf und Hartel, 1798), 67–9; cited in Bernasconi, "Who Invented the Concept," p. 18.

9. *Of the Different Human Races* (AA 2: 430); *On the Use of Teleological Principles in Philosophy,* (AA 8: 165). By way of contrast, Buffon, who was generally committed to the fixity of species, was open to the possibility of indeterminate variation. See *Histoire naturelle* vol. 4: 215–16; cf. 385–6. Ultimately, fertile progeny, and not shared looks, serves as the decisive basis for Buffonian classification.

10. Kant's insistence that the notion of purpose guide, rather than foreclose, inquiry into mechanical causes answers the (further) Baconian objection that teleological taxonomy is intrinsically unfruitful.

11. See Kant, *On the Use of Teleological Principles,* (AA 8: 161–64).

12. See Kant, *Anthropology from a pragmatic point of view,* AA 9: 321; 331: the *Bestimmung* of man is not a concept, but a practically regulative idea through which we characterize *ourselves*. Cf. *Jäsche Logic,* AA 9:25: all of philosophy can be "fundamentally" reckoned as an answer to the question, "what is man?"

13. Accordingly, Kant's conjectural account of the beginning of human history begins with a speaking couple (AA 8: 110). Reason cannot be derived from the nonrational. And material nature cannot itself be rational.

14. Kant, *Critique of Judgment*, AA 5: 400–1.

15. Kant allows nature a greater, though still fixed, fecundity where human *variety* is concerned—for example, the uniqueness of each human face: "A variety is a hereditary peculiarity . . . that does not invariably reproduce itself. . . . Concerning . . . human . . . variety, . . . we may regard nature as forming, not in full freedom, but in the same way as with racial characters, which develop . . . from original predispositions." Our ability to recognize a portrait painting as "true," even without knowing the original, indicates that "in all probability" the variety among human beings was purposively inscribed in the original stem in order to establish, and, in successive generations, to develop, "the greatest variety in order to facilitate an infinite variety of purposes, just as the difference among races establishes different, but more essential purposes." In the latter case, however, such difference, established in the most ancient times, "prevails," allowing no new forms to emerge or old ones to become extinguished. The former case, on the other hand—"at least according to our knowledge"—seems to announce "a nature inexhaustible in new characters (as much outer as inner)" (AA 8: 165–66). Kant thus allows for the possibility of, say, artistic "genius" without attributing to nature a creative "freedom" that would violate the boundary between the living and the nonliving, and, with it, the integrity of reason itself.

16. Cf. Kant, *Critique of Judgment,* (AA 5: 431–32): "Producing in a rational being an aptitude for desired *(beliebigen)* purposes in general (hence in accordance with that being's freedom) is *culture.* Hence culture is the only ultimate purpose *(letzte Zweck)* that we have cause to attribute to nature with respect to the human species." The final purpose *(Endzweck),* on the other hand, which requires no other purpose as a condition of its possibility—that is, which "is to exist necessarily"—depends on nothing other than the sheer "idea of it." Hence, only in man, and indeed, only in man as a moral subject, do we find "unconditional legislation in regard to purposes," on account of which man can be a "final purpose to which all of nature is teleologically subordinated" (5: 435–36). Racial difference marks the gap between those aptitudes that initially fit man for survival and the freedom that is the necessary condition of man's moral perfection.

17. See Susan M. Shell, "Kant as Propagator: 'Observations on the Feeling of the Beautiful and the Sublime,' " *Eighteenth-Century Studies* 35, no. 3 (2002): 455–68.

18. See Kant's unpublished "Notes on 'Observations of the Feeling of the Beautiful and the Sublime' " (1764). See *Bemerkungen in den »Beobachtungen über das Schöne and Erhabene«,* ed. Marie Rischmüller (Hamburg: Felix Meiner, 1991), 38.

19. See Kant, *Lectures on Metaphysics* [Metaphysics L] AA 28: 290–99; Metaphysics K2 AA 28: 766–77.

20. Compare Kant's insistence, in his 1793 *Lectures on Ethics* [Vigilantius], that man is at all times capable of acting virtuously (AA 27: 570). One can overcome even temperament and [empirical] character. *(Reflexionen, AA* 15: 866) On the other hand, it is difficult to acquire a [moral] character "if *Naturanlagen* do not help." The natural predisposition is "the *Fond, Grundstück. Capital.*" *(Reflexionen,* AA 15: 868)

21. Kant, *Religion within the Limits of Reason alone,* AA 6: 50–1; 161, 192; 193.

22. On the 'free use of reason' *(Freiheit des Vernunftgebrauches)* see AA 8: 160.

23. Both Karl Leonhard Reinhold and Georg Foster had accused Kant of an 'unmanly fear.' Reinhold did so in the course of defending Herder's suggestion that

all life originated from a common womb. Forster made the charge in the context of his own polygenetic hypothesis. Since Reinhold and Kant are now friends (he is the reviewer explicitly praised in Kant's essay), Kant's reversion to Herder's passage, in responding to Forster, is especially pointed.

24. *Review of Herder's 'Ideas'*, AA 8: 63.

25. Cf. John Rawls' famous claim, in a *Theory of Justice* (Cambridge, MA: Harvard University Press, 1971), that willingness to make an effort is no more imputable to an agent than are (other) natural gifts.

26. Cf. Kant, *Reflexionen,* 15: 632: "Virtue. It is in us a hybrid (*Bastart*) or *Blendling*, that is produced by the mixture of evil with the seed of the good, and therefore always has in itself something of this ignoble ancestry (*Abstammung*)."

27. In his *Review* Kant had accused Herder of straying into just such a wasteland (*Wüste*) (AA 8:64).

28. For an exploration of that impossibility, see *Perpetual Peace*, whose very title ironically invokes the nonrepresentability of what it aims at.

29. Cf. *Vorarbeiten* to *Perpetual Peace* (AA 23: 170), which includes "race," along with "language" and "religion," as factors working against the (premature) *Verschmelzung* of humanity into a single *Schlag*. "Race" is omitted in the published version.

5

Kant and Blumenbach's Polyps

A Neglected Chapter in the History of the Concept of Race

Robert Bernasconi

Until relatively recently Immanuel Kant's central role in the invention of the scientific concept of race had been largely forgotten.[1] Neglect of the relevant texts by Kant scholars, together with a tendency by scholars to impose on the late eighteenth century a more rigorous distinction between the philosopher and the scientist than existed at the time, combined to lead historians of race to focus instead on the contribution of Johann Friedrich Blumenbach. But there is another factor at work. Blumenbach's significance for the nineteenth-century discussion of race cannot be denied. Although Henrich Steffens, for example, addressed Kant's essays on race directly, albeit to reject them, they were for the most part largely forgotten until, as a result of the theoretical uncertainty provoked by Charles Darwin's *The Origin of Species*, they were once again appealed to as an intellectual resource, a position they maintained through at least the first three decades of the twentieth century.[2] If it was Blumenbach, not Kant, who was the main point of reference at the start of the nineteenth century, does that not mean that those scholars who upheld Blumenbach's significance and ignored Kant's place as the first champion of a scientific concept of race were ultimately justified in doing so?

There is a way of describing the relationship between Kant and Blumenbach that supports such a conclusion. The main stages of the narrative would be some version of the following. Kant's account of race, as he first formulated it in 1775, relied on a notion of germs or seeds (*Keime*). His account owed an unmistakable debt to Albrecht von Haller's preformationism, as did Blumenbach's account of human varieties that appeared for the first time in the very same year.[3] But in 1780 Blumenbach repudiated Haller's preformationism and introduced the idea of a formative drive (*Bildungstrieb*), which he then used to reformulate his account of human varieties. Blumenbach's observation that if one cut off the tentacles of polyps, their lost organs would grow afresh, albeit smaller, after a couple of days, decisively refuted the idea of *Keime* that had previously held sway.[4] This refutation went unnoticed by Kant, who in 1785 and 1788 restated his account of race in terms of *Keime*. Kant's scientific incompetence is revealed by the fact that in 1788 he enthusiastically referred to Blumenbach's *Bildungstrieb* without recognizing the damage it did to his account.[5] However, when Kant came to write the *Critique of Judgment*, the fact that Blumenbach had refuted the theoretical basis for his account of race had finally dawned on him: in this major work, he was silent, not only about the *Keime*, but also about race. On this basis some scholars have entertained the idea that the theory of races lost its significance for Kant in his latter years.[6] More frequently, it is maintained that Kant abandoned the notion of *Keime*, and thus his specific account of race, once he recognized the significance of Blumenbach's critique. It is Blumenbach's conception of race that was passed on to the nineteenth century.

There are a number of variations on this basic narrative; at its heart, in any event, is the idea that while Kant may have formulated his account of race at the same time that Blumenbach first presented his description of human varieties, Kant's was a formulation based on outmoded or soon to be outmoded science. To support this picture of Kant as someone totally out of his depth in the scientific world of his day, scholars also point to Kant's tendency in 1777, and subsequently, to present skin color as the basis of his account of the human races. Blumenbach took a much broader view and developed the study of anatomy, as well as the study of human skulls.[7] This fact lends support to the view that the science of race owed little or nothing to Kant, and most everything to Blumenbach.

Although this picture might be attractive to those Kantians who would prefer to see Kant's essays on race fall back into the general neglect from which they have only recently resurfaced, it cannot be sustained. In the course of this essay, I will highlight various points where this picture needs to be revised or rejected; the most decisive refutation of the picture, however, comes in the form of Christoph G. Girtanner's *Über das Kantische Prinzip für Naturgeschichte*.[8] This remarkable book, published in 1796, attempted to demonstrate that Kant's and Blumenbach's accounts of race were totally compatible. Nor did it call for strategic silence about Kant's appeal to *Keime*: Kant's *Keime* and Blumenbach's *Bildungstrieb* were presented as acting in unison. Indeed, Girtanner placed both terms together in the same sentence (e.g. KPN, 11 and 24).[9] Furthermore, although the book was dedicated to Blumenbach, the principle for organizing racial divisions was, as the title indicated, Kant's: "in the mixing of two different races of the same stem the character of each is invariably reproduced in the offspring" (KPN, 39).

Of course, there is always the possibility that Girtanner was out of his depth, and the few historians who have discussed his work have, for the most part, been somewhat dismissive of him.[10] However, in the preface to *Über das Kantische Prinzip für Naturgeschichte*, Girtanner invited Kant to confirm the interpretation offered there (KPN, 3), and, surprisingly, given Kant's usual reserve, we read in his *Anthropology from a pragmatic point of view* an extraordinary endorsement of Girtanner's work as "in keeping with my principles" (AA 7: 320). It is inconceivable that Kant would have so written had he suspected Girtanner of totally misunderstanding the relation of his account to Blumenbach's, which is precisely what many historians of science seem to ask us to believe when they set Kant's *Keime* in direct opposition to Blumenbach's *Bildungstrieb*. If Kant had abandoned the *Keime* for strong theoretical reasons, following his adoption of Blumenbach's notion of *Bildungstrieb*, then he surely would have repudiated, or at least ignored, Girtanner's study. What is more, Blumenbach cited Girtanner's book approvingly in the 1807 edition of his *Handbuch der Naturgeschichte*.[11] He would not have done so had Girtanner's confusion been as obvious to the participants in the debate as it seems to some historians of science.

Girtanner's book, together with its endorsement by the main protagonists of the debate, is sufficient to refute the conventional account that dismisses Kant's contribution as outmoded—notwithstanding that the book concedes Kant's contribution as having undergone some changes after its first formulation. But we still need to reconstruct both Kant's and Blumenbach's contributions to the formation of the concept of race. Although a number of scholars have explored their relationship at the general level, I argue here that the concept of race played a more decisive role in their relation than has previously been recognized.[12] More specifically, I explore the possibility that Kant's commitment to the concept of race led him to develop a strategy for persuading Blumenbach to adopt it. This strategy is what led him to address Blumenbach directly in "The Methodology of Teleological Judgment" in the Third Critique. Far from its being the case that Kant wavered in his conviction that he had made an important contribution to the science of his day by advocating the concept of race, it has a privileged—albeit unspoken—role in the Third Critique as an example of how to address nature. And if Kant sought Blumenbach's approval, he received it: beginning in 1797, Blumenbach explicitly employed Kant's notion of race (HN 1797, 23n).[13] Given that Kant argued that races are formed from the original stem through the realization of the relevant *Keime*, whereas Blumenbach in his account of varieties made no such claim; given, further, that Kant himself put this difference at the heart of his distinction between races and varieties, it is at first sight mysterious that Blumenbach could suddenly adopt Kant's terminology. We need an explanation.

It is true that, when Blumenbach introduced the idea of the *Bildungstrieb*, it was to displace the conception of *Keime* advocated by the preformationists. Indeed, the experiment that Blumenbach conducted with polyps repeated similar experiments that belonged to the history of the debate over preformationism. When in 1746 Albrecht Haller, who as a student had accepted preformationism, embraced epigenesis, it was after repeating on polyps an experiment Charles Bonnet had conducted the year before on freshwater worms showing that, when cut in half, the worms reformed themselves as two organisms.[14] However, in 1758 in *Sur la formation du coeur dans le poulet*, Haller announced that observation of the formation of chickens had led him to return to preformationism.[15] It was not, therefore, the mutilation of polyps that was new, though Blumenbach insisted on the story about polyps as if he was deliberately trying to create another of those myths about how scientific discoveries are made in idle moments, as in the case of Sir Isaac Newton and the apple (B 1780, 247–248). What was new was that Blumenbach had formulated a version of epigenesis that did not postulate an essential force, like that proposed by Casper Friedrich Wolff, which operated by repulsion or attraction. To highlight that novelty and to strengthen the image of himself as a scientific innovator, Blumenbach specifically presented the *Bildungstrieb*, like Newton's gravity, as a *qualitas occulta* deducible only from its effects (B 1791, 32–33).

In the first edition of *De generis humani varietate nativa*, Blumenbach adopted Haller's account of how the embryo is contained in the maternal egg, thereby restricting the role of the male seed to awakening it, which is explained by appeal to the principle of irritability (GH 1776, 6; AT, 70). Blumenbach's experiment with polyps was conducted in 1778, and, in the following year, while still maintaining his allegiance to Haller's account, he expressed doubts about the restrictions Haller placed on the role of the male semen. He did not mention polyps at this time, but he appealed to the way that in many species of animals the different sexes exhibit a different form (HN 1779, 20). However, race-mixing also played a prominent role in his argument against preformationism. In 1780, in the first version of his work on the *Bildungstrieb*, Blumenbach introduced a number of examples to make his case, including the fact that the mixing of Blacks and Whites produces mulattoes (B 1780, 259–260). The example was repeated when this essay was expanded to form *Über den Bildungstrieb und das Zeugungsgeschäfte*, and on that occasion Blumenbach explicitly announced that the existence of mulattoes contradicted "all concepts of preformed germs" (B 1781, 60–61).

That is to say, Blumenbach accepted that mulattoes exhibited in significant ways the characteristics of both parents. However, when the essay was republished in an entirely new version in 1789 the specific reference to mulattoes was missing, although the case of hybridity was introduced in a general way as contradicting the preexistence of all concepts of preformed germs (B 1791, 75–77).

The important point here is that Blumenbach's argument against preformationism does not work against Kant's account of *Keime* as he proposed it in 1775, and as he repeated it with some modifications in his subsequent essays on race in 1777, 1785, and 1788. That is to say, in 1775 it was Blumenbach alone, and not Kant, who proposed a preformationist account of human diversity such that the offspring derived only from the *Keime* of the woman and not from both sexual partners; but this same account was precisely what Blumenbach opposed in 1780 in "Über den Bildungstrieb."

Mulattoes had not been a central example for Blumenbach in 1775, as they had already been for Kant at that time. By applying Georges-Louis Leclerc Comte de Buffon's rule of species identification, Kant used the existence of mulattoes to establish the unity of the human race against polygenesis, but also to identify those features of human beings that were salient to the identification of the human races. In 1777, Kant already began to emphasize one: skin color (AA 2: 433).[16] This feature was elevated by Kant to the rank of a principle in 1785 (AA 8: 101). On his account the skin color of a child of racially mixed parents would be midway between that of the parents. That one of the central examples employed by Blumenbach to refute preformationism was also the fundamental principle organizing Kant's account of race, suggests that, when Blumenbach said that the existence of mulattoes contradicted all concepts of preformed *Keime*, he either did not know Kant's "Von den verschiedenen Racen der Menschen" or he did not think of Kant's appeal to *Keime* in those terms. It is not known when Blumenbach first read Kant's essay, but in 1781, in the second edition of *De generis humani varietate nativa*, he cited it three times (GH 1781, 50, 62, and 97). It is therefore possible, but perhaps unlikely, that it was in deference to Kant's essay that Blumenbach dropped the specific reference to mulattoes from the 1789 edition. In any event, when in section 81 of the Third Critique Kant repeated Blumenbach's complaint that preformationism does not accommodate hybrids (AA 5: 423–424; CJ, 310), he would not have expected anyone to read this as a formal repudiation of his earlier essays on race. As if to underline this point, when Kant took up the contrast between evolution and epigenesis with which Blumenbach began the 1789 edition of *Über den Bildungstrieb* (B 1791, 13–17), he also reformulated the argument so as to maintain a distinction between individual preformationism and generic preformationism (AA 5: 423; CJ, 309): it was individual preformationism, not generic preformationism, that could not accommodate the existence of hybrids (AA 5: 424; CJ, 310).

There are other indications in the *Critique of Judgment* that Kant had studied Blumenbach's arguments. Kant praised Blumenbach specifically for limiting the *Bildungstrieb* to organized matter in such a way as to give a place to mechanical laws while simultaneously acknowledging the inscrutable principle that surpasses them (AA 5: 424; CJ, 311). Kant thereby presented the *Bildungstrieb* as addressing a problem posed in section 65 of the Third Critique, which called for an account of purposes and which gave natural science the basis for introducing an accompanying teleological account (AA 5: 375–376; CJ, 255). Blumenbach was thereby cast by Kant as the theorist who exemplified in the realm of natural history the introduction of teleological causes where mechanical causes were lacking—although Kant himself had been doing precisely this in his own essays on race, and that in a more explicit way than Blumenbach had done up to this point. Eventually, in 1807, Blumenbach described the *Bildungstrieb* in Kantian terms as a mechanistic power united with a purposive (*zweckmässige*) modification (HN 1807, 19).[17]

Why was Kant so generous to Blumenbach, not just in the *Critique of Judgment*, but already in "On the Use of Teleological Principles in Philosophy" (AA 8: 179n; R, 55)? In this essay the note that introduces Blumenbach seems at first sight somewhat gratuitous. Kant inserted the footnote, into a series of quotations from Georg Foster's essay on race, at the point where the latter referred to a chain of organic beings from humans to whales and "extending, presumably, to mosses and lichens" (AA 8: 179; R, 51). Kant, who had underwritten the idea of the chain of being in the *Critique of Pure Reason*, nevertheless objected to its extension beyond animals, just as he was concerned about any tendency to minimize the uniqueness of human beings. The footnote, attached to the phrase "natural chain," reads:

> Concerning this idea, which has become very popular primarily through *Bonnet*, the memoir of Professor *Blumenbach* (*Handbuch der Naturgeschichte*, 1779, Lecture No. 7) deserves to be read. This observant, reasonable man ascribes the formative impulse (*Bildungstrieb*), by means of which he has cleared up so many issues in the theory of reproduction, not to inorganic nature, but instead only to the rank of organized beings. (AA 8: 179; R, 55)

It is only when one reads the *Critique of Judgment*, and recognizes that the *Bildungstrieb* serves as a model to Kant for the way mechanical and teleological explanations can be united, that the reference to it in the essay from 1788 becomes clear. However, that is not the end of the matter.

What adds to the enigmatic character of the footnote is the fact that although the 1779 edition of the *Handbuch der Naturgeschichte* does indeed attribute to the chains in nature only a limited usefulness (HN, 1779, 10–14), this text predates Blumenbach's introduction of the *Bildungstrieb*. Where, then, did Kant first learn about the *Bildungstrieb*; and why did he introduce it into a discussion of the chain of being? If he had learned about the *Bildungstrieb* from the brief reference to it in the second edition of *Handbuch der Naturgeschichte*, it would be surprising that he would have referred to the first edition, which in any case was the only edition he had in his personal library.[18] On the face of it, the most likely answer would appear to be that he learned about the *Bildungstrieb* from either the 1780 essay or the 1781 book explicitly devoted to the topic; further, that Kant emphasized that Blumenbach had solved certain problems and had used the term *Zeugung* to specify them suggests familiarity specifically with the 1781 text (B 1781, 3).[19] We know of no texts by Blumenbach—other than the 1780 and 1781 essays—that, prior to 1788, give sufficient detail about the *Bildungstrieb* to warrant Kant's defense of the concept.[20] It is hardly likely that Kant would have given such a ringing endorsement of Blumenbach's notion without having read about it firsthand. The reluctance of some commentators to suppose that Kant had read the 1781 essay probably derives from their unwillingness to believe that he could have maintained the language of *Keime* after having read it. Once that problem is disposed of, there is no barrier to taking that as our answer to the question. One reason why this is important is that Kant would have read there that Blumenbach had appealed to the existence of mulattoes to refute preformationism and to propose epigenesis. In other words, Kant would have been able to see how in this context Blumenbach had given a certain centrality to the existence of mulattoes, as Kant had done in his account of race, but as Blumenbach had not done in describing varieties.

When Kant rehearsed Blumenbach's arguments against evolution in favor of epigenesis or generic preformation in the *Critique of Judgment*, he explicated the latter by reference to "the productive power of the generating beings, and therefore the form of the species" as "preformed *virtualiter* in the intrinsic predispositions (*Anlagen*) imparted to the stock" (AA 5: 423; CJ, 309). This was as clear an evocation of the *Keime* as was possible without naming them explicitly. By that time Kant, who had originally distinguished the *Keime* and the *Anlagen*, had come almost to identify them (AA 8: 98, and 105). Given that references to the *Anlagen* remain prominent in the *Critique of Judgment*, this reduces the significance of the fact that Kant did not appeal to the *Keime* in the same text. Indeed, as recently as in 1785, in his anonymous review of Herder's *Ideen zur Philosophie der Geschichte der Menschheit*, Kant had stated his agreement with Herder's rejection of both evolution and the mechanism of external causes, but refused to follow Herder's lead in abandoning the *Keime*. Indeed, he insisted that his conception of "*Keime* or *Anlagen*" (another indication of their proximity in his framework at that time), did not commit him to the system of evolution (AA 8: 62–63).[21] Furthermore, the notion of *Keime* survives in some of his essays from the 1790s, thereby further refuting the narrative according to which Kant dropped all reference to them.[22]

Kant's point was that some form of preformationism was still necessary to the account of *Bildungstrieb*. John H. Zammito has recently highlighted the fact that a certain epigenesis implied a certain preformationism: "at the origin there had to be some inexplicable (transcendent) endowment, and with it, in his view some determinate restriction in species variation. Thereafter, the organized principles within the natural world would proceed on adaptive lines."[23] In fact, Girtanner already made exactly the same point with explicit reference to Blumenbach's account: the epigenesis of the individual implied the preformationism of the species.[24] It was for the same reason that Kant referred to epigenesis as generic preformationism. I do not know of any text in which Blumenbach says the same thing as clearly, but in 1797 he warned against using the notion of *Keime* in order to unify the evolution hypothesis with the doctrine of progressive formation: in such a context it was "an indeterminate empty expression" (HN 1797, 13n). Hence, it is not so much the term itself that presents a problem as the way and the context in which it is used. This is confirmed when Blumenbach himself, a few pages later, uses the term *Keime* when referring to reason and language (HN 1797, 60).

If Kant was confident that his account of race in terms of *Keime* could be reconciled with Blumenbach's *Bildungstrieb*, why then did he omit all mention of race and of the *Keime* in the *Critique of Teleological Judgment*?[25] Not having won any prominent converts to his notion of race even fifteen years after defining it, and in spite of his rigorous defenses of it against the objections of Herder and Forster,[26] it is hardly surprising that Kant did not appeal to race as evidence when he was trying to establish the framework on which the racial concept ultimately relied. But that does not mean that he was not still committed to seeing the concept adopted more widely. Kant must have seen that Blumenbach would be the best convert whom he could have attracted in order to fulfill his aim of seeing the concept of race flourish. After all, Kant already had more than one reason to believe Blumenbach ripe for conversion: by introducing the idea of the *Bildungstrieb*, Blumenbach had introduced reference to what Kant already saw as a purposive cause.

It is because the *Bildungstrieb* transcends mechanical causes that it was a useful illustration for Kant in writing "On the Use of Teleological Principles in Philosophy" and the *Critique of Judgment*. But clearly not lost on Kant was that this meant that Blumenbach had passed, in the terms that Kant himself had employed in his first essay on race, from offering a "description of nature" to giving a "history of nature." Kant insisted that the former, as an account of the condition of nature at the present time, was not able to explain the diversity of human races (AA 2: 463; DHR, 22), and that the task was not only to create artificial divisions so as to classify creatures, but also to bring those creatures under laws (AA 2: 429; DHR, 8). This was the task of natural history as Kant understood it. By incorporating the notion of *Bildungstrieb* into his account of human varieties, Blumenbach had strayed into natural history in Kant's sense; and it was Kant's strategy to use this fact to persuade Blumenbach that the latter had thereby already offered what in places amounted to a concept of race, again in the strict sense.

Kant and Blumenbach had initially used different words to discuss human diversity: race and variety respectively. To Kant, these terms represented the difference between natural history and description of nature. The question of the origin of the Negro was, on Kant's terms, a question posed not to natural description but to natural history (AA 8: 162; R, 39). Insofar as "variety" was a term of natural description, it did not belong to the appropriate realm from which to address the debate between monogenesis and polygenesis. Blumenbach and Kant from the outset agreed on the central point that human beings belonged to a single species. To this extent they were both allies against Forster. However, by addressing the question of the Negro, as Forster did, as a question of whether Negroes were a species or a variety, rather than as a question of whether Negroes were a species or a race, Foster had reformulated the question on Blumenbach's terms, and thereby rendered it, in Kant's view, impossible to resolve satisfactorily, insofar as race did not reveal itself to the description of nature. Even though we have no direct evidence that Kant had read *De generis humani varietate nativa*, and even though "variety" was a term Kant had already used in 1775 in contrast to "race" (VR, 3), perhaps with reference to Buffon, it seems likely that Kant's argument in "On the Use of Teleological Principles in Philosophy" was intended as a response to Blumenbach as well as to Forster. That is probably how it would be heard and that is the best explanation of why Kant makes so much more of the distinction between race and variety in the later work.

How well did Kant know Blumenbach's texts? When Johann Jachmann, in a letter dated October 14, 1790 that also brought the name of Christoph Girtanner to Kant's attention, told Kant that he would be bringing him a copy of the *Beyträge zur Naturgeschichte* as a gift from Blumenbach, Jachmann said that he believed Kant had already read it (AA 11: 222). This suggests that, two years later, Kant's interest in Blumenbach was well known, at least in his intimate circle. We also know that Kant had in his personal library a copy of the 1789 edition of *Über den Bildungstrieb* that Blumenbach had sent him some time during the year of its publication, and thus in time to impact the writing of the Third Critique. Kant did not write to thank Blumenbach for it until August 5, 1790, but in that letter Kant acknowledged that he had received Blumenbach's essay the previous year (AA 11: 185). With this letter Kant enclosed a copy of *Critique of Judgment*, and he seems to have been looking for Blumenbach's endorsement in much the same way that Girtanner would later look for Kant's. Kant also drew to Blumenbach's attention the fact that he had been acknowledged in the text, adding: "Your writings have taught me a great deal; indeed, the novelty of your recent unification of the two principles, the physico-mechanical and the purely teleological way of explaining organic nature, which were otherwise believed to be ununifiable, are in close proximity to the ideas that have recently exercised me and yet which need such factual confirmation" (AA 11: 185).

The division of labor this implies, whereby the maxims of reason from which one begins would be differentiated from the facts collected by following them, had already been suggested by Kant in his 1785 essay on race (AA 8: 96). However, matters are more complicated, even though Kant knew his limitations and realized how much additional reading he would need to do if he was to extend his study of race beyond humanity (AA 10: 227–230). Perhaps Blumenbach could supply the facts for Kant's theory. But, of course, such a supposition ignores Blumenbach's role as a theoretician just as it ignores Kant's command of the facts. When Blumenbach reread Kant's 1777 essay on race in preparing the 1795 text of *De generis humani varietate nativa*, he referenced it for his comments on the coldness of the touch of Indians (GH, 1795 162; AT, 223), the length of their legs (GH 1795, 243; AT, 260), the structure of the face of Mongolians (GH 1795, 190; AT, 231), and the probable origin of Native Americans (GH 1795, 315; AT, 273). Kant may not have been as great an expert as others on plants and animals, and he did not mutilate polyps, but in the course of preparing his lectures on both physical geography and anthropology he had come to know the travel literature well. However, it is an indication of the general neglect to which Kant's essays on race were subject that Girtanner highlighted Blumenbach's references to him in *De generis humani varietate nativa* as something of an exception (KPN, 3).

It seems clear that Kant, in his letter to Blumenbach of 1790, was actively seeking the latter's support for the account of the relation of mechanical and teleological purposes set out in *Critique of Judgment*. But although it cannot be proven, there is sufficient evidence to consider plausible the idea that Kant was also still seeking Blumenbach's support for his concept of race, a process begun in 1788 when Kant implicitly contrasted his account of race with the notion of variety, and then somewhat gratuitously praised Blumenbach's notion of *Bildungstrieb*. This helps to explain some of the details of the construction of sections 80 and 81 of *Critique of Judgment*. In any event, whether or not this was the intention, this was the effect. It is *as if* this was Kant's intention.

Kant believed he had factual confirmation of the purposiveness of nature in what he designated "race." One already sees a trace of this in section 80 of the *Critique of Judgment* where Kant introduced the central principle that judged "nothing in an organized being as unpurposive if it is preserved in the being's propagation" (AA 5: 420; CJ, 306). When Kant insisted that "nothing is to be taken up into the generative force that does not already belong to one of the being's undeveloped predispositions" (AA 5: 420; CJ, 306), he was still referring hereditary characteristics to the predispositions, as he had already done in 1775 (AA 2: 435; DHR, 14). That he went on to warn that we do not have knowledge of the original stock confirms the revision of the 1777 essay (AA 2: 461; DHR, 20) he had made in 1785 (AA 8: 98). Kant was evoking race, but his immediate problem was to render persuasive the principle that introduces teleology into organic beings. Even if everything natural is an example for Kant, insofar as he considered it impossible to avoid applying the concept of intention to nature (AA 5: 398; CJ, 280), the intention of nature is not always clear. Nevertheless, Kant did offer some illustrations to show that, although one can approach the parts of the bodies of animals by mechanical laws, if one conceives the body as an organized being, everything must be judged as purposive:

> Now it is entirely possible that some parts in (say) an animal body (such as skin, bone, or hair) could be grasped as accumulations governed by merely mechanical laws. Still the cause that procures the appropriate matter, that modifies and forms it in that way, and deposits it in the pertinent locations must always be judged teleologically. (AA 5: 377; CJ, 257)

These examples are not accidental. Skin color, hair texture, and bone structure, including presumably the angle of the face, were precisely what observers like Blumenbach and Samuel Thomas Soemmerring focused on in distinguishing the different human varieties. Furthermore, from the time of Kant's first essay on race, he had focused on the fact that mechanical laws provided an insufficient basis for explaining those characteristics of the human races that were transmitted through propagation: appeal to the providence (*Fürsorge*) of nature (AA 2: 434; DHR, 13), its foresight (*Vorsorge*) [AA 8: 93], was necessary. As he explained in section 68 of the Third Critique: "when we apply teleology to physics, we do quite rightly speak of nature's wisdom, parsimony, foresight (*Vorsorge*) or beneficence" (AA 5: 383; CJ, 263). The same was true of natural history. Indeed, this was what defined natural history in its distinction from the description of nature.

For Kant, skin color was the decisive example of what he was talking about. Although Kant had, in keeping with the obsessions of Northern Europeans for over a century, offered speculations about what made Blacks black, what was significant for him was that the purposiveness of their color was undeniable. Kant was clear that his appeal to iron particles (AA 2: 438; IR, 17) and later to phlogiston (AA 8: 103) were hypotheses intended to stimulate further investigations (AA 2: 440; IR, 19 and AA 8: 100). The purposefulness of the color of the Negro was another story:

> Purposefulness in an organism is the universal reason why we conclude that there is a preparation originally laid out in the nature of a creature in this design and, if this purpose is only attained later, that there are producing germs. Indeed, this purposiveness of properties is possibly in no race so clearly proven than in the Negro race. (AA 8: 102–103)[27]

Kant reiterated the point in the 1788 essay, highlighting, with reference to Soemmerring's studies, "the perfect purposefulness of the development of the Negro with reference to his motherland" (AA 8: 169; R, 44). Indeed, Kant quoted Soemmerring as saying that "one finds characteristics in the build of the Negro which make him most perfect for his climate, perhaps as perfect as the Europeans" (AA 8: 169n; R, 54n2). It seems that Soemmerring, not Blumenbach, provided the factual confirmation, at least for the principle annunciated in section 80. Race may not have been mentioned explicitly in the *Critique of Teleological Judgment*, but it nonetheless helped to sustain the argument insofar as Kant considered the skin color of Blacks as a uniquely clear example of the purposiveness of nature.

Blumenbach confirmed Kant's reading of him when in 1807 he acknowledged that the *Bildungstrieb* united purposive and mechanical causes. However, what Kant needed was an endorsement of the notion of race, and this is exactly what he received in 1797, in the fifth edition of his *Handbuch der Naturgeschichte*, when Blumenbach acknowledged that Kant had, in "On the Use of Teleological Principles of Philosophy," precisely determined the distinctions between race and varieties (HN 1797, 23n). Furthermore, Blumenbach defined race in terms that Kant would have recognized: "Race in its precise sense is a character produced by degeneration that operates through inevitable and necessary inheritance, as, for example, when Whites with Blacks produce mulattoes or when Whites with American Indians produce mestizoes" (HN 1797, 23). By contrast, using an example already found in Kant's first essay on race, Blumenbach acknowledged that when fair individuals produce children who are brunettes with dark eyes these are indications only of variations (*Spielarten*), because the characteristics are not inherited invariably (HN 1797, 23. See VR, 3). Blumenbach would never follow Buffon and Kant in regarding hybridity as a practical tool in the identification of species (GH 1795, 67–69; AT, 189. Also HN 1814, 26), but he believed hybridity decisive for formulating a theory of generation, because it showed the central role of both parents (GHV 1795, 85–86; AT, 195–196).

Blumenbach's shift in the direction of Kant's concept of race went further in the 1797 edition of the *Handbuch der Naturgeschichte* than simply adopting the term from him. He also employed, albeit without direct attribution, Kant's claim that when two races mate their offspring is necessarily an intermediate, a half-breed, a *Mittelschlag*, and, in the case of Blacks and Whites, a mulatto (HN 1797, 14). Blumenbach is here appealing to what Girtanner earlier referred to as the Kantian principle of natural history, and in Kant's stronger formulation according to which the offspring resembles both parents equally in certain specific respects.

Because skin color provided the best support for such a claim, it is no surprise to find Blumenbach, at the same time that he endorsed the concept of race, highlighting skin color—again with specific reference to Kant—and this despite his prior attention to the factors that made it somewhat unreliable (GH 1776, 54–56; AT, 110–111). Blumenbach wrote in 1795:

> We must begin with the color of the skin, which although it sometimes deceives, still is a much more constant character, and more generally transmitted than the others, and which most clearly appears in hybrid progeny sprung from the union of varieties of different color composed of the tint of either parent. (GH 1795: 115; AT, 207).

An accompanying footnote referred to Kant's essays of 1785 and 1788, as if they had been the works of a bona fide scientist.

I have tried to show that certain ostensibly puzzling features of Kant's discussions, of preformationism, epigenesis, *Keime,* and the *Bildungstrieb*, become somewhat less so if one recognizes that Kant was strongly committed to the idea of race he had proposed in 1775. It was his attempt to contribute to the science of his day and he wanted to see it prosper. This is why he rushed to its defense when it was challenged by Herder and Forster; this is why he celebrated its adoption by Girtanner. Everything in this narrative happens *as if* Kant knew that the best way to secure support for his concept of race was to persuade Blumenbach to support it: first, Kant's evocation in "On the Use of Teleological Principles of Philosophy" of the observant Blumenbach's *Bildungstrieb* at a moment when it hardly seemed necessary to do so; then, Kant's repetition of the same gesture in an even more extravagant fashion in *Critique of Judgment*; and finally, a letter praising Blumenbach for factual confirmation of Kant's ideas.

Because Blumenbach did not write another edition of *De generis humani varietate nativa* after having explicitly adopted Kant's notion of race, it is not as easy as it otherwise would have been to know how much more (other than an acknowledgment of the focus on skin color) than the word he took from Kant; but we can reconstruct their differences. Whereas Kant regarded the races as permanent divisions, Blumenbach seems never to have departed from his earlier view whereby they "ran into one another by unnoticed passages and intermediate shades" (AT, 303).[28] To be sure, Kant would not have contested that observation as one belonging to natural description; the observation, though, held a different meaning within natural history. Kant had an explanation of how the four races became established by virtue of a variety of factors, including reference to both race-mixing and only partially realized *Keime* because of migration at the significant time (AA 2: 432–441; IR, 11–20). Even in 1795, as Blumenbach was still moving toward accepting the term "race," he still questioned whether Kant was right to deny that deformities or mutilations could begin a new variety by degeneration (GH 1795 106; AT 203). But, perhaps more significantly, Blumenbach came over time to be interested in a question that Kant seems, at least officially, to have left to one side as "a daring adventure of reason" (AA 5: 419n; CJ, 305n). As Blumenbach became more focused on the evidence for the production of new species as a result of a modification of the *Bildungstrieb*, he seems to have balanced his approach by giving more order to the process and conceiving types as permanent (BN, 20–23; AT, 287–88).[29] Furthermore, even though Blumenbach did not accept hybridity as a useful tool in the identification of species, he nevertheless believed that it was decisive for formulating a theory of generation because it showed that both parents played a central role (GHV 1795, 85–86; AT, 195–196). Kant's theory of race changed in significant ways from the time of its first formulation, but the changes Blumenbach's account of human varieties underwent were more significant. Even if it was more through Blumenbach than directly from Kant that the notion of race became the preferred term for discussing human varieties, Kant's emphasis on the fixity of the races and on race mixing is strongly echoed in the nineteenth-century usage of the term and constitutes his legacy. For this reason, reference to Kant is indispensable to any history of the concept of race.[30]

NOTES

1. For a summary of the arguments see Robert Bernasconi, "Who Invented the Concept of Race? Kant's Role in the Enlightenment Construction of Race," in *Race*, ed. Robert Bernasconi (Oxford: Blackwell, 2001), 11–36. In addition to the authorities cited in that essay supporting that claim, I should add Frank William Peter Dougherty, *Gesammelte Aufsätze zu Themen der klassischen Periode der Naturgeschichte* (Göttingen: Norbert Klatt), 1996, 35.

2. Henrich Steffens, *Anthropologie*, vol. 2 (Breslau: Josef Max, 1822), 415 seq. Steffens took up a number of the questions explored in this paper, but a full consideration of his historical role must await another occasion. The return to Kant provoked by Darwin's theories can be seen in Fritz Schultze, *Kant und Darwin* (Jena: Hermann Dufft, 1875). The importance of Kant's theories of race to certain early-twentieth-century theorists is verified by O. Kleinschmidt, *Die Formenkreislehre und das Weltwerden des Lebens*, (Halle: Gebauer-Schwetzschke, 1926), esp. 82–85.

3. A photomechanical reprint of Kant's 1775 text, *Von den verschiedenen Racen der Menschen zur Ankündigung der Vorlesungen der physischen Geographie im Summerhalbenjahre 1775* (Königsberg: G. E. Hartung, 1775), has recently been published in volume three of *Concepts of Race in the Eighteenth Century*, ed. R. Bernasconi (Bristol: Thoemmes Press, 2001). Because editions of Kant do not print this text as an integral whole, but only as variations on the 1777 edition, I will cite the original here as VR. The eight volumes constituting this set contain many of the texts by Kant, Forster, Girtanner, and Blumenbach cited here, including in volume four all three editions of *De generis humani varietate nativa* (Göttingen: Vandenhoeck, 1776, 1781, and 1795). Henceforth GH followed by the year of publication. (There was apparently also a 1775 edition of GH identical to that of 1776, but I have not seen it.) The 1776 and 1795 editions were translated by Thomas Bendyshe in *The Anthropological Treatises of Johann Friedrich Blumenbach* (London: Longman, Green, Longman, Roberts, and Green, 1865). Henceforth AT.

4. J. F. Blumenbach, "Über den Bildungstrieb (Nisus formativus) und seinen Einfluss auf die Generation und Reproduction," *Göttingisches Magazin der Wissenschaften und Literatur*, 1, no. 5 (1780): 248. In 1781, Blumenbach published an expanded version, incorporating "Über eine ungemein einfache Fortpflanzungsart," *Göttingisches Magazin der Wissenschaften und Literatur* 2, no. 1, (1781): 80–89 and other additions, in *Über den Bildungstrieb und das Zeugungsgeschäfte* (Göttingen: Johann Christian Dieterich, 1781). An entirely new version was published with the same publishers in 1789 under the title *Über den Bildungstrieb* and reprinted virtually unchanged in 1791. References to these texts will be given as B followed by the year of publication.

5. Immanuel Kant, "Über den Gebrauch teleologischer Prinzipien in der Philosophie," in *Gesammelte Schriften=Akademie Ausgabe*, (Berlin: Walter de Gruyter, 1905–), 8: 180; trans. Jon Mark Mikkelsen, "On the Use of Teleological Principles in Philosophy," in *Race*, ed. R. Bernasconi (Oxford: Blackwell, 2001), 55, n6. Reference to the Akadamie edition of Kant henceforth AA followed by volume number; references to *Race* henceforth R respectively.

6. For example, Susan M. Shell, *The Embodiment of Reason* (Chicago: University of Chicago Press, 1996), 418, n 53.

7. See J. F. Blumenbach, *Geschichte und Beschreibung der Knochen des menschlichen Körpers* (Göttingen: Heinrich Dieterich, 1805).

8. Christoph G. Girtanner, *Über das Kantische Prinzip für Naturgeschichte* (Göttingen: Vanderhoek und Ruprecht, 1796). Henceforth KPN.

9. That does not mean that Girtanner did not recognize the importance of the *Bildungstrieb*. Whereas Kant simply referred to the climate as actualizing the germs,

according to Girtanner, that happens through the different directions of the *Bildungstrieb* (KPN, 11).

10. An exception is Philip Sloan in his "Buffon, German Biology and the Historical Interpretation of Biological Species," *British Journal for the History of Science* 12 (1979): 109–153. It is therefore somewhat surprising that Girtanner does not play a stronger role in his "Preforming the Categories: Eighteenth-Century Generation Theory and the Biological Roots of Kant's A Priori," *Journal of the History of Philosophy* 40, no. 2 (2002): 251.

11. J. F. Blumenbach, *Handbuch der Naturgeschichte* (Göttingen: Heinrich Dieterich, 1807), 25n. Blumenbach published many editions. I have consulted the editions published in 1779, 1782, 1788, 1791, 1797, 1807, 1821, 1825, and 1832, but unfortunately I have not seen the editions of 1788, 1799, 1803, 1816, and 1830. References to the different editions of the *Handbuch* will be given by using the abbreviation HN followed by the year of the edition.

12. In addition to the works by Philip Sloan and John H. Zammito cited below, see especially these works by Timothy Lenoir: "Kant, Blumenbach, and Vital Materialism in Germany," *Isis* 71 (1980): 77–108, "Teleology without Regrets. The Transformation of Physiology in Germany: 1790–1847," *History of the Philosophy of Science* 12, no. 4 (1981): 293–354; "The Göttingen School and the Development of Transcendental Naturphilosophie in the Romantic Era," *Studies in the History of Biology* 5 (1981): 111–203; and "Generational Factors in the Origin of Romantische Naturphilosophie, *Journal of the History of Biology* 11 (1978): 57–100.

13. Blumenbach seems to have employed the term "race" first in relation to the human species in a curious essay "Über Menschen-Racen und Schweine-Racen," *Magazin für das Neueste aus der Physik und Naturgeschichte* 6 (1789): 1–13. I have no reason to believe Kant knew of this essay, but, more importantly, this essay did not clarify the term. A significant step was already taken in 1798, when the third edition of *De generis humani varietate nativa* was translated into German; and the accompanying notes highlighted Blumenbach's adoption of the term. For more on the history of Blumenbach's adoption of the term "race," see R. Bernasconi, "Editor's Note," in *Über die natürlichen Verschiedenheiten im Menschengeschlechte* by Johann Blumenbach (Bristol: Thoemmes Press, 2001), v–vii.

14. Shirley A. Roe, *Matter, Life, and Generation* (Cambridge: Cambridge University Press), pp. 22–23.

15. Ibid., p. 26.

16. The 1777 version of "Von den verschiedenen Racen der Menschen" has been translated by Jon Mark Mikkelsen as "Of the Different Human Races" in *The Idea of Race,* eds. Robert Bernasconi and Tommy Lott, (Indianapolis: Hackett, 2000), 8–22. Here p. 12. Henceforth DHR.

17. Although this essay is indebted to a recent essay by John H. Zammito, I am not yet persuaded by his claim that the 1789 version of *Über der Bildungstrieb* "showed clearly the influence of Kant's own arguments about distinguishing mechanical from teleological explanations." "'This inscrutable principle of an original organization': epigenesis and 'looseness of fit' in Kant's philosophy of science," *Studies in History and Philosophy of Science* 34 (2003): 94. The problem is not so much that

Blumenbach does not, so far as I know, refer directly to "On the Use of Teleological Principles of Philosophy" until 1795 (HN 1797, 23n), a point which is hardly conclusive. The problem is that I do not see—or have not yet seen—the clear influence of Kant's 1788 essay on Blumenbach's 1789 text. However, by 1795 Blumenbach had embraced the terms of *Critique of Judgment* concerning the relation between the mechanical and the teleological (GH 1795, 82–83; AT, 194). By 1797, the same year in which Blumenbach adopted the notion of race, he can be found appealing to Kant's *Critique of Judgment* to find arguments against preformed *Keime* in addition to those drawn from experience (HN 1797, 13). Other references are at HN 1797, 12 with a further addition at HN 1807, 12.

18. Arthur Warda, *Immanuel Kants Bücher* (Berlin: Martin Breslauer, 1922), 27.

19. In 1780 and 1781, Blumenbach was in general more concerned than he was than in 1789 with anthropological questions, such as whether Native Americans are beardless by nature or art (B 1781, 66–68).

20. There were also two Latin editions that I have not seen from 1785 and 1787 under the title *De nisu formativo et generationis negotio nuperae observationes.*

21. For an English translation of this important passage see Immanuel Kant, *Political Writings*, trans. H. B. Nisbet, (Cambridge: Cambridge University Press, 1995), 217. Kant also seems to equate the *Keime* and *Anlagen* in his "Bestimmung des Begriffs einer Menschenrace" (AA 8: 98 and 105).

22. An assessment of this evidence can be found in Philip Sloan, "Preforming the Categories," pp. 250–251.

23. Zammito, "'This inscrutable principle of an original organization,'" p. 88. I fully accept Zammito's solution and his assessment that it has not hitherto been fully understood.

24. Peter McLaughlin, "Blumenbach und der Bildungstrieb. Zum Verhältnis von epigenetischer Embryologie und typologischem Artbegriff," *Medizinhistorisches Journal* 176 (1982): 369.

25. The term race does appear in the *Critique of Aesthetic Judgment* at AA 5: 234; CJ, 82.

26. Johann Gottfried von Herder denied that there were races: *Ideen zur Philosophie der Geschichte der Menschheit,* ed. M. Bollacher, (Frankfurt: Deutscher Klassiker, 1989), 256; trans. Tom Nenon, "Ideas on the Philosophy of the History of Humankind," in *The Idea of Race*, eds. Robert Bernasconi and Tommy L. Lott (Indianapolis: Hackett, 2000), 26. Georg Forster equated "race" and "variety": "Noch etwas über die Menschenvassen," *Kleine Schriften aus Philosophie und Naturgeschichte,* ed. Siegfried Scheibe, *Werke*, vol. 8 (Berlin: Akademie, 1991): 152.

27. I am indebted to Jon Mark Mikkelsen for permission to use his translation of this essay.

28. Johann Friedrich Blumenbach, *Beyträge zur Naturgeschichte,* Erster Theil, zweite Ausgabe (Göttingem: Heinrich Dieterich, 1806), 69; trans. AT, 303. Henceforth BN.

29. J. F. Blumenbach. *Beyträge zur Naturgeschichte* p. 20. I am indebted here to Timothy Lenoir, "The Göttingen School and the Development of Transcendental Naturphilosophie in the Romantic Era," p. 139.

30. An earlier version of the paper was given in April 2001 in New Orleans at the Conference of the American Society of Eighteenth Century Studies under the title "Kant and Blumenbach on the *Bildungstrieb*." I am grateful to both Philip Sloan and John H. Zammito for their comments on that occasion.

6

Race, Freedom and the Fall in Steffens and Kant

Mark Larrimore

In 1822, the romantic mineralogist, *Naturphilosoph* and theologian Henrich Steffens published his lecture cycle on *Anthropologie*. Defining "anthropology" as "philosophy in the most extended sense," Steffens moved from the cataclysmic geological history of the Earth through the arising of the plant and animal kingdoms to human history. Why all this should be part of "anthropology" was explained in terms of "race": "the truly highest problem of anthropology is: How can the freedom of the most degenerate (*verwahrlosesten*) races be saved?"[1] For Steffens, it was in the "races" that the paradox of freedom subjected to nature could most clearly be seen. How could human beings, the free flower of nature, have become enslaved to nature? Neither a physiological account of nature nor a merely metaphysical analysis of freedom could make sense of this paradox. Only a "spiritual" understanding of humanity's place in nature could account for it, Steffens argued. Race was in fact the consequence of sin.[2]

Steffens' view is of interest to an understanding of early German race thinking not because it was influential (it was not), but because it reveals underlying questions and assumptions already present when Immanuel Kant

91

invented the concept of race.[3] Steffens in fact asserted that his own view was most nearly anticipated by Kant. This surprising claim turns out to be almost plausible if all of Kant's scattered discussions of race and the races are taken into account. The fact that Kant could be read in this way nearly half a century after his invention of race, meanwhile, shows that the "scientific" concept of race had not yet displaced the theological and other categories from which it originally emerged.

My aim in this essay is broader than just complicating our understanding of Kant's thinking on race and the races. With Steffens' help, I hope to provide a sense of an intellectual climate in which race had not yet made the shift from *explanans* to *explanandum*, a climate in which monogenesis implied a theological and not merely a historical narrative. Steffens helps us see that Kant's theory of race presupposed and mobilized earlier accounts of human difference, from the Fall and theodicy to the theory of the temperaments. It is only against the background of these common assumptions that we are able to see what really distinguished Kant's view from Steffens' (I shall call it the "rhetoric of freedom"), and to discern the forgotten "pragmatic" intentions of Kant's fateful writings on race.

STEFFENS

Norwegian-born Henrich Steffens (1773–1845) gravitated toward German-speaking lands through his study of mineralogy and *Naturphilosophie* (the latter with F. W. J. Schelling, who became a close friend). Steffens' oeuvre extended from geological studies to analyses of Germanness in the face of the French challenge (he was the first civilian to join the march against Napoleon in 1813), from works in the philosophy of religion to several novels and a ten-volume autobiography. He presented the problem of the races as the key to the convergence of Christian theology, pagan mythology, and science in works of several genres: *Caricaturen des Heiligsten* (1819–21), a theory of the state; *Anthropologie* (1822); and the section on "teleology" of his *Christliche Religionsphilosophie* (1839).

Building on Johann Gottlieb Werner's understanding of geological history as involving several radically distinct stages and on Schelling's idea that the histories of nature and freedom were in a profound sense one, Steffens argued that human beings were the last of many stages of creativity in a nature working towards freedom. Humanity literally represented the fusion of the kingdoms of nature.[4] "Do you want to know nature?" Steffens asked in an essay published in 1821; "Turn your glance inwards and you will be granted the privilege of beholding nature's stages of development in the stages of your spiritual education. Do you want to know yourself? Seek in nature: her works are those of the self-same spirit."[5]

The Place of Race in "Anthropology"

Anthropology for Steffens was philosophy "in its most extended sense" (1:1). It encompassed all the physical sciences as well as a very real anticipation of revelation.

> We will venture in this essay in a threefold direction in regarding man
>
> 1. as the endpoint of an infinite past of nature (*developmental history of the earth, geological anthropology*);
>
> 2. as midpoint of an infinite present (*organic epoch of Earth, physiological anthropology*);
>
> 3. as starting point of an infinite future (*spiritual revelation of the divine in everyone, psychological anthropology*). (1:16)[6]

Half of the *Anthropologie* was taken up with "geological anthropology," in which Steffens attempted to demonstrate that the center of the Earth was metallic. As such, it was the locus of magnetism, the inorganic form of what in the organic realm appeared as death and in the spiritual as evil. Steffens thought that geological anthropology disclosed the true relationship of freedom and nature:

> [N]ature, where she presents herself in fully pure form—the clearly recognized, all enlivening liberating image of eternal love which confirms every spiritual nature in its kind—*is* freedom and the science of nature only becomes anthropology, indeed an anthropology is only then possible, when we recognize the seeds of freedom, the hidden site of self-unfolding spirit in nature itself. (2:13)

Steffens thought the Bible and the mythology of the world's most ancient peoples told the same story. Human history was but the final chapter in a narrative which long predated the emergence of human beings. The drama of humanity's fall and its ultimate redemption was at once recapitulation and dénouement of a timeless struggle.

For Steffens, freedom did not stand in conflict with nature as good to evil: both good and evil were already present in nature before the emergence of freedom. Geology confirmed that the world had once been paradisiacal, created by "innocence," and was being completed by human beings, whose freedom did not put them at odds with nature but at its "midpoint."

> The creating will of the Creator produced heaven and Earth and the days of Creation show us the eventual uncovering of his glory, as he

wanted to reveal it to us. He created humans, in order that the whole inner order of the Creation should find its point of unification in them. All other creations were bound to narrow particular circles of the general existence, and for just that reason, because they were tied in some particular direction, the inner unity of the whole creation could find no midpoint through them. Man was torn entirely from this circle. Not torn in some one-sided direction, which only received its significance through its relation to another, he was placed in the free middle, so that all other shapes should relate to his as the scattered rays of all external objects do to the sun. The human form was not just a *mid*point of all animals, but also an equilibrium [*Gleichmaaß*] of all animals and plants; and not just an ordering midpoint of all emergent life, but also an equilibrium of life and all elements; and not just a midpoint of all terrestrial life, but also an equilibrium of all celestial bodies. Thus, the form of man [is] *purely* separated from each individual thing, from every final relation, precisely because it is related in an infinite way to all. (1:286–87)

But since human beings were *free*, their succumbing to nature still had to be explained. This was where Steffens introduced the language of race.

Steffens found that the problem posed by the races was that of the relation of freedom to nature in its "most difficult" form (1:11).[7] A metaphysical account of the nature of freedom could not make sense of the apparent forfeiture of freedom Steffens saw in the non-European peoples he described as races. An entirely materialist natural science, meanwhile, would be driven to polygenesis, since a merely physical account could not make sense of the fact that these peoples seemed to have taken on the character of different climates in the past, but did so no longer (1:387).[8] The moral degeneration of the races, which Steffens took for granted, seemed to raise insuperable theodicy problems for divine justice.[9] Only a science attentive to the spiritual—a science which recognized freedom at work in a nature gradually unfolding—could confirm the unity of humanity, and justify the ways of God. Steffens' *Anthropologie* was thus not only a theory but also a theodicy of race.

That the races had forfeited their freedom did not for Steffens mean that all human beings had. Not everyone was a member of a race. For Steffens, the races designated only the outermost of three concentric rings of diffusion as human beings radiated outward from the Himalayan paradise where their history had begun. The races comprised only Malaysians, Mongolians, Africans, and North Americans, and were to be distinguished from "*ur*-historical peoples" (Egyptians, most Asians, Peruvians, Mexicans) and "historical peoples" (Greeks, Romans, Germans) (2:428–34). The five groups—four races and the historical peoples—corresponded to the five human "varieties" Johann

Friedrich Blumenbach listed in 1788 and relabeled as "races" in 1795, following Kant.[10] Blumenbach's "Caucasians"—peoples in Asia, North Africa,
and North America who, despite differences in form and color, nonetheless
"seem to agree in many things with ourselves"[11]—corresponded to what
Steffens called the "historical peoples."

In not regarding this collection of peoples as a race, Steffens made explicit what was implicit in many earlier accounts. Human history was understood as the story of a fall, but one in which not all peoples had fallen equally
far from wholeness. "All peoples, in distancing themselves from the seat of
their common origin, lose spiritual capacities to the same degree that their
bodily degeneration [*Verbildung*] increases" (2:411), Steffens wrote; degeneration admitted of degrees. The theodicy question remained: why should
certain peoples have been—have made themselves—vulnerable to degeneration in this way? It was here that "anthropology" came in. Steffens' natural
history was attentive to the way nature itself—in inorganic processes like
magnetism and electricity, just as in organic ones like reproduction and irritability—expressed what in humanity appeared as free personality (1:196).The
processes in question were opposed but usually in some kind of balance. It
was when balance was lost that things went wrong, in nature as in freedom.

The inorganically and organically prefigured imbalance that led people to
leave their Edenic state was something Steffens called "reflexion" (1:372).
Reflexion was the "self-interest" (*Selbstsucht*) of an "earthly reason" which
wanted to reduce that which was "self-contained in its unity to the isolated,
to something not only externally separate, but also internally distinct" (1:360–
61).[12] Reflexion worked by taking an individual out of the context of all the
other individuals with which it was historically, organically, and mystically
bound up, and seeking a specious "universality" by hypostatizing it. Forgetting that he was the "midpoint" of nature, man had tried to understand himself only in terms of himself. Forgetting (or denying) that he was related to
nature as its "free middle" (1:286), he had come to *contrast* himself with
nature. Yet since nature was only his *own* nature exploded, he had lost sight
at once of nature and of himself, of nature *and* of freedom. In this way the
evil—the merely physical—in him had overwhelmed the spiritual.

But the Fall brought about by reflexion was a fortunate one. The Fall into
race was irreversible (for human beings), but the stage of reflexion was necessary for humanity's coming to self-consciousness as the center and equilibrium of all things. Steffens put it in the framework of salvation history,
glossing the *Selbstsucht* of earthly reason as original sin (*Erbsünde*). All
human beings—not just the "races"—had fallen from wholeness, but ultimate
redemption was assured. The anthropology which disclosed this could be no
more than prologue, however. Asked Steffens at the book's end: "Where is
the human knowledge which could loose the fetters" of man enslaved to

nature through his own refusal to acknowledge his place in it? "Is there an earthly power, which can fight with all the horror of the abyss and overcome it?" Steffens' answer was that everything he had described had no more than "Old Testamental significance." The full and final answer was to be found in Jesus Christ (2:455).

Temperament and Human Destiny

Human nature itself contained the prophecy of Christ, however. Indeed, Steffens argued that it was precisely his "spiritual" understanding of the races that pointed to the wholeness and perfection of man (and thus of nature), which was the nature of Christ. The proof was given in Steffens' analysis of temperament, the culmination of the section on "pyschological anthropology." The four temperaments were the key to Steffens' whole anthropology.[13] They constituted the grid for the three concentric rings of human diffusion and for the—now empty—center where paradisiacal wholeness once had been.

The four temperaments functioned as a scheme for the races, the outer-most ring of human diffusion. In the races, Steffens saw in "one-sided separation" what interpenetrated in the infinitely varied individual personalities of the members of historical peoples (2:441). Steffens found it "superfluous" to spell out the "obvious" race-temperament correlations of Mongolians with the melancholy, Malaysians with the choleric, Africans with the sanguine, and Native Americans with the phlegmatic (2:441). The races emerged from that loss of complexly balanced human nature which resulted when one of humanity's constituent "seeds" overwhelmed all the others, destroying the equilibrium that constituted freedom.[14]

But these "seeds," correlated to the temperaments, also pointed back toward the center of the human map, to the once and future perfection of man. "If we put the temperaments together, we discover in them the surviving organs of a higher organization of the species" (2:445). Steffens thought that the one-sided separation of the races recapitulated and confirmed humanity's calling to be the "midpoint" of creation. Once his German readers saw these linkages, he thought, they would recognize their kinship with all human beings, even with the *verwahrlosesten*, for all human beings were defined by distance from the center. All were imbalances, and could be understood only in terms of the balanced whole of humanity revealed in pieces by the races, as indeed by the natural world as a whole.[15] Recognizing the stultified humanity in the races would make clear that nobody would be free until everyone was,[16] and that nobody could be freed without the saving grace of Jesus Christ. Steffens' anthropology, which started in geology, ended in the forecourt of theology.

Remarkably, Steffens claimed to have found the ingredients for his view of race in the work of Immanuel Kant. This was a rather unlikely claim of pedigree, not least because *Naturphilosophie* was generally anti-Kantian.[17] Kant wrote from the very heart of "reflexion," Steffens conceded, but was the first to intuit the significance of the "mystical origin of original sin" for an understanding of race (2:415).[18] In this Kant had come as close as anyone had to understanding the "spiritual" meaning of race, Steffens thought, as also in his discovery that the races developed as the germination of seeds (*Keime*) common to all human beings.

> From two directions, whose original unity he did not suspect, *Kant* indicated the source from afar from which we can understand the emergence of the races. In the separation in which these directions appear in Kant, they cannot of course solve the riddle. . . . But in regarding this [fall] as only a human deed, . . . in mistaking the primordial extratemporal act of nature which, one in and with the spiritual [act], generated the original sin, he could of course not recognize in it the principle of raciation. (2:415)

Had Kant but understood the "seeds" of race *spiritually*, as elements of a human nature forming the "midpoint" of nature, rather than as merely physical elements of human nature, Steffens asserted, he would have been in a position to see the whole picture of the Fall and redemption exhibited by race.

KANT

Kant was not a *Naturphilosoph* in disguise or in aspiration, but Steffens' claim of a Kantian pedigree for his understanding of race as the consequence of the Fall is harder to dismiss than one might think. We no longer see the interpretive possibilities in Kant's views which encouraged Steffens, but many of Steffens' views do indeed correspond to positions Kant took or left available. Many but not all of these shared positions were common to German enlightenment thinking about human diversity and its significance. Reading Kant through Steffens provides a valuable supplement to our inevitably anachronistic *Fragestellungen*. Explaining how and why Steffens nevertheless got Kant wrong shows long overlooked intentions behind Kant's invention of race.

Steffens claimed that Kant had come close to seeing the true significance of race "from two directions." The two directions were presumably (1) Kant's appropriation of the biblical account of the Fall in his semi-serious "Muthmaßlicher Anfang der Menschengeschichte" (published in the *Berliner*

Monatsschrift in January 1786), and (2) his three essays on race: "Von den verschiedenen Racen der Menschen" (revised edition, 1777); "Bestimmung des Begriffs einer Menschenrasse" (which appeared in the *Berliner Monatsschrift* in 1785, just two months before the "Muthmaßlicher Anfang"); and "Über den Gebrauch teleologischer Principien in der Philosophie" (1788).[19] All four writings were readily available in collections of Kant's essays,[20] as were the further discussions of the Fall in *Die Religion innerhalb der Grenzen der bloßen Vernunft* (1793/4) and of race in Friedrich Theodor Rink's edition of *Immanuel Kants Physische Geographie* (1801). It was not as arbitrary as it might seem to read these two bodies of work together. Both projects were nontheological defenses of monogenesis, and both involved a fall. I will discuss Kant's retelling of the story of the Fall first, as Genesis was the matrix both for the theories of human diversity which preceded race and—as Steffens helps us see—for race itself.

"Conjectural Beginning of Human History"

Kant's 1786 essay was a conjectural reconstruction of the early history of humanity based on our experience of human nature and the demands of freedom. Kant suggested that this conjectural history squared with Genesis 2–6:17. The essay was perhaps primarily a parody of Johann Gottfried Herder's efforts to confirm the cosmogony of Genesis through a poetic study of nature, but Kant did more than show that one could reconstruct the narrative of Genesis from many directions. Kant's philosophy of freedom led him to emphasize different aspects of Genesis. Kant started his conjectural prehistory thus:

> Unless one is to indulge in irresponsible conjectures, one must start out with something which human reason cannot derive from prior natural causes—in the present case, the existence of man. Moreover, it must be man as an adult, because he must get along without the help of a mother; it must be a pair, in order that he may perpetuate his kind; and it must be a single pair. (This is necessary in order that war should not originate at once, what with men being close to each other and yet strangers. Also, if there were an original diversity of descent [*Abstammung*], nature could be accused of having ignored the most suitable means to bring about the highest end intended for man, namely, sociability; for undoubtedly the descent of all men from a single family was the best arrangement to that end.) (AA 8: 110/54)

The assumptions called into service here, from the anti-Aristotelian rejection of man's need to be raised from childhood to the reduction of women's existence to reproduction, could occupy an entire essay. It is surely unsurprising that readers like Georg Forster saw these assumptions as no more than ad hoc arguments designed to defend a biblical conclusion without biblical or scientific arguments.

Kant went on to conjecture that this original couple must have fallen into freedom by disregarding instinct, "that voice of God which is obeyed by all animals" (AA 8:111/55). The circumstances of the Fall were insignificant, and there was nothing sinful about it. It made possible and indeed inevitable many more (and now sinful because knowing) misuses of freedom, but the Fall had been a fortunate one. It was the only way a history of freedom *properly used* could have been jump-started. The only way human beings could have become aware of their freedom was by realizing that they were capable of choosing not to heed the voice of nature, and this could happen only when humankind acted *knowingly* against nature.[21]

Kant proceeded to help himself to the narrative implications of the Fall:

> Morally, the first step from this latter state was therefore a fall; physically, it was a punishment, for a whole host of formerly unknown ills were a consequence of this fall. The history of nature therefore begins with good, for it is the work of God, while the history of freedom begins with wickedness, for it is the work of man. For the individual, who in the use of his freedom is concerned only with himself, this whole change was a loss; for nature, whose purpose with man concerns the species, it was a gain. (AA 8:115–16/60)

The "conjectural history" provided no warrant whatsoever for the conclusion that the Fall should have called forth physical evil as punishment. Kant nevertheless went on to claim that he had provided a philosophically respectable understanding of the Fall that worked as a defense of providence with respect to moral *and* phyical evil (AA 8:121–3/66–8). The essay ends:

> This, then, is the lesson taught by a philosophical attempt to write the most ancient part of human history: contentment with Providence, and with the course of human affairs, considered as a whole. For this course is not a decline from good to evil, but rather a gradual development from the worse to the better; and nature itself has given the vocation to everyone to contribute as much to this progress as may be within his power. (AA 8:123/68)

The conclusion seemed encouraging. The problem of evil had been solved, and progress in human affairs seemed assured. Like many of Kant's essays, however, the "Conjectural beginning" did not end in a grand finale so much as trail off in a series of codas pointing in different directions. In an earlier section entitled "The End of History [*Das Ende der Geschichte*]"[22] (AA 8:118/ 63), Kant's actual reconstruction of Genesis ended with the *destruction* of a humanity prematurely unified and at peace. Kant there conjecturally imagined original humanity's sliding into ever greater moral corruption, until "the human species became unworthy of its destiny, which is not to live in brutish pleasure or slavish servitude, but to rule over the earth" (AA 8:120/65). He added a parenthetical reference to Genesis 6:17, which his readers would have known: "For my part, [says God,] I am going to bring a flood of waters on the Earth, to destroy from under heaven all flesh in which is the breath of life; everything that is on the Earth shall die."

The Rhetoric of Freedom

It is easy to forget that the biblical anthropogony to which monogenetic theories of human diversity appealed involved a lot more than just the idea of a single pair of parents. The framework for Christian (as for Jewish and Islamic) maps of cultural difference had long been Genesis' account of the division and dispersion which resulted from sin. The diffusion of the sons of Noah across the globe was probably the most important.[23] Christian accounts led ineluctibly to the need for a *second* Adam, a redeemer of ever-stumbling humanity. Why did Kant end his account with the Flood, rather than with Noah or his sons (let alone with Christ)?

Herder had ended his account of the "oldest document of humankind" with Noah and his sons, asserting that the Adam-to-Noah story represented a "complete cycle," the pattern for the rest of human history.[24] This resonated with Herder's understanding of all human cultures and eras as wholes, each in its own way of vital and final significance, and none merely a means to the *telos* of the species. Kant thought human history had not yet achieved anything of final significance, and might never do so. The only hope lay in developments which nature seemed to be furthering by vice and war. Kant's 1784 "Idee zu einer allgemeinen Geschichte in weltbürgerlicher Absicht" found conflict *necessary* for moral progress. Lazy men sought concord, but nature knew better what was good for the species. Were it not for the fruits of strife, Kant argued, human beings, "good-natured as the sheep they herd, . . . would not fill the empty place in creation by achieving their end, which is rational nature" (AA 8:21/16–17).[25]

Herder objected to Kant's view of race in the second volume of his *Ideen zur Philosophie der Geschichte der Menschheit* in 1785. Kant's response in the second of his reviews of the *Ideen* was harsh: "if the happy inhabitants of Tahiti, never visited by more civilized nations, were destined to live in their quiet indolence for thousands of centuries, one could give [no] satisfactory answer to the question why they bothered to exist at all."[26] It was a kindred point Kant was making when he spoke of humanity's having become "unworthy of its destiny" in his 1786 counterappropriation of Genesis (AA 8:120/65). If human history was no more than the repetition of the Adam-to-Noah cycle, humanity would have failed to achieve its *telos*. Kant's conjectural beginning of human history thus gave reason to fear that the experiment of humanity might end in failure. The optimistic note on which the essay ended is misunderstood if we don't notice that the bulk of the essay gave at least as much reason to fear as to hope.

All of Kant's considerations of the possibility of moral progress in human history were similarly Janus-faced, however. The rhetoric of Kantian freedom *requires* that no clear answers be given to such questions. The counterpoint of voices in a key passage of the 1784 "Idea" can serve as illustration. "Man is an animal which . . . requires a master," Kant wrote there; "But whence does he get this master? Only from the human race (*Menschengattung*). But then the master is himself an animal, and needs a master. . . . The highest master should be just in himself, and yet a man" (AA 8:23/17). It is in this context that Kant made the famous claim that "from such crooked wood as man is made of, nothing perfectly straight can be built" (AA 8:23/17–18). To a reader like Steffens, Kant's description of this "most difficult" problem will have seemed to be clearing the way for Christology: fallen man cannot save himself. Yet just a page before, Kant had described how "trees in a forest," through competition for sunlight, enable (and force) each other to "achieve a beautiful, straight stature" (AA 8:22/17). Could human beings, warped and twisted by vice, ever make good? Since making good would require the self-birthing of freedom,[27] only the stalemate of individually compelling cases for *yes* and for *no* could make possible hope's *maybe*.

Hope-enabling equivocation appeared in each of Kant's accounts of the apparent emergence of freedom. Almost everything in human affairs was "paradoxical," he wrote (AA 8:41). Nature wisely wished discord where men preferred concord (AA 8:21), yet this was no guarantee of a good outcome: the democratic end result of a history of discord would be the same for men as it would be for a "nation of devils" (AA 8:366). As Kant summed up the point in *Anthropology*:

Nature within man tries to lead him from culture to morality and not (as reason prescribes) from morality and its law, as the starting point,

to a culture designed to conform with morality. And this course inevitably *perverts* his tendency and *turns it against* its end. (AA 7:328/188)

Christian notions of a paradoxically fortunate fall fit well with this rhetoric of freedom. That reason and freedom could be discovered only through an initial misuse seemed at once to promise freedom and to guarantee its impossibility. The first Adam's capacity for good was rendered notional by the Fall until the (first) coming of the second Adam, Christ. Until the Second Coming of this second Adam, however, the world and human nature were at once fallen and redeemed. One can see Kant's Janus-faced equivocations as inflected by Lutheranism, but one can also see Kant as making strategic use of Lutheran paradox in the service of the rhetoric of freedom.

Kant put the point more clearly, if not more perspicuously, in *Religion within the Limits of Reason Alone.*[28] Man might have had a prior "predisposition" to good, but his actions resulted from his "propensity" to evil (AA 6:32ff). This may seem no more than the familiar *yes* and *no* on whether man was by nature good. The way Kant went on to argue that "radical evil" could be overcome, however, was theologically quite sophisticated. The problem of the "Idea" (including the "crooked wood"; cf. AA 6:100) returned here, but a new form of socialization, besides that of competing trees in a forest, turned out to be key. Only through participation in an "ethical commonwealth" like the church could man's better nature make a place for itself in his life. Yet of this kingdom, Kant wrote cryptically, "God himself must be the founder" (AA 6:152).

The correlate to this Janus-faced history was an account of human action and motivation which built in a deliberate opacity. No act was unambiguously that of someone free. Every act exhibiting conformity with the moral law could be no more than "legal," and could in fact manifest no freedom at all. In our own cases we should always assume the worst. As we shall see, the "pragmatic" considerations of human difference in the second part of Kant's *Anthropology*—including the discussion of "the character of race"—produced an analogous opacity.[29] The paradoxical rhetoric of freedom may be all that stands between Kant's understandings of human nature and race and Steffens' appropriations.

Kant on Race

Kant's view of race was not monolithic. That there were many layers to Kant's view should be no surprise: Kant invented the concept of race after two decades of lectures on geography and on anthropology which involved discussions of the peoples he would, after 1775, designate as races. I have elsewhere argued that his view was a palimpsest: it pasted several different teleological accounts of what race allegedly accomplished on top of a set view of the hierarchy of peoples.[30] To Steffens and other later readers, this discussion of particular races was a vital part of the theory. What to us may seem Kant's incomplete sealing-off of his theory from his vicious empirical views will have seemed to Steffens and others, for whom race was not merely a theoretical question but a question of world-historical import, a deliberate leaving-open. That the white race was morally superior to the others was in the air; Kant needed no more than to leave an opening for it. In what follows, I will emphasize the openings which made Steffens' appropriation plausible.

It seems clear that Kant had views similar to Steffens' as he lectured and wrote on race and the races. Yet the most "Kantian" feature of Kant's view of race is distinct, both from a theological-historical reading like Steffens' and from modern readings which see Kant as engaged only in a discussion about scientific "classification."[31] The views Steffens attributed to Kant were in fact commonplace. Kant should be understood not so much to be endorsing them as appropriating them for his philosophy of freedom.

What might be called Kant's official view of race disavowed the need to know the actual history of the races. Tracing this history was dismissed as, at best, a "secondary project" (AA 8:91). The official view was most consistently expressed in the essay of 1785, where Kant affected a completely theoretical interest in race. Herder had claimed that any use of the language of race concerning human beings inevitably treated human beings as if their animal natures were more important than their humanity.[32] In response, Kant argued that the theoretical concept of race rested solely on the alleged necessity of the heritability of "racial" traits (AA 8:99, 101). But Kant also commended it as a solution available entirely a priori to problems facing humanity precisely and only when human nature was understood in terms of its final destiny, freedom.

Kant's starting point was his discovery in 1775 of a kind of human trait which (he thought) inherited exceptionlessly, inevitably producing "half-breeds" when people with differences in these traits mixed. These traits were determinative of what Kant called "races," which contrasted with "variations" (*Spielarten*), whose traits descended unpredictably; with "varieties" (*Varietäten*), whose traits descended unpredictably; and with special "stocks" (*Schläge*), whose traits were necessarily heritable but did not endure over many generations (AA 2:430–39).[33] Since humanity was destined to populate a globe characterized by many different climates, nature must have found a way for human beings to acclimatize without changing their fundamental natures as human beings. "Consequently," Kant argued already in 1775, "numerous seeds (*Keime*) and natural predispositions (*Anlagen*) must lie ready in human beings either to be developed or held back in such a way that he [man] might become fitted to a particular place in the world" (AA 2:435/14). As people interacted with a given climate, the relevant "seed" unfolded, "stifling" the others (AA 2:441/21). This stifling in turn explained why racial acclimatization no longer occurred, and it was thus the key to Kant's defense of monogenesis against polygenetic objections to climate theory.

Kant radicalized his claims in 1788 in response to Georg Forster's accusation that he was misrepresenting his sources. Kant now asserted that his theory didn't *need* empirical evidence. Race might or might not exist in the world, but the *concept* existed in the mind of any observer trying to think how "to unite the greatest multiplicity of generation with the greatest unity of descent" (AA 8:164/40–1). Of course this was a different teleological argument than the official view. The end in question was not the spreading of peoples over all the Earth, but the development of infinitely many different individuals. And what accomplished this wasn't really race at all but "variety." Race alone demonstrated "necessity" (AA 8:99), and was thus exhibit A for the "natural history" (*Naturgeschichte*) that Kant claimed could replace the "description of nature" (*Naturbeschreibung*) (AA 2:434n/13n; 8:110n; 8:161/38). The infinity of future types of human beings, however, was assured by the mixing of people with traits which inherited *less* predictably.

In the 1788 essay Kant asserted that nature achieved its ends through both "race" *and* "variety."

> The variety [*Varietät*] among people of the same race was in all probability laid in the original genus to establish—and in successive generations, to develop—the greatest multiplicity to the end of infinitely different purposes just as purposively as was race difference [laid] to achieve fewer but more essential purposes. (AA 8:166/42)

This was the only point Kant recapitulated in the abbreviated discussion of "The Character of Race" in the *Anthropology* of 1798. In fusing different races, he there asserted, nature aimed at *"assimilation"* (*Verschmelzung*). When it came to "family stock and the varieties or variations" (*Familienschlag und den Varietäten oder Spielarten*) within a race,

> it has made the exact opposite its law: that is, nature's law regarding a people of the same race (for example, the white) is not to let their characters constantly approach one another in likeness . . . but instead to diversify to infinity the members of the same stock and even of the same clan, in both their bodily and spiritual traits. In which case there would finally appear only one portrait, as in prints taken from the same engraving—but instead to diversify to infinity the

members of the same stock and even of the same clan, in both their bodily and spiritual/mental traits [*im Körperlichen und Geistigen*].— It is true that nurses try to flatter one of the parents by saying: "The child gets this from his father and that from his mother"; but if this were true, all forms of human generation would have been exhausted long ago. And since it is the mating of dissimilar individuals that revives *fertility*, propagation would be brought to a standstill. (AA 7:320/182)

Kant on the Races

It is not clear why mixing people of different races would interfere with this proliferation to infinity of bodily (and *spiritual/mental!*) traits.[34] To understand why Kant should have thought so, we need to attend to his particular estimations of the peoples he called "races." In geography lectures before and after his development of his theory of race, Kant presented a hierarchy of peoples which claimed a *qualitative* difference between Europeans and the rest of humanity. Steffens will have known this hierarchy from *Physical Geography*, where Kant wrote: "Mankind is at its greatest perfection in the race of Whites. Yellow Indians have a lesser talent. Negroes are far below this, and the lowest stand a part of the American peoples."[35] The white denizens of temperate zones were "more beautiful, hard-working, humorous, moderate in their passions, and smarter than all others." These people—who included "the Romans, the Greeks, the old nordic peoples, Genghis Khan, the Turks, Tamerlane, the Europeans after Columbus' discoveries"—had always educated and militarily dominated the others (AA 9:316–18).

The notes on which Friedrich Theodor Rink based his edition of the *Physical Geography* may have predated 1775 (AA 9:509ff), but the same scale of peoples surfaced in Kant's 1788 essay on race. All races had the "ability to work," he asserted there, but a "drive to activity" was something the Native American and Black races lacked. These peoples were adequately outfitted for survival in their own climates, but no amount of time spent in more strenuous climes could strengthen their "drive to activity," as demonstrated by the reported reluctance of gypsies and free Blacks living in northern climes to do strenuous work (AA 8:174n).[36] Now that all *Keime* had stopped developing, the (nonwhite) races would never push themselves to action, while Whites, whose "drive to activity" was innate, could not lose this drive even if they went to the areas where people of lesser drive were at home. Since effort was required to achieve freedom,[37] how could the nonwhite races contribute to the settlement of all the Earth with republics of free

citizens? Kant's answer seemed to be that they couldn't, and didn't need to—
for Whites *could*.

Because it has not fallen as far from the tree, the white race seemed on
Kant's account not to have lost the use of any of its moral *Keime* and *Anlagen*. The idea that "Whites" were immediate and substantially unchanged
descendents of the earliest human beings was a commonplace,[38] and the 1775–
77 essay shows it was a view to which Kant was at least at one time open.
"[W]e cannot hope now to find anywhere in the world an unchanged example
of the original human form," Kant noted—just before adducing reasons to
conclude that original humanity had been composed of the "white brunettes"
who inhabit the parts of the world most moderate in climate, between the 31st
and 52nd parallel in the Old World (AA 2:440/19):[39]

> The happiest mixture of the influences of colder and warmer regions
> as well as the greatest wealth of terrestrial creatures are found here
> and this is also where human being must diverge least from their
> original form, since the human beings living in this region are [*sic!*]
> already well-prepared to be transplanted into every other region of
> the Earth. (AA 2:441/19–20)

The use of the present tense here suggests that Kant in 1775–77 thought
that Whites—precisely because they were *not* a "race"—could still settle in
all climates.[40]

While Kant tidied up his use of language by 1785 ("Even the character
of the whites is just the development of one of the original tendencies," AA
8:106), the idea that the articulation of races was necessary in order that there
be people capable of settling in every climate was undermined clearly in both
of the later essays, too. The seeds which begat races were needed, Kant noted
in 1785, "at least *for the first epoch* of humanity's propagation (*Fortpflanzung*)"
(AA 8:98; italics mine). And in 1788 Kant emphasized that those same seeds
were indispensable *"for the first general populating of the earth"* (AA 8:169/
44; italics in original). Why a *first* population of the Earth should have been
necessary at all was far from clear. The implication that the denizens of
temperate climes could *still* be transplanted rendered the official view of why
race was necessary otiose.

Together with the claim that the stifling of *Keime* that generated the races
fatally handicapped the prospects for autonomy of all but the Whites, Kant's
account seems to suggest that the *Keime* were never intended by nature to work
alone but only in concert with each other. White brunettes could even now
expect to settle every part of the globe without falling into race. The people
reshaped by raciation simply—tragically—had set out *too soon*.[41] The destiny
of humanity would be achieved, if at all, by the *second* settlement of the world.

This picture of the not-quite-raced character of (at least some) Whites was clearest in a "summary" Kant added when he revised his first essay in 1777:

Stem Genus:
White brunettes
First race, very blond (northern Europe) of damp cold
Second race, copper-red (America) of dry cold
Third race, black (Senegambia) of damp heat
Fourth race, olive-yellow (Indians) of dry heat (AA 2:441/20)

That Kant didn't think of the Whites as a race was confirmed by the surprising terminological sloppiness of this essay written expressly to introduce terminological rigor. Kant here called Whites a "race" but also a "Schlag" and a "Geschlecht"[42]—terms he had just carefully defined "race" *against.* At one point he explicitly says that Whites and Native Americans are not a "real race" at all (AA 2:441).[43] Further, the "blond" varied from "brunettes" only as a "variation (*Spielart*)" (AA 2:430/9), and so presumably was not a "race" either.

The official view of races as climatically attuned variations of the same unchanging human nature seemed to have no *intrinsic* connection to a white-supremacist view of world history. Yet Kant's attempts to present it in neutral terms was undermined by explicit and implicit appeals to substantive views of the relative abilities and the different historical roles of the races. His view of a hierarchy of races peeked through in 1777 and 1788—together with the concession in the essays of 1785 and 1788 that race was *not* the only way human beings could spread over the whole world. These slippages make clear why Kant could have considered—although he never published—the view that "all races will be extinguished (Americans and Negroes cannot govern themselves. Thus are good only as slaves) except that of the white" (AA 15.2:878).[44] Kant did not stop ranking the various "peoples" of the world when he started calling them "races" and the slow evisceration of his official view's nonracist account of the "necessity" of raciation makes it understandable that Steffens should have thought Kant's white-supremacism remained essential to his view.

RACE, TEMPERAMENT, AND HUMAN DESTINY

Beyond Kant's official view lay a picture of human diversity strikingly similar to Steffens'. For Kant, as for Steffens, race seems to be the consequence of a fall from a state of at least possible perfection, a geographical diffusion from a common center mapped onto a diagram of the four temperaments.

There were numerous differences of detail between Kant's and Steffens' views, but diagramming their accounts of the Fall into race makes clear that they worked from the same underlying schema of human difference.

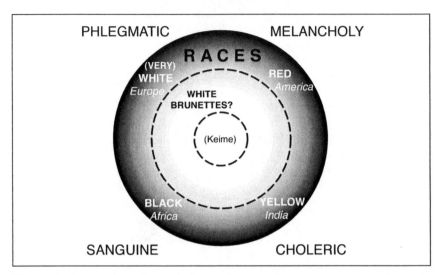

Figure 1. A mapping of correlations of geography, temperament and race in the 1777 version of Kant's "Von den verschiedenen Racen der Menschen"

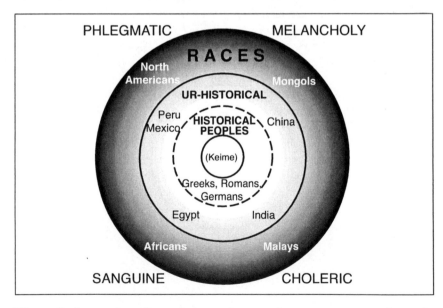

Figure 2. A mapping of correlations of geography, temperament and race in Henrich Steffens' *Anthropologie*

Those people who fell farthest were the "real races." They no longer had more than a notional capacity to achieve the human *telos*, and neither could nor needed to contribute to human history, which had always been the work of others. Nonwhites had lost the use of important *Keime* and *Anlagen*, while Whites—or some of them at least—still had access to them all.

Although Kant and Steffens divided humanity up differently and correlated peoples and temperaments differently, it is striking that the same schema underlay their views. However, the most important difference between Kant's and Steffens' ways of historically and geographically mapping human diversity lay in their differently sharp boundaries. For Steffens, "historical peoples" were clearly distinguished from the "races," but they also were still too one-sided to achieve the full freedom of love. Although history might yet be made, the point of Steffens' *Anthropologie* was that the center truly was lost, and that all of humanity (not just the *verwahrlosesten*) was so crippled by the Fall that only Christ could save it. By contrast, the uncertainty of the frontiers on both sides of the history-making Whites (with the center and the "real races") was part of Kant's rhetoric of freedom. I argued above that the rhetoric of freedom requires that accounts of progress in human history be equivocal, and accounts of human acts and motivations ambiguous. Kant's fuzzy boundaries combined elements of each of these. His White readers and listeners were left in the air: were they "raced"—that is, ruined—or not? Could they make meaningful progress toward freedom or not?

Anthropology from a pragmatic point of view (1798) made the role played by race in Kant's rhetoric of freedom clear. Kant had promised in his preface to deliver a "pragmatic" (as opposed to a "physiological") anthropological view of race (AA 7:120/3–4),[45] but the abbreviated section on "The Character of Race" seemed too short to do much of anything. And yet, as mentioned above, Kant reasserted the 1788 essay's argument for the teleological utility of "races" *and* "varieties": nature's wise plan involved maximal mixing of the latter and minimal mixing of the former (AA 7:320/ 182). Analogous appeals to a kind of providential purpose in human diversity ended all the discussions in the "Anthropological Characteristic." Accounting for "what nature makes of man" in teleological terms led to "what man can and must make of himself": "physiological" anthropology passes the torch to the "pragmatic" (AA 7:119/3).

We have seen, however, that Kant's teleological projections into the human past and future were always equivocal. Man *might* be on his way to becoming a true "citizen of the world (*Weltbürger*)" (AA 7:120/3), but the achievement of freedom was not and could not be assured. In the "Anthropological Characteristic" Kant mobilized received categories of human difference and the standard judgments as to their relative merit not only to ratify these differences, but also to turn the screws on people who thought they had transcended their natural dispositions.

I have argued elsewhere that Kant's discussion of temperament served just this purpose.[46] "Temperament" was a middle category between *Naturell*, which was explained in terms of what nature makes of man, and *Charakter*, which concerned what man makes of himself. The temperaments in turn were broken down into temperaments of "feeling" and "activity" through a distinction analogous to the one Kant had made between *Naturell* and *Charakter*. Any kind of temperament looked to be *Naturell* from one side and *Charakter* from another, so determining whether the temperamentally characteristic motivations and actions of a person were free or not turned out to be impossible. *Naturell* was not destiny, but constant effort and vigilance were necessary to transcend it. This opacity was not a weakness of the category of temperament. It was, rather, its indispensable contribution to the moral life.

The Place of Race in Pragmatic Anthropology

Race seemed to be a similarly unstable category in Kant's *Anthropology*. The discussion of the "Character of Race" was juxtaposed with the section "The Character of the Species." The former was brief and abbreviated, but student lecture notes confirm that Kant discussed the hierarchy of races here (AA 25.2:1187–88). About the "Character of the Species," however, Kant found there was not much one could say. One would need to be able to compare humanity to other free earthly beings, an impossibility as on this planet man alone was potentially free. The argument was parallel to the juxtaposition of temperament and individual character.

These discussions were followed by a final section called "Main Features of the Description of the Human Species' Character." (As in Kant's essays, it was unclear whether this was a coda to the immediately preceding discussion or to the whole work.) Here Kant suggested that there *was* a sense in which humanity could be seen as having a "character" as one member of a larger set of beings. Intriguingly, this amounted to seeing the whole human species as a race.

> The question can be raised, whether our species should be considered a *good* race or an *evil* one (for we can also call it a *race,* if we conceive of it as a species of rational *terrestrial beings* in comparison with rational beings on other planets, as a multitude of creatures originating from one demiurge); and then I must admit that there is not much to boast about in it. If we look at man's behavior not only in ancient history but also in contemporary events, we are often tempted to take the part of *Timon* the misanthropist in our judgments; but far more often, and more to the point, that of *Momus,*

who considers foolishness rather than evil as the most striking trait of character in our species. But since foolishness combined with a lineament of evil (which is then called offensive folly) is an unmistakable feature in the moral physiognomy of our species, the mere fact that any prudent man finds it necessary to conceal a good part of his thoughts makes it clear enough that every member of our race is well advised to be on his guard and not to reveal himself *completely*. (AA 7:331–2/91–92)

This extension of the concept of race is something different from any of Kant's earlier uses, but entirely compatible with the terminological opacity and instability I have explored.

Kant asserted throughout his life that human beings, while the only rational beings on Earth, were not the only rational beings in the universe.[47] In the *Groundwork* of 1785, Kant had declared speculative comparison with extraterrestrials invidious. Here, however, he revived it in order, I think, to play the kind of is-he-or-isn't-he? game with race that he had earlier played with temperament. What of the (nonwhite) races? I don't think he was thinking about them at all here, but only about those (white) peoples who he believed still possessed the potential to make history.

Suggesting that in the larger scheme of the universe, human beings of every kind were just one race among others was supposed to kindle fear that this whole race would suffer the fate of the (nonwhite) races on Earth: the irrevocable loss of any meaningful potential for freedom.[48] Even if not a "real race" in the terrestrial scheme, Whites might turn out to be part of a "race" after all in the cosmic scheme. This was precisely the kind of equivocal account the rhetoric of freedom demanded. So while Kant might in fact have believed that the borders between the "real races" and Whites were every bit as rigid as Steffens alleged they were, that would be no more than "physiological anthropology." A *pragmatic* anthropological account of race mobilized empirical and theoretical considerations on race for the sake of what man might make of himself—that part of man, that is, which was still capable of doing so.

In pragmatic anthropology, Kant emphasized his official view only for strategic purposes, and even then sloppily. From the way he discussed the particular races his readers and auditors learned that the white race was *qualitatively* different from the others. It was not just that the white race had different *Triebfedern* at the ready than did the others (the official view). Each other race *lacked* (the use of) specific *Triebfedern*, while Whites still had use of *all*. Only the other races were defined by the one-sided articulation of *Keime*. The picture Kant painted actually corresponded very well with Steffens' claim that the races exhibited in "one-sided separation" what mixed in the infinitely varied individual personalities of the members of "historical peoples." For both Kant and Steffens, Whites differed from the rest of humanity as center from periphery, as balance from imbalance, as completeness from incompleteness—and so were not really a race.

Temperament and German Destiny

Steffens' concept of a "free middle" applies remarkably well to Kant. Steffens distinguished those human beings still (more or less) in the "free middle" from those who had lost the "equilibrium" that put man above nature. As we have seen, what revealed the underlying shared humanity of the "historical people" and the "races" was temperament, whose components Steffens identified with the "seeds" of race.

Although he didn't make a point of it, this is another way, and perhaps the most profound one, in which Steffens' view of the races illuminates Kant's. I have mentioned already that Kant was devoted to the theory of the temperaments.[49] I want now to suggest that the theory of the four temperaments was Kant's matrix at least for the early conceptualization of race which Steffens claimed as a forebear. This should be no surprise, as Kant clearly thought in temperamental terms of the peoples he eventually called races throughout his career. Reading Kant through Steffens suggests that temperament may also have been the matrix for Kant's understanding of race: the scheme of the four temperaments achieved all the things a monogenetic account of human diversity needed to accomplish.

The clearest indication of the indebtedness of Kant's conceptualization of race to the theory of the temperaments came in the 1777 "summary" quoted above. There I did not mention one of the most striking features of the "summary"—the fact that it did not in fact summarize the arguments of the essay at all. *Its* four "races" corresponded to Kant's later view, but not to the particular "races" and not quite "races" discussed in the essay itself. As John H. Zammito shows in this volume, Kant encountered empirical evidence undermining his division of races soon after publishing the 1775 essay. Arguably, the "summary," with its modified list of "races," was supposed to provide a defense of Kant's understanding of race which would immunize the theory of race against inconvenient facts—something we know Kant would do in his subsequent years.

The role of the summary appended to Kant's essay was simply to look familiar. This was what a scheme of human difference was *supposed* to look like. Look again at Kant's summary. It suggested there were just four *possible* kinds of peoples, defined by the moisture and temperature of the climates which allegedly precipitated their unfolding. There was no reason to think the old world conveniently divided into a grid of hot and cold, moist and dry zones. The plausibility of the picture came instead from the fact that this correlation evoked one of the longest standing understandings of temperament:

Sanguine	Warm and Moist
Choleric	Warm and Dry
Melancholy	Cold and Dry
Phlegmatic	Cold and Moist[50]

Readers who followed up the implied correlations of temperament and race would find them confirmed in Kant's concrete descriptions in the lectures on geography and anthropology (and in their early fruit, 1764's *Beobachtungen über das Gefühl des Schönen und Erhabenen*). But Kant was not just unthinkingly reproducing the prejudices of the day. Linnaeus had just in 1758 added temperament to his influential foursome of human types.[51] Kant turned Linnaeus' correlations on their heads, asserting that Africans were not phlegmatic but sanguine—and Europeans not sanguine but phlegmatic. These were claims of considerable moment. As Monika Firla has shown, Kant's descriptions of the " 'national character' of 'the Africans' " accepted the view of Africans as constitutionally incapable of making distinctions of value—part of the discourse of fetishism which William Pietz has shown was a key component of the ideology of the slave trade.[52] As we will see, classifying Europeans as "phlegmatic" was significant, too.

The theory of the temperaments had two things to offer Kant's complicated understanding of race and of the races. First, the idea of a humanity divided into different temperaments, each a stably *different* ratio of the *same* elements, was a perfect model for the official view and for the account of a species which, though divided into permanent-seeming difference, still shared a common human nature. No other available account of human diversity could offer this. Second, the specific temperaments as Kant had come to understand them by the mid–1770s had a feature parallel to his 1777 understanding of Whites as not a "real race." The phlegmatic temperament had for many years been little more than a cipher in accounts of the temperaments (including Kant's own account in 1764). The phlegmatic seemed defined not by the preponderance of some element or humor or motive, but by the relative *lack* of all of them.

At the very same time that he developed his theory of race, however, Kant concluded that this made the phlegmatic temperament qualitatively different from the other temperaments and, at least when understood "in a good sense," an escape from the one-sidedness of temperament. What Kant at this point started to call *phlegma in significatu bono* (phlegma in a good sense) was a stable *equilibrium* of motives.[53] Unlike "phlegma as weakness," which was characterized by the absence of motives (Linnaeus' view), he who had "phlegma as strength" had all *Triebfedern* but was ruled by none.[54] At some point between his anthropology lectures of 1775–76 and 1777–78, Kant started to call this "the best of all temperaments" (AA 25.2:801, 821).

In a striking way, phlegma's status as the temperament that transcended temperament—it was characterized by balance, where the others were characterized by imbalances of various kinds—paralleled other contemporary developments in Kant's thinking. The analogy with Whites, the race that transcended race because it still had all the *Triebfedern* which have been variously "stifled" in the "real races," is clear enough. But Kant during this period also stopped describing the German national character as a kind of pastiche of the character and temperament of other nations. The German temperament was now phlegmatic—in a good sense, naturally. Indeed, Kant's claim in the *Metaphysik der Sitten* (1797) that everyone had a "duty" to develop moral "apathy" (AA 6:408)—a term which had been clearly correlated in his work with "phlegma"—can make even the timing of the invention of autonomy seem related here.

In each of these cases, an original harmonious mixture of *Keime, Triebfedern,* and *Anlagen*—that which fit the original humans for rationality and for freedom in every clime—was lost in various imbalances. The original completeness remained only (if at all) in one group, a group of phlegmatic Whites—and most particularly phlegmatic Germans—superficially *primus inter pares* but really different from the others *qualitatively*. Students who learned to understand their national character in these terms would have known to transport into Kant's discussions of their "racial" status a similar understanding of their *qualitative* superiority. Balance was no guarantee of the achievement of the human *telos*, of course. But Germans, at least, had a fighting chance to justify the existence of the human race.

CONCLUSION: FREEDOM AND FALLENNESS

Reading Kant's views of race through the lens of Steffens' *Anthropologie* has uncovered continuities even more profound than those Steffens claimed. Kant implicitly and Steffens explicitly offered a way of understanding human diversity as the result of a fortunate fall from wholeness—a fall which was superficially egalitarian in form but whose results were nationalist and racist in content. Both thinkers saw humanity as marked by the consequences of this fortunate fall into race. Both thought the consequences less dire for some peoples than for others.

Steffens marked a difference between races and "historical peoples," but suggested that all human beings were lost without the grace of Christ. Kant's view was superficially more neutral. However, his discussions of the particular races suggest that he operated with an analogous distinction. Yet Kant refused to use the concept of race in this way in what I have called his official view, where he argued for a theory of race divorced from all empirical study of the races and their history, as well as in his pragmatic anthropology, where the rhetoric of freedom demanded that no view could justify resting on one's "racial" or national laurels. The elements Steffens brought together in his theodicy of race served Kant's purposes precisely by being kept ambiguously apart. The pragmatic anthropology designed to sustain Kant's ethics required the failure of all historical as well as philosophical theodicies.[55]

Kant's and Steffens' theories of race were composed of many of the same elements. These included not only white supremacist and German nationalist convictions, but also the theological and temperamental accounts of human diversity from which Kant first derived his four-race scheme in the 1770s. Kant's view can be fully distinguished from Steffens' only if we appreciate the "pragmatic" manner in which he appropriated these elements. Steffens overlooked the "pragmatic" intention of Kant's view of race entirely. But he was not the only one to do so. The ambiguous decoupling of empirical and theoretical work on race (and on human difference more generally) required by Kant's rhetoric of freedom has been overlooked by physical anthropologists from Kant's time to our own. Steffens mistook Kant's "pragmatic" view for a theodicy of race. In taking sublime ethical exhortation for detached scientific classification, theorists of race have misunderstood the "pragmatic" intentions of Kant's theory of race no less seriously.

NOTES

1. Henrich Steffens, *Anthropologie*, 2 vols. (Breslau: Josef Max, 1822), 10. (Future references to this work will be made in text.) The term *verwahrlost* can connote neglect, desolation, depravity, and degeneration. That degenerations are what Steffens had in mind was suggested by his use of the language of deformity (*Verbildung*); see *Anthropologie* 2:404, 408, 411. Introducing the same argument in 1819, Steffens had discussed the "furchtbare Verworfenheit," the "Versunkenseyn" and "Verzerrung" of the "races." Cf. *Caricaturen des Heiligsten*, 2 vols. (Leipzig: F. A. Brockhaus, 1819, 1821), 1:47.

2. I omit scare quotes from "race" and "the races" in the rest of this essay.

3. Robert Bernasconi, "Who Invented the Concept of Race? Kant's Role in the Enlightenment Construction of Race," in *Race*, ed. Robert Bernasconi (Malden, MA and Oxford: Blackwell, 2001), 11–36, 11.

4. For the importance of Werner's Mining Academy in Freiberg for *Naturphilosophie*, see Nicholas A. Rupke, "Caves, Fossils and the History of the Earth," in *Romanticism and the Sciences*, ed. Andrew Cunningham and Nicholas Jardine (Cambridge: Cambridge University Press, 1990), 241–59, 250–52.

5. Steffens, "Ueber die Vegetation," in *Schriften: Alt und Neu* (Breslau: Josef Max, 1821), 2:10, quoted in the introduction to *Romanticism and the Sciences*, 3.

6. This formula appeared also in *Caricaturen* 1:39 and *Christliche Religionsphilosophie*, 2 vols. (Breslau: Josef Max, 1839), 1:277.

7. Cf. *Caricaturen* 1:46f.

8. Cf. *Christliche Religionsphilosophie* 1:223.

9. "If we call the chance which favors some and subjects others to the deepest reprobation (*Verworfenheit*) grace, then grace itself is contemptible, indeed the highest injustice, and in this miserable excuse of an uncomprehending piety, which if it were entirely consistent would dissolve in complete nonsense, God appears as distorted (*verzerrt*) as man is sacrificed (*Preis gegeben*)" (*Caricaturen* 1:27).

10. See *On the Natural Variety of Mankind*, 3rd ed., trans. in *The Anthropological Treatises of Johann Friedrich Blumenbach . . .*, trans. and ed. Thomas Bendyshe (London: Longman, Green, Longman, Roberts, & Green, 1865), 269. Blumenbach's five are taken over also in Christoph G. Girtanner, *Ueber das kantische Prinzip für die Naturgeschichte. Ein Versuch diese Wissenschaft philosophisch zu behandeln* (Göttingen: Vandenhoek und Ruprecht, 1796; repr., Bruxelles: Aetas Kantiana, 1968), 59.

11. Blumenbach, *On the Natural Variety of Mankind*, 1775 ed., *Anthropological Treatises*, 99, and 3rd ed. (1795), *Anthropological Treatises*, 269.

12. In Steffens' earlier patriotic writings "*Reflexion*" had been defined as the simultaneous "negation both of mankind's unconscious starting state and its conscious end state," as Werner Abelein has put it, and was linked with France and the Enlightenment. The world-historical role to be played by Germans, the only people in the world with "paradisiacal memories," was defined as the struggle against "*Reflexion*." See Abelein, *Henrik Steffens' politische Schriften. Zum politischen Denken in Deutschland in den Jahren um die Befreiungskriege* (Tübingen: Max Niemeyer, 1977), 103. For the linkage with the French, see Steffens, *Die gegenwärtige Zeit und wie sie geworden, mit besonderer Rücksicht auf Deutschland*, erster Theil (Berlin: Reimer, 1817), and Abelein, *Henrik Steffen's*, 102.

13. Steffens glossed the sanguine, melancholy, choleric and phlegmatic as the *enjoying, yearning, active,* and *passive* (*genießendes, sehnsüchtiges, thätiges, leidendes*) temperaments. See *Anthropologie* 2:441.

14. Steffens correlated the compass directions with vices. In this way the forms of desire traditionally correlated to the temperaments explained why different peoples were drawn in different directions once they left the Himalayan paradise (2:428).

15. Steffens at once expanded and contracted *Naturphilosophie*'s picture of man's place in the world. The understanding of man as the "midpoint" of the natural kingdoms of water, plants, animals and insects was only a more ambitious form of this argument. But Steffens also reproduced it *within* human nature through the temperaments.

16. Cf. *Caricaturen,* 1:27.

17. Kant was invoked already in *Caricaturen,* 1:49, and later in *Christliche Religionsphilosophie* 1:292. Steffens' teacher and friend Schelling referred to Kant's

race essays of 1785 and 1788 in his *Erster Entwurf eines Systems der Naturphilosophie. Zum Behuf seiner Vorlesungen* (Jena and Leipzig: Christian Ernst Gabler, 1799), 56, taking up the distinction there made between *Rasse, Varietät,* and *Spiel.*

18. Steffens thought Kant's "trefflicher Sinn," which "viel höher stand als sein System" (Steffens, *Caricaturen,* 1:49), was undoubtedly rooted in the "paradisiacal memories" to which he was heir as a German.

19. All references to Kant's works are to the still growing *Gesammelte Schriften=Akademie Ausgabe* (Berlin: Walter de Gruyter, 1905–), referred to in text as AA. I will refer to (while modifying) Emil L. Fackenstein's translation of the 1786 essay in Immanuel Kant, *On History,* ed. Lewis White Beck (Indianapolis: Bobbs-Merrill (LLA), 1963), 53–68; and Jon Mark Mikkelsen's translations of the essays of 1777 and 1788 in *The Idea of Race,* ed. Robert Bernasconi and Tommy L. Lott (Hackett Readings in Philosophy) (Indianapolis and Cambridge: Hackett, 2000), 8–22; and *Race,* ed. Bernasconi, 37–56, respectively. (No translation of Kant's second essay on "race" has been published.) For Kant's *Anthropology,* I refer to *Anthropology from a pragmatic point of view,* trans. Mary J. Gregor (The Hague: Martinus Nijhoff, 1974).

20. Each had been republished several times. Kant's first two race essays appeared in *Immanuel Kants frühere noch nicht gesammelte kleine Schriften* (Linz: n. p., 1795). All four essays here discussed appeared in *Kants sämmtliche kleine Schriften* (Königsberg and Leipzig [actually Jena]: n. p., 1797–98) and *Kants vermischte Schriften* (Halle: Renger, 1799).

21. The argument is consonant with the much-misread arguments in the *Grundlegung* (published shortly before this essay) which led Friedrich Schiller and others to think that for Kant duty was *always* the opposite of happiness. In fact, Kant thought the interests of long-term prudence and moral law generally coincided. This was why the gradual loss of awareness of the quality of one's motives which Kant later dubbed "radical evil" was such a danger. Without moments where one's motives were experienced as distinct, it would be impossible sincerely to believe that one chose maxims autonomously rather than heteronomously.

22. This could also be translated as "the end of the story" (as Ted Humphrey does); doubtless Kant was playing on the two possibilities.

23. See Don Cameron Allen, *The Legend of Noah: Renaissance Rationalism in Art, Science, and Letters* (1949; repr., Urbana, IL: University of Illinois Press, 1964). The African slave trade led to a new European vogue for the long-forgotten "curse of Ham."

24. The story of Noah completes "der *Cirkel der ersten Welt,* das erste *Räthsel* und *Riesenvorbild der ganzen Menschengeschichte.* Die letzten Zeiten der Welt sollen seyn, wie die Tage des Noah." See *Aelteste Urkunde des Menschengeschlechts,* 4.3.3; in *Herders Sämmtliche Werke,* ed. Bernhard Suphan, vol. 7 (Berlin: Weidmannsche Buchhandlung, 1884), 168. The argument of *Aelteste Urkunde* is reprised in book 10 of *Ideen* (part of 1785's volume 2).

25. AA 8:21; trans. Lewis White Beck in *On History,* 16–17.

26. AA 8:65; trans. Robert E. Anchor in *On History,* 50.

27. See Susan M. Shell, *The Embodiment of Reason: Kant on Spirit, Generation, and Community* (Chicago: University of Chicago, 1996).

28. The problematic of "radical evil" was introduced already in early 1792.

29. I analyze the representative fuzziness in the discussion of temperament in my "Substitutes for Wisdom: Kant's Practical Thought and the Tradition of the Temperaments," *Journal of the History of Philosophy* 39, no. 2 (April 2001): 259–88, 278–80. I argue that this ambiguity is most explicitly theorized in Kant's discussion of "parerga" in "Parerga: Rhetorical freedom, hope, and human diversity in Kant" (forthcoming).

30. See my "Sublime waste: Kant on the destiny of the 'races'," in *Civilization and Oppression*, ed. Catherine Wilson, (*Canadian Journal of Philosophy Supplementary Volume* 25, Calgary: University of Calgary Press) 1999 (See note 19), 99–137, esp. 115–16.

31. Robert Bernasconi and Tommy L. Lott, introduction to *The Idea of Race*, vii; Bernasconi, "Who Invented the Concept of Race?", 21.

32. Johann Gottfried Herder, *Ideen zur Philosophie der Geschichte der Menschheit* 7:1; see *Zweiter Theil* (Riga und Leipzig: Johann Friedrich Hartknoch, 1785), 80.

33. In "Sublime waste" I translated *Spielart* as "sport" and *Schlag* as "stamp," following the translation "On the Different Races of Man" in *This is Race: An Anthology Selected from the International Literature on the Races of Man*, ed. Earl W. Count (New York: Henry Schuman, 1950), 16–24. Mary J. Gregor uses the same translations in *Anthropology from a Pragmatic Point of View*, quoted above.

34. Nature had gone to great lengths to keep the "races" apart through cataclysms and the abiding discomfort felt by anyone in a climate different from the one in which his "racial" character had emerged. In Kant's own time, as slavery and colonialism brought the "races" into intimate contact, Kant's understanding of "races'" and "varieties" in the context of a "pragmatic anthropology" constitutes a new argument for a ban on miscegenation. See Robert Bernasconi, "Kant as an unfamiliar Source of Racism" (paper presented at the New School for Social Research, April 17, 1998), and my "Sublime waste," 112–13, 123–35.

35. Kant made explicit in lectures: only Whites have "all incentives (*Triebfedern*) and talents" (AA 25.2:1187).

36. Kant's sources here are David Hume and a pro-slavery essay, sources he used despite having access to less partial information; see Monika Firla, "Kants Thesen vom 'Nationalcharakter' der Afrikaner und der nicht vorhandene 'Zeitgeist'," in *Rassismus und Kulturalismus: Mitteilungen des Instituts für Wissenschaft und Kunst* 52, no. 3 (Wien: IWK, 1997), 7–17.

37. The significance of the presence or absence of *Eifrigkeit* is discussed in Susan M. Shell's "Kant's Concept of a Human Race," in this volume.

38. Buffon thought the "temperate" climate was the home not only of the "most beautiful" people in the world, but also where one ought to expect to see man's "original color." Cf. Buffon, *Allgemeine Historie der Natur nach allen ihren besonderen Theilen abgehandel* II/1 (Hamburg and Leipzig: Georg Christian Grund & Adam Heinrich Holle, 1752), 313. Blumenbach's list of "races" in his 1775 *De Generis Humani Varietate Nativa* began with the "first . . . which is also the primitive one," the "race of Europe." Cf. *The Anthropological Treatises . . .* , 99. For his part, Kant in 1775 claimed that one could "without any prejudice" suppose that the original was white because of the greater "perfection (*Vollkommenheit*)" of this color (2:551), but replaced the claim in 1777 with an explanation of the color(lessness) of the white kind

(*Geschlechte*) appealing to its optimal dissolution of iron in the body, "thereby proving both the perfect mixing of these juices and the strength of this human stock in comparison to the others" (AA 2:441/19).

39. For Kant, "brunette" referred to brownish "skin color (with its result, eye and hair color)" (AA 8:68).

40. Kant noted in *Anthropology* that Germans were especially well suited for settling in other lands (AA 7:317/179–80). See Susanne Zantop, *Colonial Fantasies. Conquest, Family, and Nation in Precolonial Germany, 1770–1870* (Durham and London: Duke University Press, 1997), 96.

41. I argue this claim in "Sublime waste," 121–23.

42. See my "Sublime waste," 102–105.

43. Mikkelson mistranslates "Wir können diese (he's just discussed Native Americans and Europeans) also zum wenigsten als eine Annäherung den wirklichen racen beizählen" as "We can, therefore, at least take all this as a tentative account of the origins of the real races" (20).

44. This most infamous of Kant's claims appears only in a hard-to-date note (Reflexion #1520), and was, so far as we know, not Kant's considered view. That it makes such good sense of the loose ends in Kant's published views must surely give us pause, however.

45. "Eine solche Anthropologie, als Weltkenntniß, welche auf die Schule folgen muß, betrachtet, wird eigentlich alsdann noch nicht pragmatisch genannt, wenn sie ein ausgebreitetes Erkenntniß der Sachen in der Welt, z.B. der Thiere, Pflanzen und Mineralien in verschiedenen Ländern und Klimaten, sondern wenn sie Erkenntniß des Menschen als Weltbürgers enthält.—Daher wird selbst die Kenntniß der Menschenrassen als zum Spiel der Natur gehörender Producte noch nicht zur pragmatischen, sondern nur zur theoretischen Weltkenntniß gezählt."

46. See my "Substitutes for Wisdom," esp. 277–80.

47. See especially the "Anhang, von den Bewohnern der Gestirne" in 1755's *Universal Natural History and Theory of the Heavens* (1:351–65). Extraterrestrials appeared even in the *Critique of Pure Reason* (A 825/B 853).

48. Kant's discussions of race and other forms of human difference were often in the register of the sublime.

49. See my "Substitutes for Wisdom." Harro Wilhelm Dircksen *Die Lehre von den Temperamenten, neu dargestellt* (Nürnberg & Sulzbach: Seidel, 1804), 62, credited Kant and Christoph Wilhelm Hufeland with having saved four-temperament theory from oblivion.

50. Johann Heinrich Zedler's *Grosses Vollständiges Universal-Lexicon*, for instance, reported that the sanguine, choleric, phlegmatic, and melancholy temperaments are often referred to as *humidum calidum, calidum siccum, frigidum humidum, frigidum siccum*, respectively. See article "Temperament des Leibes," vol. 42 (Leipzig & Halle: Zedler, 1744), 763–77, 765. This correlation goes back at least to the Hippocratic "On the nature of man."

51. See *Caroli Linnaei . . . Systema Naturae per regna tria naturae, secundum classes, ordines, genera, species, cum characteribus, differentiis, synonymis, locis* (Holmiae: n. p., 1758; Landmarks of Science Microprint), 1:20–2; also *A General*

system of Nature through the three Grand Kingdoms of Animals, Vegetables, and Minerals, trans. W. Turton, 7 vols. (London: Lackington, 1802–6), 1:9.

52. See Firla, "Kants Thesen vom 'Nationalcharakter' der Afrikaner..."; William Pietz, "The problem of the fetish, IIIa: Bosman's Guinea and the enlightenment theory of fetishism," *Res* 16 (Autumn 1988): 105–23.

53. Kant had had the ingredients of his mature celebratory view of the phlegmatic to hand for a decade before he put them together. A non-temperamental *phlegma in significatu bono* was discussed in the text for Kant's lectures on ethics, Alexander Baumgarten's *Ethica philosophica* (1751), section 249, reprinted at AA 27:938. Kant's exploration of the distinction between "equilibrium" and "indifference" in "Versuch den Begriff der negativen Größen in die Weltweisheit einzuführen" (1763) seems to be the key to splitting the phlegmatic into a strong and a weak form (AA 2:171–80). See my "Substitutes for Wisdom," 274–5.

54. See my "Substitutes for Wisdom," 281–2.

55. The importance of theodicy's failure for Kantian ethics is discussed in my "Autonomy and the invention of theodicy," in *New Essays on the History of Autonomy: A Collection Honoring J. B. Schneewind*, ed. Natalie Brender and Larry Krasnoff (Cambridge: Cambridge University Press, 2004), 61–91.

III

Race in the Sciences of Culture

7

The German Invention of *Völkerkunde*

Ethnological Discourse in Europe and Asia, 1740–1798

Han F. Vermeulen

Anthropology is characterized by a fundamental distinction between the physical study of the human species (physical anthropology or anthropobiology) and the sociocultural study of humankind (social or cultural anthropology). As the term anthropology is in use for both approaches, it is vital to distinguish between them for historical purposes. The American historian of anthropology George W. Stocking, Jr. calls anthropology "the hybrid study of human culture and nature," describing it as "a hybrid discipline uniting at least two distinct scholarly traditions: the natural historical and the social theoretical (with input as well from various lines of humanistic inquiry)."[1] This statement is in accord with the American "four-fields approach," which, together with archaeology and linguistic anthropology, links the two traditions in a common study program. In Europe, however, physical and cultural anthropology have developed separately and, even today, are seen as separate branches of learning. Both studies are generally regarded as having emerged in the mid-nineteenth century, parallel to and influenced by evolutionism. The papers collected in the present book demonstrate that this dating is false as far as physical and philosophical anthropology are concerned. I shall adopt the same position and argue that sociocultural anthropology also emerged much earlier than has been assumed, namely, during the eighteenth century.

Ethnography is one of anthropology's most important components and, in fact, its distinguishing feature. This applies especially to cultural and social anthropology: the terms "cultural anthropology" and "social anthropology" were introduced as new names for a study previously called "ethnology" (*Völkerkunde*) or "ethnography." This process of name-changing took place in the United Kingdom during the 1870s,[2] in France and the United States during the 1880s, in the Netherlands after World War II, and in Germany after the fall of the Berlin Wall (1989). From the 1920s, thanks to the Malinowskian revolution, ethnography has come to be regarded as being characterized by long-term fieldwork in a foreign society. Nowadays, ethnography is the single most important term in the anthropological vocabulary; it is characteristic for fieldwork-based research conducted by cultural and social anthropologists. As we shall see, "ethnography" is also the oldest of the ethnos-concepts, originating from eighteenth-century praxis as a study of peoples and of nations.

The history of anthropology has been studied in great detail by a variety of scholars, but studies on the history of ethnography are rare.[3] Ethnography as a descriptive study is subordinated to "anthropology," a broader term denoting the "study of man," of mankind or humankind. The term "anthropologia," dating back to the sixteenth century (first reported in 1501), has been employed since the mid-nineteenth century (1860 in France, 1871 in the United Kingdom) as an encompassing concept: an umbrella term, so to speak, for a group of studies dealing with humankind and its diversity. Generally, however, "anthropology" came to stand for the physical study of man, particularly on the European continent, whereas cultural or social anthropology was denoted as "ethnology" (*Völkerkunde* in German-speaking countries, *volkenkunde* in Dutch). Lately, since 1989, the term "ethnology" has been abandoned by cultural and social anthropologists—leaving the term free for appropriation by students of folklore (*Volkskunde*), which is now referred to as "European ethnology."

Recent research has demonstrated that ethnography and ethnology emerged much earlier than has been assumed, namely, in the second half of the eighteenth century rather than in the mid-nineteenth. The concept "ethnographia" first surfaced in 1767 and 1771 (in the latter case as *Ethnographie*); the terms *Völkerkunde* and *Volkskunde* in 1771 and 1776, respectively. "Ethnologia," meanwhile, appeared in 1781–83 and "ethnologie" in 1787.[4] Contrary to the standard account, this development took place not in Scotland, the United States, or France, but in German-speaking areas including Austria, Switzerland, and what later became Germany. These terms first arose in the work of German historians associated with the Second Kamchatka expedition (1733–43) working in Russia and the Siberian parts of Asia, and—a few decades later—in that of German-speaking historians connected to the University of Göttingen (Germany) or operating in Vienna (Austria) and Lausanne (Switzerland).

On the basis of these new datings of strategic concepts in anthropology, we must revise the history of anthropology, including ethnology and ethnography. Michèle Duchet, in her celebrated *Anthropologie et histoire au siècle des Lumières* (1971, 2nd ed. 1995), concentrated on the anthropological discourse of French philosophers such as Georges-Louis Buffon, Voltaire, Jean-Jacques Rousseau, Claude-Adrien Helvétius, and Denis Diderot. She also identified an "ethnological discourse,"[5] but was able to identify only one of the authors contributing to that discourse: the Swiss Protestant French- and German-speaking theologian Alexandre-César Chavannes, who used the term "ethnologie" in 1787 and 1788. Chavannes, working at Lausanne, saw "ethnologie" as part of a larger study or anthropology, which he called "a new science" (*une science nouvelle*) or "general science of man" (*science générale de l'homme*).[6]

In this essay I shall present central- and eastern-European ethnological discourse in relation to the anthropological discourse discussed in the present book. My thesis is that an ethnological discourse developed during the eighteenth century alongside, and partly in opposition to, the anthropological discourse, subsequently defined as either the philosophical or the physical study of man. The relevance of this thesis is clear: if a discourse on peoples and on nations (*Völker*) developed alongside a discourse on race and on races; if, further, this discourse developed even earlier than the racial discourse, which is the subject of the present book, then we have to reflect on its origins. Cultural and social anthropology are direct offshoots of ethnology, and the study of cultured groups is widely pursued today. What, then, is the relationship between these two discourses? How do they affect one another?

Concentrating on those German-speaking historians working in Russia, Germany, Austria/Hungary, and Switzerland who have dealt with ethnography and ethnology as a nascent discipline, I shall in the following discuss four stages in a process lasting half a century. I shall then concentrate on the discipline's relations with anthropology, particularly as applied by the philosophers Immanuel Kant and Johann Gottfried von Herder, and shall conclude by presenting some conclusions on ethnological discourse in eighteenth-century Europe and in Asia.

1. THE INTRODUCTION OF "VÖLKER-BESCHREIBUNG" (1740)

A possible prototype of ethnography was the German concept "Völker-Beschreibung," denoting a descriptive study of peoples (*Völker*). This term occurred some thirty years earlier than "ethnography," not in Germany but in the Russian Empire. In fact, the concept "Völker-Beschreibung" first appeared in Siberia, where it was used by German-speaking explorers such as Gerhard Friedrich Müller (in 1740) and Peter Simon Pallas in 1781.

Gerhard Friedrich Müller (1705–1783), a historian educated at Leipzig, had traveled to St. Petersburg in 1725, where he was invited to become a junior member of the Russian Academy of Sciences. He taught Latin, history, and geography at the academic *gymnasium*, attended sessions at the Russian Academy, and worked in the Academy's library and archives. He edited several journals and was appointed professor of history at the Academy in 1731. Müller was present as secretary when the extensive collections of Daniel Gottlieb Messerschmidt (1685–1735) were catalogued in the Russian Academy of Sciences in 1728. Messerschmidt had been the first Western explorer of Siberia and had traveled through the eastern parts of the Russian Empire as far as its Chinese and Mongolian frontiers (1720–27). The impressive collections of "indigenous natural-historical objects and rarities" he acquired were included in the Imperial *Kunstkamera* (*Kunstkammer*), founded at St. Petersburg in 1713–14. A few years after Messerschmidt's return, Müller embarked on the Second Kamchatka expedition (1733–43). Directed by Vitus Bering, this expedition would take Müller to the heart of Siberia, albeit not to Kamchatka itself. During this trip, Müller assembled huge collections pertaining to the history, geography, and linguistics of the Siberian peoples, in addition to ethnographical and archeological artifacts.

Müller's reputation is based on his publications in the fields of Siberian history and geography. By contrast, his ethnographic work has hardly been published and is almost unknown in the West. Müller published very little on Siberian ethnography, and the ethnographic artifacts, including Siberian costumes he collected in northern Asia, were destroyed by a fire in the *Kunstkammer* in 1747. Recent research in Russia and East Germany reveals, however, that Müller not only collected artifacts, but also made ethnographic inquiries along the way, the results of which he recorded in a separate logbook. This journal was recently published as *Nachrichten über Völker Sibiriens (1736–1742)*.[7] These ethnographic fieldnotes served as the basis for Müller's systematically arranged description of Siberian peoples (*Beschreibung der sibirischen Völker*).[8]

Thanks to these works, it has finally become clear that Müller dealt not only with the history and geography of Siberia, but also, and quite extensively, with the ethnography of Siberian peoples. Müller's interest in this subject is also demonstrated by the instructions, at least six, which he wrote for his own assignment and for those of his assistants and his successor.[9] The last instruction, dated June 1740, is the most important. Having been underway for seven years, Müller requested that he be replaced for health reasons.

Then, in Surgut, on the borders of the Ob river, he wrote an elaborate instruction for the "geographical and historical description of Siberia" to be carried out by his successor, Johann Eberhard Fischer (1697–1771), a German historian and linguist. The sixth and final part of this document dealt with "the description of manners and customs of peoples" (*Von Beschreibung der Sitten und Gebräuche der Völcker*). In it Müller summed up in 923 points all aspects to be studied by Fischer and his assistants in Siberia. Starting with the outward appearance of peoples, including physical characteristics, Müller moved from language to cultural subjects, including religion. The editor Fjodor Russow called this sixth part "ethnographisch" but Müller himself summarized it as "Völker-Beschreibung."[10] Thus, apart from studying the history and geography of Siberia, Müller also collected ethnographic artifacts (including textiles), made ethnographic inquiries among Siberian peoples, and wrote a systematic study of those peoples on the basis of his own field recordings and those of his assistants.[11] In addition, and in order to arrive at such a "Völker-Beschreibung" of Siberia, Müller summarized his ethnographic findings in an extensive catalogue (1740), a veritable "Notes and Queries" consisting of almost one thousand questions waiting to be answered in Siberia.

2. THE EMERGENCE OF "ETHNOGRAPHIA" (1767–1775)

It took less than thirty years for ethnography, the neo-Greek equivalent of the term "Völker-Beschreibung," to surface in Germany. In 1767 the term "ethnographia" occurred in a short history of Swabia (*Prolvsio scholastica qva Sueviae veteris*) written in Latin by Johann Friedrich Schöpperlin (1732–1772), a historian and head of a *gymnasium* at Nördlingen (Swabia). Following a description of the Swabian people and their history, Schöpperlin remarked: "Ethnographia haec potius dicenda est, quam geographia Sueviae veteris, quam nunc brevissime subiicimus," meaning: "This (the preceding) must rather be called the ethnography than the geography of ancient Swabia, which we shall now briefly represent."[12] The idea was that for the study of the ancient history of Swabia ethnography was crucial, rather than geography, as the ancient inhabitants of that area were still migrating. The term "ethnographia" was coined from the Greek words "ethnos" (people, *Volk*) and "graphein" (to write). Its introduction was an important innovation in the field of history. The distinction Schöpperlin made between "ethnographia" and "geographia" is clear-cut, and it could confirm Hans Fischer's hypothesis that the term *Ethnographie* was coined by analogy to the word *Geographie*.[13] In a journal he coedited at Nördlingen, Schöpperlin returned to the parallellism between geography and ethnography: "In geography proper, as far as she is recently distinguished from ethnography [. . .]."[14] This indicates that the term "Völker-Beschreibung" had become known on a wider scale since 1740. Schöpperlin used "ethnographia" more or less in passing, as if it spoke for itself. He did not claim its coinage, nor did he provide its definition. He did, however, use it in important contexts, contrasting it with geography while reserving it a special place as a new discipline in historiography.

Four years later August Ludwig Schlözer (1735–1809), an up-and-coming historian at Göttingen, introduced the term "Ethnographie" in his *General History of the North* (*Allgemeine Nordische Geschichte*), published at Halle in 1771. In this book, Schlözer presented a new outline of the history of the European and Asiatic North in an attempt to supplant earlier "myths" with fresh new ideas on the origin, kinship, and migration of the Nordic nations. Those nations in the European part of this enormous area were divided in five large groups, in fact language groups, which Schlözer spoke of as "Haupt- und Stammvölker." These included not only the Germanic, Slavic, Lettish, and Finnish peoples, but also the Samoyeds; the latter also partly belonged to Europe due to their location west of the Urals—which Schlözer, following Müller, suggested as a boundary between Europe and Asia. For the Asiatic part of the north, Schlözer mentioned no fewer than twenty-two peoples, which we nowadays would call ethnic groups but which Schlözer called "Völker"; these groups he, following Leibniz and Müller, distinguished on linguistic grounds.[15]

In this context, Schlözer introduced the concepts "Völkerkunde" (ethnology), "Ethnographie" (ethnography), "ethnographisch" (ethnographic), and even "Ethnograph" (ethnographer). He did not present a definition of these terms, but from the context in which he used them, and on the basis of contemporary sources, it seems clear (1) that "Ethnographie" was seen as the equivalent of the German term "Völkerkunde" (a study of peoples); (2) that it occurred in contrast to such terms as "Kosmographie," "Chronographie," "Geographie," "Biographie," "Technographie," and "Hydrographie;" and (3) that the meaning of "ethnographisch" was more or less equivalent to ethnography's present-day meaning as a descriptive study of peoples or nations, of cultures or societies. Thus, we may conclude that "Ethnographie" in Schlözer's view was a generalized science of peoples, empirical and descriptive as well as holistic and universal.[16] If there was to be a study of peoples (*Völkerkunde*), all peoples of the world should be included and, in principle, all aspects should be dealt with.

Of special interest here is the concept "ethnographisch," which Schlözer introduced in his monograph of 1771 and in a later book titled *Vorstellung seiner Universal-Historie* (Göttingen 1772, 2nd ed. 1775). In the latter, a manual for students, Schlözer devised an "ethnographical method" as one of the four methods of history[17]—basically, a history of the world arranged according to peoples. "Following the ethnographical method," Schlözer wrote, "world history would have as many chapters as there are separate peoples."[18] In the preface to the second edition Schlözer estimated that "between 150 and 200 peoples" exist, adding: "We need a description of each." Therefore, at least 150 or 200 ethnographies should be written in order to arrive at a genuine world history.

It is likely that Schlözer formed the connection between Schöpperlin and Müller, as he had been in contact with both. Schlözer was a relative of Thilo and had been Müller's assistant for half a year at St. Petersburg. He had lived in Müller's house in 1761–62, until he found his own specialization: the ancient and modern history of Russia.

3. THE EMERGENCE OF "VÖLKERKUNDE" (1771–1775)

In addition to "Ethnographie" and "ethnographisch," Schlözer introduced *Völkerkunde*, another concept of scholarly importance. This term, even if it has lately been losing ground to "ethnology" and especially to "social anthropology," is still in use as the name of the discipline of (sociocultural) anthropology in Germany. Schlözer used the term *Völkerkunde* both in his monograph *Allgemeine Nordische Geschichte* (1771) and in *Vorstellung seiner Universal-Historie* (1772). Although "ethnographisch" is the most important and in any case longest lasting of these terms, it is clear that by coining the term "Völkerkunde," Schlözer elevated the descriptive work of Müller and of others to a higher, more general level.

Völkerkunde as such means "knowledge of peoples," and Schlözer contrasted it with *Weltkunde*, the "knowledge of the world." In his *Allgemeine Nordische Geschichte*, Schlözer showed little respect for the *Weltkunde* of the ancient Greeks and Romans: "Their ethnology could not reach beyond their cosmology" [*Ihre Völkerkunde konnte nicht weiter als ihre Weltkunde gehen*], adding that their cosmology ended at the Rhine, Danube, Don, and Tigris rivers; in the same context, he wrote about the ignorance of the Greeks in regard to cosmology (*Welt-Unkunde der Griechen*).[19] More respect, according to Schlözer, was due the ancient Persians who had under Cyrus founded the first "world empire," which implied "the first large state union of humankind." The Persians had united four principal peoples from the Ancient World as well as peoples from three continents, bringing the kingdoms of the Assyrians, the Babylonians, and the Medes within a single state.[20] With the Romans, history had become somewhat "world historic"; with Cyrus and the founding of the Persian Empire, "the world itself had become world historic." "Only since then did humankind join in closer union and acquaintance."[21] Although the object of such a *"Völkerkunde"* was *all* peoples, only a selection of peoples could be discussed in a systematic world history, which would focus on the interconnection of peoples and of states. Peoples who had founded states were, according to Schlözer, more advanced than those peoples without a state insofar as the former party had connected other peoples. Therefore, the study of the former was more essential both to arriving at that process of increased connection (*Verbindung*) which occurs partly through conquests; and to arriving at a greater *Verkettung* of the world, namely, at that process of increased concatenation on a global scale which we, since the fall of the Berlin Wall, call "globalization."[22] Schlözer was one of the first world historians to pay close attention to this process of increasing interconnectedness, and it is highly significant that he introduced the terms *Ethnographie* and *Völkerkunde* in this context.

The second source in which the concepts *Völkerkunde* and *Ethnographie* appeared, and the first in which they were expressly equated with each other, was an overview of geography (*Abriß der Geographie*) by Schlözer's senior colleague, the historian Johann Christoph Gatterer (1727–1799). This book is dated 1775 but it appeared in 1778, even if the relevant sections occur in passages that were printed in 1775. Gatterer spoke of "Menschen- und Völkerkunde (Anthropographia und Ethnographia)," giving the subject a place in his classification of geographical sciences. He divided geography in four main chapters, including physical geography (*Gränzkunde*), geography proper (*Länderkunde*), political geography (*Staatenkunde*), and ethnology (*Völkerkunde*). The latter category was combined with anthropology (*Menschenkunde*), thereby linking both the anthropological and the ethnological discourses. Gatterer formulated his views on the classification of geographical sciences as follows:

> The entire description of the Earth, with and without respect to the division in ancient, middle and new [periods], can conveniently be brought, I think, under four main categories or sciences: (1) the study of boundaries [*Gränzkunde (Horismographia)*], (2) the study of countries [*Länderkunde (Chorographia)*], (3) the study of states [*Staatenkunde (Poleographia* or *geographica Politice)*], and (4) the study of people and peoples [*Menschen- und Völkerkunde (Anthropographia* and *Ethnographia)*]. As we deal with geography here, it stands to reason that these four artificial terms are to be taken in their geographical meaning, not in their historical, political or statistical sense.[23]

That Gatterer classified the new discipline of *Völkerkunde* in the domain of geography is remarkable, as Schlözer had given it a place in the historical domain and had even designed an "ethnographical method" as one of the four methods of history (see above). The reason for this reordering was probably that Gatterer was aware that some peoples, including "wild peoples" (*wilde Völker*), do not have a written history (as he wrote in 1773);[24] this made their treatment within the discipline of history problematic. However, as Gatterer regarded geography as an auxiliary discipline of history, it was to be expected that the results obtained by ethnography—within the domain of geography— would find their way back into the mother discipline of history, from which ethnography had just been split off.

Gatterer also presented a first table of contents of the combined *Menschen- und Völkerkunde*, which should deal with people according to: (1) the human body, both in terms of stature and of color; (2) languages; (3) religions; (4) natural products; (5) culture (*Kultur*); (6) trade; and (7) geography.[25]

Schlözer and Gatterer were the first two historians to use the concept *Völkerkunde*, not only in what later became Germany, but also worldwide. The University of Göttingen occupied a central place in the scholarly network of Germany, connecting western Europe and the Americas with eastern Europe and Asia. That the concept *Völkerkunde* was coined in the context of a study of peoples introduced by Müller in Siberia (1740) and by Schöpperlin in Swabia (1767) places this fact in a much brighter light. The next step was to move from a descriptive study of separate peoples towards a general science of the same.

4. From "Ethnographia" to "Ethnologia" (1767–1787)

Several years after the concepts *Völkerkunde* and *Ethnographie* had been introduced, the concepts *Volkskunde* and *Ethnologie* appeared. In Germany the term "Volks-Kunde" first surfaced in the journal *Der Reisende* (The Traveller), published in 1782 by Friedrich Ekkard, a close collaborator of Schlözer's.[26] It reappeared in 1787 in an article by Joseph Mader in Prague, and in 1788 in a Stuttgart chronicle by the popular poet C. F. D. Schubart.[27] Although none of these authors supplied a definition for *Volkskunde*, its meaning was probably the same as *Völkerkunde* in the singular, that is a study of a (one) people, as opposed to the study of more than one people or even of all peoples.

In the Netherlands, however, the term *Volkskunde* appeared even earlier, namely, in the work of the Dutch physician and natural historian Johannes le Francq van Berkhey (1729–1812). Le Francq used the term in volume three of his *Natuurlyke historie van Holland* (published at Amsterdam in 1776), in which, at the end of a chapter on children's games, he writes: "The foregoing expositions will suffice, I trust, to open up this subject. Its study still seems to lack in our *Volkskunde* [in the study of our people] and, in my opinion, is here highly appropriate."[28] There may have been a connection with Göttingen scholars again, as Le Francq later adapted an introduction to natural history for children, written by George Christian Raff and published in Göttingen (*Naturgeschichte für Kinder,* 1778), for a Dutch readership as *Natuurlyke historie voor kinderen* (1781).

More fundamental was the term "Ethnologie," which many scholars suppose was first used in 1787 by Alexandre-César Chavannes (1731–1800), professor of theology in Lausanne. This reference has been known for more than a century in France and Switzerland.[29] However, an earlier, even more important reference to the term, discovered by Ján Tibensky, a historian from Bratislava (Slovakia), in 1978, has long been neglected in western Europe.[30] Tibensky found out that the concept "ethnologia" already occurred in a work by the historian and librarian Adam Ferenz Kollár (1718–1783) on the History and Constitutional Law of the Kingdom of Hungary, written in Latin (Vienna, 1783). The importance of this discovery is not only that Kollár introduced this term earlier than Chavannes (the term may have been common in the intervening years), but Kollár also supplied a definition, different from the one given by Chavannes, which comes close to the (implicit) meaning of *Ethnographie* given by Schlözer. Chavannes's definition was general in scope. He defined *ethnologie* as "the history of peoples progressing towards civilization" [*l'histoire des progrès des peuples vers la civilisation*],[31] and saw ethnology as a part of anthropology, or "the general study of man."[32] This definition fit well within the conceptual scheme of the Enlightenment and its theory of stage-like progress. But Kollár, four years earlier, defined "Ethnologia" in a quite different way:

> Ethnology, which I have mentioned occasionally above, is the science of nations and peoples, or, that study of learned men in which they inquire into the origins, languages, customs, and institutions of various nations, and finally into the fatherland and ancient seats, in order to be able better to judge the nations and peoples in their own times.[33]

This means that Kollár, writing from Vienna, the capital of the Austrian-Hungarian multinational state, generalized Schlözer's view, extending "ethnologia" to peoples and to nations (*populis* and *gens*). His list of topics included the origins, languages, customs, (legal) institutions, and "ancient seats" of nations; and he added that ethnology's aim was also a practical one: to improve evaluations of nations and of peoples in their own day and age. Earlier, in his annotations to Petrus Lambecius, Kollár had written ". . . Graecos ultra Istrum ac Tanaim in geographicis admodum parum, in ethnologicis nihil omnino vidisse" [beyond the Danube and the Don the Greeks noticed very little in geography and nothing in ethnology].[34] This view comes close to what we observed earlier in Schöpperlin, Schlözer and Gatterer.

In fact, the meaning of Schlözer's *Ethnographie* was very similar to Kollár's *Ethnologia*; both concepts referred to a historical description of peoples. However, Kollár added "nations," as he referred to ethnology as *notitia gentium populorumque*, that is, the study of nations and of peoples. The main object of this study was to arrive at reliable information on "the origins of nations," or, as Schlözer called it, *origines gentibus*. This was an old problem; but new was the linguistic method used in order to arrive at information on the early history of peoples of which no documented history existed.

We find in the *Ethnographie* and *ethnologia* presented by Schlözer and Kollár a very different kind of ethnology from that presented in Chavannes's *Ethnologie*. This difference was expressed by Vitomir Belaj in the following way: whereas the definition by Chavannes "puts an emphasis on the understanding of the laws of the general development of mankind," Kollár's definition places it "on the ethnic characteristics of the culture of a certain group of people (*gens*)." While Kollár's "criteria are cultural" and his orientation is historical, Chavannes's "subject matter is 'people' as a political, i.e. sociological category"; and Chavannes's "aim is to reconstruct the universal cultural development of all mankind."[35] Belaj also pointed at the different conceptions of *Volk* implicit in these definitions of ethnology: in the definition of Kollár the "ethnic characteristics" of a group of people are considered important; in that of Chavannes, the concept "people" became a sociopolitical category or "another word for a certain stage of development in the hierarchy of universal history" (ibid.).

In Kollár's view, as in Schlözer's, ethnology and anthropology are not explicitly related. In their views on history, and how it should be reformed, there is a need for a philosophically informed discourse on human development, but not for a study of the physical differences among people and between humans and other animals. This is striking, as such a connection does occur in Gatterer's and Chavannes's work. It also occurs, explicitly, in the historical and philosophical work of Johann Gottfried Herder.

5. The View of Herder

Alongside the view of Schlözer and Kollár on the one hand, and that of Chavannes on the other, there was a third perspective on ethnology—an even more appealing one. This view, developed by the philosopher and historian Johann Gottfried Herder (1744–1803), was influential in the northern and eastern parts of Europe, particularly through his *Ideen zur Philosophie der Geschichte der Menschheit* (4 vols. 1784–91) and his later *Briefe zur Beförderung der Humanität* (1793–97). Herder's ideas on the originality of the "folk-life," as expressed in national songs or "Volkslieder," which he began collecting in

1772, added to the rise of nationalism in eastern Europe, particularly in Poland and Bohemia.[36] Herder's star rose again in the early twentieth century, when Franz Boas used Herder's vision in his successful attempts to found (modern) ethnology in the United States.[37] Herder's work has remained important ever since as one of the major sources of anthropological thinking.[38]

Whereas for Schlözer *Volk* was a taxonomical unit, a subgroup of the larger unity of humankind, Herder regarded *Volk* as something natural and organic in which humanity expressed itself. These differences are essential, since Schlözer was a staunch adherent of the Enlightenment, in particular of the German *Spätaufklärung*, whereas Herder belonged to the avant-garde of that countermovement to the Enlightenment called *"Frühromantik,"* which in the early nineteenth century resulted in Romanticism proper (*Hochromantik*). Already in 1772 Herder attacked not only Schlözer's concept of "ethno-graphisch," which he found "difficult" and ugly,[39] but also Schlözer's view on world history and especially his implicit assumption that humankind was progressing through specific stages of civilization towards some penultimate goal: "Where is that one great endpole? Where is the straight way leading to it? What does 'progress of the human race' mean? Is it Enlightenment?"[40]

Schlözer reacted with a second volume of his *Vorstellung* in 1773,[41] but could offer very little in reply to Herder's main critique. Schlözer had taken great pains to distinguish between the different definitions of *Volk* current at the time. In his *Allgemeine Nordische Geschichte* (1771) and *Vorstellung seiner Universal-Historie* (1772), Schlözer distinguished between a "geo-graphic," a "genetic" (or historical), and a "political" definition of *Volk*, summarizing his views by stating that in the first definition people are regarded as making up a class of peoples (in the Linnaean sense); in the second as belonging to a tribe (*Stamm*); and in the third as forming a state.[42] He con-cluded his exposition with the remark: "It would be difficult to imagine how fertile and important these distinctions will be for a critique on [ancient] ethnology [i.e., on the knowledge of peoples]."[43]

Further reactions by Herder to Schlözer's work are few. Herder simulta-neously worked on his own project of writing a world history, to which purpose he contributed part of his travel journal (1769), a fragment on the teaching of the subject (*Grundriß des Unterrichts in der Universal-historie*; 1773, unpublished at the time), and his essay *Auch eine Philosophie der Geschichte zur Bildung der Menschheit* (1774; its title is intentionally sarcas-tic). Especially in his later works, the *Ideen zur Philosophie der Geschichte der Menschheit* (1784–91), and *Briefe zur Beförderung der Humanität* (1793–97), Herder put forward a relativist, almost pluralistic vision of world history in which peoples are regarded not as objects in an "aggregate," as Schlözer had suggested, but as the "most noble part of humanity" (*edelsten Teil der Menschheit*), possessing an inherent value of their own. A people's value, indeed their specificity was not to be judged by reference to the stage (or phase) which they occupied.

In his work, Herder consistently seems to have avoided the term *Ethnographie*. He occasionally used the term *Völkerkunde* but never again *ethnographisch*. His ethnological view, expressed in the sixth book of his *Ideen*, was deeply entrenched in his anthropological vision of humankind and of *Völker* as the bearers of humanity. Instead, Herder preferred more poetic phrases such as a "painting of nations" [*Gemälde der Nationen*] or "a painting of the diversity of our species" [*ein Gemälde der Verschiedenheit unseres Geschlechts*].[44]

Ironically, Herder, who is generally accepted as a founder of anthropology, while not accepting Schlözer's term *Ethnographie*, contributed to nationalism in Europe, whereas Schlözer, a real patriot (in the sense of a *citoyen* or *Weltbürger*), introduced the new science of peoples or of nations—without any real influence on nationalism as it later developed.[45] Was *Völkerkunde* therefore a descriptive reflection on the condition of peoples or of nations, a reflection that developed *before* the phenomenon of nationalism had reached such a magnitude as to become visible on the world screen? Or have certain protoforms of this social process escaped our attention?

The relation between "Nation" and "Volk" seems relevant in the context of current discussions on ethnicity as a broader, more general phenomenon than nationalism. The question is: how was it possible that that study of nations dubbed *Völkerkunde* was conceived before the political movement of European nations gained momentum?

During the following years in Germany and in surrounding countries, the subject of *Völkerkunde* was developed most intensively in combination with "Länderkunde" or geography. From 1781 onwards, several journals were founded which carried the combination of "Völker- und Länderkunde" (or vice versa) in their title and contents.[46] The concept *Völkerkunde* became popular in the form of "Staaten-, Länder- und Völkerkunde," that is in combination with political history and geography; and it is noteworthy that the ethnographical method which Schlözer designed remained part and parcel of the historiographical paradigm up to the work of Leopold von Ranke.

Even more striking is that one finds the term *Ethnographie* in the work of such historians as Schöpperlin, Schlözer and Gatterer, but not in the work of philosophers such as Herder and Kant.

6. RELATIONS BETWEEN ETHNOLOGY AND ANTHROPOLOGY

The first historian to deal with the relations between ethnology (or ethnography) and anthropology (anthropography) was Gatterer. As we have seen, he spoke of "the study of people and peoples" (*Menschen- und Völkerkunde*),

Anthropographia and *Ethnographia*, giving each subject a place in his classification of geographical sciences (1775). Gatterer expressly linked the two subjects, obviously aware of the great opportunities for the "science of man" (not yet exclusively physical but also philosophical) in his day and age.

Schlözer did not comment on anthropology as such, although he agreed with Georges-Louis Buffon that only varieties, and not races, exist. Müller, as we have seen, dealt with the physical characteristics of Siberian peoples in his "Völker-Beschreibung," thereby including physical anthropology in ethnography. However, not only historians such as Gatterer and Müller were aware of the links between these two approaches. The same applies to Johann Friedrich Blumenbach (1752–1840), one of the founders of physical anthropology or, as he preferred to call it, the "natural history of man." Shortly after presenting his dissertation "On the Natural Varieties of Humankind" [*De generis hvmani varietate nativa*] at Göttingen in 1775,[47] Blumenbach published a sketch of anthropology (concerned with medical anthropology) and an article on "Diversity in Humanity" in which he described drawings of several varieties of people.[48] Three years later, Blumenbach compiled a catalogue of the Academic Museum of Göttingen, including a category "Kunst Sachen" (*artifacts*) totaling sixty-six items. By that time, he had been appointed extraordinary Professor of Medicine as well as Inspector of the Museum. On August 27, 1781, Blumenbach wrote to the government in Hannover asking for "some of the superfluous foreign natural curiosities" acquired during James Cook's third voyage (1776–80). George III, King of Great Britain and Ireland and Elector of Hannover, ordered a shipment of 350 items, predominantly of an ethnographic nature, to be shipped from London in December that year.[49] This unexpected high-quality gift enhanced the reputation of the University of Göttingen as a center of eighteenth-century South Seas artifacts, stimulating Blumenbach's interest in ethnography. During his long life, Blumenbach combined this interest with his main subject: anthropology. He published little on ethnological subjects (e.g., an article on the "Abilities and Manners of Savages"),[50] but maintained his position as director of the Göttingen Academic Museum until his death.

By contrast, the best-known philosopher of the German Enlightenment, Immanuel Kant (1724–1804), does not seem to have taken notice of these new developments in the field of ethnology. The concepts ethnography and ethnology do not figure in his work, with one exception (see below). This is surprising, as Kant was teaching anthropology at Königsberg during the winter semester from 1772–73 until 1795–96, alternating with lectures on geography during the summer semester. Kant was aware of Herder's historical work and that of Schlözer; he studied Gatterer's work on geography. It is unlikely that he could have overlooked the many references to a new study of nations and of peoples in the German literature. The history of terminology shows that these terms were so popular during the 1780s and 1790s,[51] that they could hardly have escaped Kant's attention. We may therefore assume that ethnography, as a descriptive study of peoples, was deemed unworthy to be included in Kant's *Anthropology from a Pragmatic Point of View* (1798)[52]—as if in his philosophical accounts of "man" the study of *Volk/Völker*, and of ethnicity as such, did not need to be incorporated. If this is true, Kant was not "culture conscious" in the sense Alfred Louis Kroeber and Clyde Kluckhohn (1952) imputed to the term.[53]

Another explanation for Kant's negligence, that he was not familiar with the new discipline of *Völkerkunde*, is not very likely. In his review of Herder's second volume of *Ideas* (1785), Kant used the term "ethnographic" when summarizing Herder's view that "a collection of new ethnographic illustrations" would be needed.[54] However, as we have seen, Herder avoided the term ethnography in his work and preferred to speak of a "painting of nations" or "a painting of the diversity of our species."

Several years ago, Emmanuel Chukwudi Eze deplored the fact that Kant's views on race had been dismissed by then-recent scholarship: in Howard Caygill's *Kant Dictionary* (1995), the entry "race" is lacking.[55] I would add that of importance here is Kant's failure to acknowledge the contemporary, growing body of work on ethnography and on ethnology in his work regarding (philosophical) anthropology. This failure on Kant's behalf is, at some level, detrimental to our scholarship inasmuch as his work is regarded as the summation of the German Enlightenment and forms the basis of most recent studies on eighteenth-century philosophy in the United States. John H. Zammito claims that (philosophical) anthropology was born out of philosophy in the work of Kant and of Herder during the late 1760s and early 1770s.[56] This claim may be true, but it neglects the part played by ethnography and by ethnology in German Enlightenment thinking—a neglect which partly resulted from Kant's failure to acknowledge what was going on in central and eastern Europe, as well as from Herder's refusal to adopt innovative terminology.

Indeed, the mainstream of eighteenth-century German ethnological thinking was not voiced by Herder—his influence is of a later date. Mainstream summaries were provided by authors such as Theophil Friedrich Ehrmann (1762–1811), a compiler and translator of travel accounts. Ehrmann presented the earliest overview of "Völkerkunde" (1787) and returned to the subject several times.[57] To the important journal *Allgemeines Archiv für Ethnographie und Linguistik*, published at Weimar in 1808, Ehrmann contributed a summary of general and special ethnology (*allgemeinen und besonderen Völkerkunde*),[58] making clear that the first term refers to a general, comparative study of peoples (*Ethnologie*), whereas the second is a descriptive study of a people or of several peoples (*Ethnographie*). This distinction would remain essential until the 1920s.

In a separate article in the same journal, Ehrmann went into the field of (biological) anthropology, presenting an overview of the most important "varieties of mankind." Following Blumenbach, he wrote several paragraphs to supplement a map of human races according to skin color. In the title of that article, Ehrman speaks of "main diversities of peoples" (*Hauptverschieden-heiten der Völker*); in the subtitle, though, he refers to the map of "human races" (*Menschen-Rassen*).[59] This confusion is significant. The map is in color and five main "diversities" are distinguished. In pink are engraved the Europeans (excepting the Lapps and Finns), West-Asians and North Africans (the Caucasian variety); in yellow: the East- and South-Asians (excepting the Malay peoples), Finns, Lapps, Eskimos, inhabitants of Greenland, and inhabitants of part of the North-West Coast of America (the Mongolian variety); in black: the Africans (the Ethiopian variety), excepting the North Africans; in brown: the Americans (the American variety), excepting the most northerly inhabitants; in red: the Malays from Malaysia and the Indonesian Islands, as well as the Australians (the Malay variety).

The map is a symbol of Western industriousness and shows the eighteenth century's triumph: the geographical discovery of the world is almost complete. All continents are in place, with their locations fairly correct though not yet definite. Africa is too small, the northern parts of America, Asia, and Europe too large; Oceania is in place; however, the interior of many continents remains uncharted. Over these geographical boundaries is woven a web of physical-anthropological categorization in which Lapps and Finns are located outside the Caucasian variety and brought under the Mongolian variety; and in which West Asians and North Africans are brought into the Caucasian family, thereby separating North Africans from the Ethiopian variety that subsequently includes only African Blacks. Interesting is the Malay variety, which, separated from the Asians, includes both the Australian Aborigines and the original population of New Zealand. All this is indeed based on Blumenbach's system as set forth in the second edition of his thesis (1781), wherein the human species is divided into five "varieties" instead of four, acknowledging the Malayan (Austral-Asian) as the fifth.[60]

In Ehrmann's work we have the clearest example that both studies, ethnology and anthropology, were formulated alongside each other, albeit in separate branches of learning. This suggests a conception of the world inhabited by people living in groups, which are called "Völker" or "Volksstammen" (tribes) as subcategories of humankind, which can also be subdivided in human "races" (varieties). Whereas the earlier ethnographers were historians, geographers, and linguists, the physical anthropologists were physicians and anatomists. The philosopher Kant was neither, and for this reason his anthropological work is not relevant to the current overview of ethnology.

7. CONCLUSIONS

The concepts *ethnographia*, *Völkerkunde*, and *ethnologia*, together with related concepts such as *Völkerbeschreibung* and *Volkskunde*, all appeared in Russia, Germany, and Austria-Hungary within a relatively short time span (1740–1783). This ethnological discourse, a way of thinking in terms of peoples (*Völker*), quickly spread to such other countries of Europe as Switzerland, the Netherlands, France, Bohemia, and England, as well as to the United States. The consequences of this discovery are yet to be integrated into the existing views on the history of anthropology as a whole. It appears that all the concepts mentioned above referred to a new and separate field of knowledge, namely, the history and contemporary condition of nations and of peoples (*Völker*), or ethnic groups.

The emergence of this new ethnological discourse was clearly related to the universalistic tendencies of the Enlightenment. It also had to do with processes of state-formation and nation-building in the German-speaking countries and in the Russian and Austrian/Hungarian empires. A third factor was the increasing amount of knowledge regarding peoples recently discovered in Siberia and in other areas of Europe, Asia, and Oceania. The growing knowledge of peoples in the world was incorporated in history and in geography as developed at the University of Göttingen. Schlözer and Gatterer incorporated field studies by Müller and by others into their writings, raising the discussion to a theoretical level. How many peoples exist? What is a people (*Volk*)? Which peoples should be included? What aspects of these peoples should be studied? Kollár extended the argument of Müller and Schlözer, and generalized the problem, drawing on a more pressing subject at hand: the management of ethnic diversity in the Austro-Hungarian Empire.

Shortly after its introduction in Göttingen, *Ethnographie* met forceful critiques formulated by such early Romantics as Herder, who developed a new concept of *Volk* and who claimed that a particularistic approach was necessary to do justice to the inherent value of nations and of peoples (their culture). Herder devised a new view of peoples unfolding towards humanity (*Humanisierung*), and he avoided the new vocabulary as did his teacher Kant, who ignored the topic altogether. Herder's views entered American anthropology in the early twentieth century through the work of Franz Boas, who heralded Herder's vision of peoples unfolding towards humanity and becoming (more) human.

Relevant to the German invention of race is the fact that the ethnological discourse was developed alongside that anthropological discourse in western Europe and in the United States in which philosophical or physical comments were given on human "races" and "race" in general. While the latter, "anthropological" tradition has received a great deal of the limelight, ethnological discourse has largely gone unnoticed in recent scholarship. This new way of thinking in terms of peoples and of cultures (nations, as such, without a political meaning) has been overlooked not only in France, England, the United States, and even partly in Russia, but also in Germany. These processes deserve more attention, for "nations" are not the same as "races"—even if the concept anthropology seems to include both.

Philosophical anthropology may have been born out of philosophy, as Zammito claims. Yet, ethnography and ethnology, as forerunners of sociocultural anthropology, were born out of an ethnological praxis: they resulted from attempts to understand a dazzling diversity of "peoples" and "nations" in Europe and Asia, particularly those brought together in multinational states such as Russia and Austria-Hungary. These attempts dealt both with the present state of these nations and with the historical analysis of their origins, languages, migrations, and states. Sociocultural anthropology, in the form of ethnography and ethnology, resulted during the eighteenth century from the theoretical and practical need to study these processes in order to grasp important aspects of the world.

ACKNOWLEDGEMENTS

This essay summarizes chapters from a forthcoming book on the same subject. Earlier versions were presented at the conference "The German Invention of Race" at Harvard University, Cambridge, MA, May 4–6, 2001; at the Max-Planck-Institute for Social Anthropology at Halle/Saale, June 13, 2001; and (in German) at the biannual conference of the German Ethnological Society (*Deutsche Gesellschaft für Völkerkunde*, DGV) at Göttingen, October 8, 2001. I am indebted to James W. McAllister (Leiden University), Sara Goff (Cambridge, MA) and Ken Wallace (Tantallon, Nova Scotia) for their active support. I thank James McAllister and Peter Richardus (Leiden) for improving the English of this paper.

NOTES

1. George W. Stocking, Jr., "Anthropology," in *Dictionary of the History of Science,* eds. W. F. Bynum, E. J. Browne, and Roy Porter. (Princeton: Princeton University Press and London: Macmillan, 1981), 19–21, esp. 19.

2. George W. Stocking, Jr., "What's in a Name? The Origins of the Royal Anthropological Institute, 1837–1871." *Man* (n.s.) 6, no. 3 (1971): 369–390.

3. Exceptions are: Peter Pels and Oscar Salemink, eds., *Colonial Ethnographies,* special issue of *History and Anthropology* 8, no. 1–4 (1994); Jan van Bremen and

Akitoshi Shimizu, eds., *Anthropology and Colonialism in Asia and Oceania* (London and Richmond: Curzon Press, 1999); Barry Alan Joyce, *The Shaping of American Ethnography: The Wilkes Exploring Expedition, 1838–1842* (Lincoln: University of Nebraska Press, 2001).

4. Han F. Vermeulen, "The Emergence of 'Ethnography' ca. 1770 in Göttingen," *History of Anthropology Newsletter* 19, no. 2: 6–9; "Frühe Geschichte der Völkerkunde oder Ethnographie in Deutschland 1771–1791," in *Völkerkunde Tagung 1991,* eds. M. S. Laubscher und B. Turner. (München: Akademischer Verlag München, 1994), 1: 327–344; "Origins and Institutionalization of Ethnography and Ethnology in Europe and the USA, 1771–1845," in *Fieldwork and Footnotes. Studies in the History of European Anthropology,* eds. Han F. Vermeulen and Arturo Alvarez Roldán (London: Routledge, 1995), 39–59; "Enlightenment Anthropology," in *Encyclopedia of Social and Cultural Anthropology,* eds. Alan Barnard and Jonathan Spencer (London and New York: Routledge, 1996), 183–185; Justin Stagl, "August Ludwig Schlözers Entwurf einer 'Völkerkunde' oder "Ethnographie" seit 1772," *Ethnologische Zeitschrift Zürich* 2 (1974), 73–91; *Kulturanthropologie und Gesellschaft. Eine wissenschaftsoziologische Darstellung der Kulturanthropologie und Ethnologie* 2, Auflage (Berlin: Reimer, 1981); *A History of Curiosity. The Theory of Travel 1550–1800* (Chur: Harwood, 1995).

5. Michèle Duchet, *Anthropologie et histoire au siècle des Lumières: Buffon, Voltaire, Rousseau, Helvétius, Diderot* (Paris: François Maspero, 1971), 12. (Repr. Paris: Flammarion, 1978), 2nd edition, with a postscript by Claude Blanckaert (Paris: Albin Michel, 1995).

6. Alexandre-César Chavannes, *Essai sur l'éducation intellectuelle avec le Projet d'une science nouvelle* (Lausanne: Isaac Hignou, 1787); *Anthropologie ou science générale de l'homme, pour servir d'introduction à l'étude de la philosophie et des langues, et de guide dans le plan d'éducation intellectuelle* (Lausanne: Isaac Hignou, 1788).

7. Eugen Helimski and Hartmut Katz, eds., Gerhard Friedrich Mueller, *Nachrichten über Völker Sibiriens (1736–1742)* (Hamburg: Institut für Finnougristik/ Uralistik, 2003).

8. This *Beschreibung,* begun in 1736 or 1737 and finished during the 1740s, has been retrieved from the Rgada archives at Moscow by Aleksandr Christianovi Elert from Novosibirsk. See A. C. Elert, "Die Völker Sibiriens in der Sicht Gerhard Friedrich Müllers," *Berliner Jahrbuch für Osteuropäische Geschichte* 2 (1996): 37–54.

9. See Gudrun Bucher *"Von Beschreibung der Sitten und Gebräuche der Völcker." Die Instruktionen Gerhard Friedrich Müllers und ihre Bedeutung für die Geschichte der Ethnologie und der Geschichtswissenschaft* (Stuttgart: Franz Steiner Verlag, 2002).

10. "Instruktion G. F. Müller's für den Akademiker-Adjuncten J. E. Fischer (1740): 'Unterricht, was bey Beschreibung der Völker, absonderlich der Sibirischen in acht zu nehmen,' in Fr. Russow, *Beiträge zur Geschichte der ethnographischen und anthropologischen Sammlungen der Kaiserlichen Akademie der Wissenschaften zu St.-Petersburg/Sbornik muzeja po antropologii i etnografii poi imperatorskij akademij nauk'/Publications du musée d'anthropologie et d'ethnographie de l'Académie impériale des sciences de St.-Pétersbourg* Bd. I (St.-Pétersbourg, 1900), 37–109, esp. 83.

11. Gerhard Friedrich Müller, *Beschreibung der sibirischen Völker* will be published in a Russian and a German edition by Wieland Hintzsche and Aleksandr Chr. Elert in two parts at Halle: Verlag der Frankeschen Stiftungen, in the series "Quellen zur Geschichte Sibiriens und Alaskas aus russischen Archive."

12. Johann Friedrich Schöpperlin, "Prolvsio scholastica Sveviae veteris per temporvm periodos descriptae primas lineas exhibens. Ad svpplendam Speneri Notitiam Germaniae" (Nordlingae: n. p., 1767), in *Kleine Historische Schriften*, ed. Böckh (Nördlingen: bey Karl Gottlob Beck, Zweyter Band, 1787 hrsg.), 412–449, esp. 439. See Han F. Vermeulen, "Ethnographia 1767" *Anthropology Today* 16, no. 5 (2000): 27 (Letter to the Editor).

13. Hans Fischer, "Völkerkunde," "Ethnographie," "Ethnologie": "Kritische Kontrolle der frühesten Belege." *Zeitschrift für Ethnologie* 95, no. 2 (1970): 169–182, esp. 170.

14. Johann Friedrich Schöpperlin, Review of J. C. Martini, *"Einleitung in die alte Erdbeschreibung"* (Teil 1, 1766), J. F. Schöpperlin and A. F. Thilo, eds., *Magazin für Schulen und die Erziehung überhaupt* 4, no. 3 (1770): 274.

15. August Ludwig Schlözer, *Allgemeine Nordische Geschichte* = Fortsetzung der Algemeinen Welthistorie der Neuern Zeiten . . . Dreyzehnter Theil. Halle, bey Johann Justinus Gebauer (Algemeine Welthistorie, vol. 31 Historie der Neuern Zeiten, vol. 13), 1771, 292–344, 391–436.

16. Han F. Vermeulen, "Anthropology in Colonial Contexts: The second Kamchatka expedition (1733–1743) and the Danish-German Arabia expedition (1761–1767)," in *Anthropology and Colonialism in Asia and Oceania,* eds. Jan van Bremen and Akitoshi Shimizu (London and Richmond: Curzon Press, 1999), 13–39; "Ethnographie und Ethnologie in Mittel- und Osteuropa: Völker-Beschreibung und Völkerkunde in Russland, Deutschland und Österreich (1740–1845)," in *Europa in der Frühen Neuzeit. Festschrift für Günter Mühlpfordt,* ed. Erich Donnert (Köln/Weimar/Wien: Böhlau, Band 6, 2002), 397–409.

17. August Ludwig Schlözer, *Vorstellung seiner Universal-Historie* (Göttingen und Gotha: bey Johann Christian Dieterich, 1772), 98–99; *Vorstellung der Universal-Historie,* Zwote, veränderte Auflage, 2 vols. (Göttingen: bey Johann Christian Dieterich, 1775), I: 292–294. See also Stagl, "Entwurf," 1974.

18. Schlözer, *Vorstellung seiner Universal-Historie* (1772), 101, *Vorstellung der Universal-Historie* (1775), 295.

19. Schlözer, *Allgemeine Nordische Geschichte* (1771), 286, 291.

20. Schlözer, *Vorstellung der Universal-Historie* (1775), 14, 16, 276.

21. Schlözer, *Vorstellung der Universal-Historie* (1775), 270–271 n.*.

22. Willem Frederik Wertheim, "Globalisation of the Social Sciences: Non-Western Sociology as a Temporary Panacea," in *Tales from Academia: History of Anthropology in the Netherlands,* eds. Han F. Vermeulen and Jean Kommers (Nijmegen: NICCOS/Saarbrücken: Verlag für Entwicklungspolitik, 2002), 267–296.

23. Johann Christoph Gatterer, *Abriß der Geographie* (Göttingen: bey Joh. Christian Dieterich, 1775). Erster Theil [published in 1778; no further volumes published], pp. 4–5. Also quoted in Fischer, "Völkerkunde," (1970), 170.

24. Johann Christoph Gatterer, *Ideal einer allgemeinen Weltstatistik* (Göttingen: im Vandenhökischen Verlag, 1773), 16.

25. Johann Christoph Gatterer, *Abriß der Geographie* (1775: xviii–xxxvi).

26. Uli Kutter, "Volks-Kunde—Ein Beleg von 1782." *Zeitschrift für Volkskunde* 74, no. 2 (1978): 161–166; Kutter, *Reisen—Reisehandbücher—Wissenschaft. Materialien zur Reisekultur im 18. Jahrhundert.* Mit einer unveröffentlichten Vorlesungsmitschrift des Reisekollegs von A. L. Schlözer vom W[inter]S[emester] (1792/93) im Anhang (Neuried: Ars Una [Deutsche: Hochschuledition 54], 1996).

27. Helmut Möller, "Volkskunde, Statistik, Völkerkunde 1787. Aus den Anfängen der Volkskunde als Wissenschaft," *Zeitschrift für Volkskunde* 60, no. 2 (1964): 218–232.

28. Johannes le Francq van Berkhey, *Natuurlyke historie van Holland*, 9 vols. (Te Amsterdam: by Yntema en Tieboel, 1769–1811) 3 (1776): 1457. Ton Dekker, *De Nederlandse volkskunde. De verwetenschappelijking van een emotionele belangstelling* (Amsterdam: Uitgeverij Aksant, 2002), 6, was the first to point out this earlier Dutch reference to *Volkskunde*, but incorrectly provided the year 1773 for this quotation.

29. Paul Topinard, "Un mot sur l'histoire de l'anthropologie en 1788." *Revue d'Anthropologie*, 3ᵉ série, tome 3 (1888): 197–201; Topinard, *L'Homme dans la nature* (Paris: Félix Alcan, 1891; repr., Paris: Jean Michel Place 1991). See Gérald Berthoud, "Une 'science générale de l'homme.' L'oeuvre de Chavannes," in Berthoud, *Vers une anthropologie générale. Modernité et altérité* (Genève/Paris: Librairie Droz, 1992), 257–268.

30. Ján Tibensky, "Barokovy historizmus" a zaciatky slovenskej slavistiky ["Baroque Historism" and the Beginnings of Slovak Slavonic Studies], in *Stúdie z dejín svetovej slavistiky do polovice 19. storoèia* (Bratislava: VEDA, 1978), 93–124. This reference became known to the West during the conference of the European Association of Social Anthropologists (EASA) in Prague, August 1992. See Vermeulen, *Fieldwork and Footnotes*, 57).

31. See note 6.

32. See note 6.

33. Adam F. Kollár, *Historiae ivrisqve pvblici Regni Vngariae amoenitates* [Amenities of the History and Constitutional Law of the Kingdom of Hungary], 2 vols. (Vindobonae: typis a Bavmeisterianis, 1783), I: 80.

34. Adam F. Kollár, Annotations to Petrus Lambecius, *Commentarii de avgvstissima Bibliotheca Caesarea Vindobonensis*. Editio altera opera et studio Adami Francisci Kollárii, 8 vols. (Vindobonae: n. p., 1776–82) esp. vol. 7 (1781): 322, note A. Quoted in Justin Stagl, "Rationalism and Irrationalism in Early German Ethnology: The Controversy between Schlözer and Herder, 1772/73." *Anthropos* 93, nos. 4–6 (1998): 521–536, esp. 523 note 15.

35. Vitomir Belaj, "Plaidoyer za etnologiju kao historijsku znanost o etni cim skupinama/An Argument for Ethnology as a Historical Science Concerning Ethnic Groups," *Studia Ethnologica* 1 (1989): 9–17, esp. 15.

36. Peter Drews, *Herder und die Slaven. Materialien zur Wirkungsgeschicht bis zur Mitte des 19. Jahrhunderts* (München: Sagner, 1990).

37. Franz Boas, "The History of Anthropology." *Science*, n.s. 20, no. 512 (October 21, 1904): 513–524. Reprinted in *Readings in the History of Anthropology,* ed. Regna Darnell (New York: Harper and Row, 1974), 260–273; and *The Shaping of*

American Anthropology, 1883–1911: A Franz Boas Reader, ed. George W. Stocking, Jr. (New York: Basic Books, 1974), 23–36.

38. Åke Eberhard Berg, "Johann Gottfried Herder (1744–1803)," in *Klassiker der Kulturanthropologie: von Montaigne bis Margaret Mead,* ed. Wolfgang Marschall (München: C. H. Beck, 1990), 51–68, 320–323.

39. Johann Gottfried Herder, Review of A. L. Schlözer, *Vorstellung seiner Universal-Historie* (Göttingen und Gotha: Johann Christian Dieterich, 1772), in *Frankfurter gelehrte Anzeigen,* no. 60 (July 28, 1772): 473–478, esp. 475; reprinted in *Herders Sämmtliche Werke,* ed. Bernhard Suphan, vol. 5 (Berlin: Weidmann, 1891), 436–440.

40. Herder, Review of Schlözer, 476.

41. August Ludwig Schlözer, *Vorstellung seiner Universal-Historie,* zweeter Teil (Göttingen und Gotha: bey Johann Christian Dieterich, 1773).

42. August Ludwig Schlözer, *Vorstellung seiner Universal-Historie* (1772), 101–104; *Vorstellung der Universal-Historie* (1775), 295–297.

43. ———, *Vorstellung seiner Universal-Historie* (1772), 104; *Vorstellung der Universal-Historie* (1775), 297–298.

44. Johann Gottfried Herder, *Ideen zur Philosophie der Geschichte der Menschheit,* 4 vols. (Riga und Leipzig: bei Johann Friedrich Hartknoch, 1784–91) 2:7 and 2:6, respectively. Repr. in *Herders Sämmtliche Werke,* ed. Bernhard Suphan, vol. 13–14 (Berlin: Weidmann, 1887, 1909). English translation: *Outlines of a Philosophy of the History of Man,* trans. T. Churchill (London: printed for J. Johnson, by Luke Hansard, 1800).

45. Otto Dann, *Nation und Nationalismus in Deutschland 1770–1990* (München: C. H. Beck, 1993), 3rd expanded ed. 1996.

46. See Fischer, "Völkerkunde"; Vermeulen, Frühe Geschichte "Origins and Institutionalization."

47. Johann Friedrich Blumenbach, *De generis hvmani varietate nativa,* Illvstris facvltatis medicae consensv pro gradv doctoris medicinae dispvtavit d. XVI Sept. MDCCLXXV h.l.q.s. Ioann. Frider. Blvmenbach, Gothanvs (Goettingae: typis Frid. Andr. Rosenbvschii, 1775) (mandatory publication; the commercial edition appeared as *De generis humani varietate nativa liber cum figuris aeri incises* (Goettingae: apud vidvam Abr. Vandenhoeck, 1776); 2nd ed. 1781; 3rd ed. with a letter from Joseph Banks, 1795.

48. Anonymous [Johann Friedrich Blumenbach], Verschiedenheit im Menschen-Geschlecht, in *Goettinger Taschen-Calender vom Jahr 1776* (Göttingen: bey Ioh. Chr. Dieterich, October 1775), 72–82.

49. Manfred Urban, *200 Jahre Göttinger Cook-Sammlung* (Göttingen: Institut und Sammlung für Völkerkunde, 1982); Urban, The Acquisition History of the Göttingen Collection/Die Erwerbungsgeschichte der Göttinger Sammlung, in *James Cook: Treasures from the South Seas—Gaben und Schätze aus der Südsee. The Göttingen Cook/Forster Collection—Die Göttinger Sammlung Cook/Forster,* eds. Brigitta Hauser-Schäublin and Gundolf Krüger (Munich and New York: Prestel-Verlag, 1998), 56–85.

50. Johann Friedrich Blumenbach, "Einige zerstreute Bemerkungen über die Fähigkeiten und Sitten der Wilden," in *Göttingisches Magazin der Wissenschaften und*

Litteratur, eds. Georg Christoph Lichtenberg and Georg Forster, 2. Jahrgang, 6 (Stück: n. p., 1782), 409–425.

51. Vermeulen, see note 46.

52. Immanuel Kant, *Anthropologie in pragmatischer Hinsicht* (Königsberg: bey Friedrich Nicolovius, 1798); *Kant's Vorlesungen*, hrsg. von der Akademie der Wissenschaften zu Göttingen, *Kant's gesammelte Schriften* Band 25, Vierte Abteilung, Vorlesungen Band 2: *Vorlesungen über Anthropologie*, bearbeitet von Reinhard Brandt und Werner Stark. Band 2,1–2,2 (Berlin: Walter de Gruyter & Co., 1997).

53. Alfred Louis Kroeber and Clyde Kluckhohn, *Culture: A Critical Review of Concepts and Definitions* (Papers of the Peabody Museum of American Archaelogy and Ethnology, Harvard University, vol. 47, no. 1, 1952); paperback (New York: Vintage Books/Random House, 1963).

54. Quoted in Emmanuel Chukwudi Eze, ed., *Race and the Enlightenment. A Reader* (Oxford: Blackwell, 1997), 66.

55. Eze, ed., *Race and the Enlightenment*. 3; Howard Caygill, *A Kant Dictionary* (Oxford: Blackwell, 1995).

56. John H. Zammito, *Kant, Herder, and the Birth of Anthropology* (Chicago: University of Chicago Press, 2002).

57. Theophil Friedrich Ehrmann, "Kurze Uebersicht der Völkerkunde," in *Neues Magazin für Frauenzimmer,* ed. David Christoph Seybold (Straßburg und Leipzig: Verlag der Akademischen Buchhandlung, 1787–90), Band 3, Stück 9, September 1787, pp. 241–258; Ehrmann, "Über die Völkerkunde," in *Bibliothek der neuesten Länder- und Völkerkunde. Für Geographie-Freunde*, 4 vols. (Tübingen: n. p., 1791–1794), Band 2, 1792.

58. T. F. E. [Theophil Friedrich Ehrmann], "Umriss der allgemeinen und besonderen Völkerkunde," in *Allgemeines Archiv für Ethnographie und Linguistik,* hrsg. von F. J. Bertuch und J. S. Vater (Weimar, im Verlage des Landes-Industrie-Comptoirs, 1808), Band I, no. 1, 9–25.

59. ———, "Skizzirte Uebersicht der Hauptverschiedenheiten der Völker, in Betreff der Leibesfarbe (Mit einer Charte der Menschen-Rassen)," in *Allgemeines Archiv für Ethnographie und Linguistik,* eds. F. J. Bertuch and J. S. Vater, I(1) (1808): 26–39.

60. Johann Friedrich Blumenbach, *De generis humani varietate nativa liber cum figuris aeri incisis. Editio altera longe auctior et emendatior,* 1st ed. 1775–76 (Goettingae: apud vidvam Abr. Vandenhoeck, 1781).

8

Gods, Titans, and Monsters

Philhellenism, Race, and Religion in Early-Nineteenth-Century Mythography

George S. Williamson

Hesiod's *Theogony* describes the birth of the Greek gods, who descend from a common source in Chaos but are divided by parentage and generation. His narrative culminates in the battle between the Titans and the Olympians. The Titans are the children of Heaven and Earth and represent an older generation of deities. The Olympians, led by Zeus, represent the new breed of gods. The battle rages ten years before Zeus enlists the monstrous, many-armed and many-headed Hecatoncheires to help him defeat the Titans, who are banished to Tartarus, a place "as far beneath the earth, as earth is far beneath the heavens."[1]

Hesiod's text was a favorite source for the mythographers of the late eighteenth and early nineteenth centuries, in part because it served as a reminder of the fundamental instability of the Olympian pantheon—both for the ancient Greeks and for their modern, Philhellenist disciples. Having established ancient Greece as a timeless ideal of beauty and of freedom, the Philhellenists would struggle to hold this position against challenges from advocates of "Oriental," "Germanic," or biblical traditions. Aspects of this

147

process have been described by Anthony La Vopa, Anthony Grafton, and Suzanne Marchand.[2] But while these scholars have focused primarily on factors internal to scholarship, the struggle between the Philhellenes and their challengers often spilled outside disciplinary boundaries to affect broader debates concerning politics, religion, and race.

The linkages between philological debate and the theological-political controversies of the nineteenth century were particularly evident in the bitter dispute surrounding Friedrich Creuzer's *Symbolik und Mythologie der alten Völker* (2nd ed., 1819–23). In this four-volume work, Creuzer argued that Greek mythology had emerged from an earlier religious symbolism, which had been imported into Greece by priestly emissaries from India and Egypt. The *Symbolik* set off a firestorm of controversy that would attract the attention of Goethe, G. W. F. Hegel, and F. W. J. Schelling, as well as of publicists and journalists in Germany and abroad. At stake in this dispute was the question, highlighted by Martin Bernal in *Black Athena*, of the relationship of "white," "European" Greece to other, non-European cultures, particularly that of Egypt.[3] Indeed, although Bernal has almost nothing to say about Creuzer, the outcome of the *Symbolik* affair proved decisive in securing the theory of Greek cultural autochthony within the field of classical philology, if not necessarily within German scholarship as a whole. But the problem of race was not simply a matter of geographic origin: it also appeared at the level of the mythological representations themselves. For not only did the *Symbolik* threaten the national integrity of Greece; it also undermined the Philhellenists' understanding of Greek religion as revolving around the naked white bodies celebrated in Phidias's statues and Homer's epics. By emphasizing an alternative realm of half-animal or monstrous deities, Creuzer challenged the cultural primacy of neohumanism and its accompanying values of beauty, freedom, and reason.

The symbolic-racial dimension of the Creuzer affair cannot be fully comprehended if we adopt an internalist perspective and treat it simply as a scholarly debate within the field of philology.[4] As Schelling noted later, "One felt in this question that it was a matter of more than merely mythology."[5] On the other hand, we are not much better served if we focus one-sidedly on the question of cultural origins, designating one group of scholars as "enlightened" and their opponents as "Romantic" or "reactionary." To understand the complexities and ambiguities of racial thinking in the *Symbolik* controversy, it is necessary instead to address the specific configuration of aesthetic, theological, and political concerns that shaped the scholarly discourse on ancient mythology in the decades after 1815. For it was the theological-political dimension that turned an academic dispute into a full blown cultural controversy and that helped to bring the issue of race into the heart of German mythography.[6]

The father of German Philhellenism, Johann Joachim Winckelmann, viewed Greek sculpture as both an aesthetic and a religious ideal.[7] While the biblical God existed in an infinite space beyond the realm of appearances, the Greek deities were fully present in their monuments. "Every sacred sculpture," he wrote in his *History of Ancient Art* (1764), "was filled with the godhead that it represented."[8] The artists who brought these sculptures to life enjoyed aesthetic freedom and public esteem, which reflected the broader political freedoms of the *polis* (the problem of slavery was conveniently overlooked). Winckelmann drew a sharp contrast between the situation in ancient Greece and that prevailing in ancient Egypt, where no such freedoms existed and art had remained at a comparatively low level. In this scheme, the naked body of Greek sculpture became a symbol of freedom and autonomy in art, politics, and religion that was valid even in the modern era. In establishing this ideal, Winckelmann challenged not only the eighteenth-century *Ständestaat*, but also orthodox Christianity—which had subordinated art to liturgy, covered up the naked body as an embarrassment, and confined its statues to the interior of the church. His image of the Greeks would become crucial for a strain of aesthetic-republican thought in Germany that became particularly influential with the outbreak of the French Revolution.[9]

In his *Letters on the Aesthetic Education of Mankind* (1795), Friedrich Schiller reformulated Winckelmann's ideas in the context of Kantian philosophy and in light of the Revolution's excesses. Schiller praised the organic relationship between art, religion, and public life that had characterized ancient Greece, and he traced this quality to the fundamental humanity of the Greek gods. At the same time, he emphasized the distinction between the Greek gods and the divinities of the "Orient," which included Egypt and most of the Middle East. Alluding to the *Theogony*, Schiller wrote, "The monstrous divinity of the Oriental, which rules the world with the blind strength of a beast of prey, shrinks in the imagination of the Greeks into the friendly contours of a human being. The empire of the Titans falls, and infinite force is tamed by infinite form."[10] For Schiller, the oriental "monster" evoked a form of "oriental" despotism, whereas the "friendly" Greek gods evoked a republican, if not necessarily democratic, public life.[11]

Philhellenist republicanism reached a utopian crescendo in the writings of Friedrich Schelling, a Jena Romantic who stood close to Schiller in his aesthetic and religious tastes. In his *Lectures on the Method of Academic Study* (1802) and in his unpublished lectures entitled *Philosophy of Art* (1803), Schelling described the Greek gods as the actual appearance of the divine in the finite realm. The gods were not just real "for the believer" but real in themselves, and their anthropomorphic form reflected the "symbolic significance of the human body as an image of the universe."[12] It was the divine presence of the gods in sculpture, tragedy, and festivals that was the foundation of the Greeks' "publicness" (*Oeffentlichkeit*) and the guarantee of their free-doms. At the same time, Schelling was more willing than Winckelmann or Schiller to concede a legitimacy to "Oriental" mythology, which strived from "the finite into the infinite."[13] This "Oriental" element had formed the basis of the Christian religion, which involved a similar striving for the infinite. As a result, however, there could be no complete merger of finite and infinite in Christianity as there had been in ancient Greece. Instead, the experience of the divine was confined to churches, while political life was controlled by individual dynasties. The best hope for the future was that idealist philosophy would usher in a "new mythology," which would bring about a renewal of aesthetic and public life in Europe.

Schelling's type of aesthetic republicanism, which envisioned an internal transformation of public life by means of art and mythology, was by its very nature fragile. In particular, it was premised on the intellectual's retaining a certain autonomy from broader social and political forces. For this reason, Schelling hoped that the French Revolution would inspire rather than dictate the course of cultural change in Germany. Instead, the Revolution came to Germany in the form of Napoleon's invading armies, leading to the destruc-tion of the old *Reich* and its replacement by a French-dominated Confedera-tion of the Rhine. One result of these developments was a split in the German image of ancient Greece: political liberals, particularly those students and intellectuals associated with the *Burschenschaften*, upheld the Winckelmannian image of Greece as a model for political and social transformation along national lines; a second group, hostile to radical political change, began to question the established image of ancient Greece and, in effect, to "Christian-ize" or "orientalize" it; and a third group sought to mediate these contradic-tory positions with an image of Greece that emphasized the values of order, piety, tradition, and nationality. These fault lines would become fully evident only after the defeat of Napoleon in 1815 and the outbreak of the Creuzer affair in the 1820s.

The notion that the roots of European civilization lay in the "Orient" was by no means new to the late eighteenth century. What was unique about the "Oriental Renaissance" was that its center of gravity was India and Persia, rather than Israel. This view received scholarly support in the 1780s from Sir William Jones, a British imperial official in India and specialist in Sanskrit language, and it was soon taken up by Johann Gottfried Herder. By the early 1800s, German writers like Johann Arnold Kanne, Joseph Görres, and Friedrich Schlegel had published works asserting the primacy or at least the deep antiquity of Indian culture.[14] By emphasizing the religious and essentially non-Western roots of modern civilization, this scholarship called into ques-tion the legacy of Greek republicanism and—by implication—the authority of its modern admirers. Yet it challenged this dominance not with appeals to biblical authority, but with tools already forged by the neohumanists: linguistic analysis, historicist scholarship, and a devotion to aesthetic ideals. Within the philological guild, much of the new Orientalism could be dismissed as the work of amateurs or outsiders. But this would not be the case with Friedrich Creuzer (1771–1852), who since 1804 had held the chair of philology and ancient history at the University of Heidelberg.

In *Symbolik und Mythologie der alten Völker* (1st ed, 1810–1812; 2nd ed., 1819–1823), Creuzer overturned Winckelmann's image of Greek culture by emphasizing the primacy of religious symbolism over aesthetic beauty.[15] The origins of Greek mythology, he argued, lay not in the political and aesthetic freedoms of the *polis*, but rather in revelations bestowed upon an ancient priestly class. These priests were the bearers of an esoteric symbolism (*Symbolik*), which they brought with them from India and Egypt via Thrace and the island of Samothrace.[16] In defending this thesis, Creuzer cited Herodotus, who had argued for the Egyptian origins of the Greek gods, but whose authority had subsequently been neglected. "Did the nations of the past only deliver elephant teeth, gold and slaves to one another? And not knowledge, religious practices and gods? . . . One should not close one's eyes when trustworthy Greek guides themselves point to the foreign homeland and foreign origin of a doctrine."[17] Unlike Herodotus, Creuzer believed that the original home of Greek mythology lay in India, yet he shared the ancient historian's emphasis on the common ownership of gods in the ancient world.

Creuzer maintained throughout *Symbolik und Mythologie* that he was offering a genuinely "religious" (as opposed to a rationalist or purely aesthetic) interpretation of Greek myth. In his view, the stories and legends of Greek mythology had originated from neither the fears and confusion of primitive humans nor the imagination of ancient bards. Instead, they were derived from a divine revelation, which took the form of an original symbolism. In the symbol there was an "incongruence of essence with form" and "an overflow of the content in comparison with its expression," which provided a momentary intuition of the nature of the universe.[18] Creuzer claimed to have discerned a profound *Naturphilosophie* in the ancient symbolism, which described the creation of the cosmos in terms of an interaction of male and female potences or deities. Far from being strictly anthropomorphic, these earliest gods often took the form of androgynous or half-animal beings. Dionysus, for example, appeared on ancient coins as a slaughtered steer or as a bull with a human head. This emphasis on animal symbolism narrowed the gap that Winckelmann had established between the Greek deities and the half-animal deities of Egyptian and Indian mythology. The fact that the Egyptian hieroglyphs had not yet been decoded made it possible for Creuzer to interpret them as a series of symbols, which had provided the basis for Greek religion.

According to Creuzer, the ancient symbolism inspired an intense and often highly sexualized religious life, which included elaborate liturgies, enlarged phalluses, and orgies. "What the civilized person modestly and carefully hid in social life was viewed as religious in name and likeness by the sensibility of the natural man, and consecrated in the public liturgy."[19] Yet Creuzer maintained that the core doctrines of this *Symbolik*—including its notions of creation and its idea of a suffering Dionysus—anticipated the fundamental doctrines of Christianity. For Creuzer, therefore, Christianity was the true successor to ancient Greek mythology. By contrast, the Homeric epics, the sculptures, and the tragic drama of the republican period were hollow echoes of an earlier, deeply pious stage of Greek culture.

Creuzer's *Symbolik und Mythologie* inspired an immediate reaction among classical philologists, but the controversy reached the peak of its intensity after the Congress of Vienna.[20] Scholars in Leipzig, Göttingen, and Königsberg argued that the systems of *Naturphilosophie* and the mystery cults that Creuzer saw as constituting the origins of Greek mythology were actually the products of a later, post-Homeric era. In addition, they complained that by positing a common religious symbolism, Creuzer had ignored the very real differences—in language, climate, and nationality—between ancient Greece and ancient Egypt and India. But alongside and reinforcing these scholarly criticisms was a sense that Creuzer had redrawn the image of antiquity along lines favorable to the Holy Alliance, and that he had thereby undermined ancient Greece as an aesthetic and political ideal.

This sentiment was most forcefully expressed by Creuzer's Heidelberg colleague, Johann Heinrich Voss.[21] Voss was a generation older than Creuzer. Best known as a poet of the Göttingen Grove, he had translated the Iliad and the Odyssey into German, a feat that Hegel later compared to Luther's translation of the Bible.[22] A man given to strong, often violent, opinions, Voss saw himself as defending a tradition of Protestant enlightened patriotism that was under attack by partisans of Romantic mysticism and clerical reaction. Heinrich Heine, an admirer of Voss, described him as "a lower Saxon peasant like Luther. He lacked all chivalry, all courtesy, all graciousness."[23] In his *Antisymbolik* (1824–26), Voss rejected any connection between the "Homeric gods" and the "rot" and "slime" of Egypt and India, and he implied that Creuzer had spent too much time in the Oriental "sun." What most exercised Voss, however, was Creuzer's connection of the Olympian gods to various half-human deities from India and Egypt. "Listen up, old Homer! Your virgin Pallas Athena is the Indian *Bhavani*, a hideous man-woman! Out of the triangle of her female *Yoni* arises a male *Lingam* of creation, which in Indian also means *Phallus*. From this secret *Phallus* she got the name *Pallas*, which can be used as male or female."[24] For Voss, Creuzer's theory threatened not only the national integrity of Greece, but the very "humanistic" quality that had made ancient Greece so appealing to Winckelmann and Schiller and to their liberal disciples in the early nineteenth century.

In general, Voss found Creuzer's derivation of Greek culture from India no less objectionable than its derivation from Egypt: for him both were part of an undifferentiated "Orient." This symbolic geography calls into question Martin Bernal's sharp ideological and moral distinction between the "Ancient" (Egyptian) model of Greek origins and the "Aryan" (Indian) model.[25] That is not to gainsay the racial overtones of Voss's polemic, but instead to argue that it turned less on a distinction between Egypt and India than on a general hostility to the "Oriental," which was grounded in a combination of aesthetic, theological, and political sentiments. By undermining the centrality of the Olympian gods, Creuzer was undermining the integrity of the individual (male) subject and, with it, the liberal project itself. For an old patriot like Voss, who had approved of the nationalist gathering at the Wartburg and now supported the left liberal party of Karl Rotteck and Karl Welcker in Baden, the *Symbolik* seemed like a manifesto of political reaction.[26]

In order to express his objections to the *Symbolik*, Voss relied to a large extent on the rhetoric of confessional conflict. Identifying Protestantism with political and intellectual freedom, he accused the Lutheran Creuzer of being part of a vast, crypto-Catholic conspiracy. Most commentators have passed by these accusations in silence, or with an embarrassed comment about religious prejudice. But while there was no real conspiracy, it is true that at this time a considerable number of Protestant and Catholic intellectuals found themselves attracted to baroque Catholicism and its notions of liturgy, imagery, and authority. Moreover, the works by the Catholic Joseph Görres and the convert Friedrich Schlegel on Asian languages and mythologies suggested that the new Orientalism was indeed closely linked with a resurgence of interest in Catholicism among Romantic intellectuals.[27] Nor was this trend confined to Germany: Louis de Bonald and Joseph de Maistre, architects of French "traditionalism," were inclined to the new Orientalism; de Maistre, in particular, posited an eternal and unchanging wisdom that had originated in the East and that had been passed down through the institutions of the Roman Catholic Church.[28] For his part, Voss believed he was upholding the spirit of Protestant Christianity in his attacks on Creuzer and his allies.[29]

Yet what divided Creuzer's supporters from his critics was less confession per se than a growing division in German intellectual culture between advocates and opponents of a conservative, distinctly south-German style of Romanticism. Creuzer and his allies in Heidelberg and Munich were highly critical of the eighteenth-century traditions of rationalism and classicism, and yet they remained open to a universalizing narrative of the history of religion. At the conceptual level, the Creuzerian "symbol" pointed to powers of revelation and authority that lay outside the grasp of human manipulation or comprehension, and which defied liberal-humanist norms through their manifestation in expressly "unbeautiful" forms. At the same time, Creuzer's *Symbolik und Mythologie* entailed an effort to appropriate not only classical Greece, but also the nonclassical Orient and the Middle Ages into a Christianizing economy of world history. While this scheme of history reinforced certain ideas emerging within Catholic traditionalism, it drew its legitimacy from the secular realms of history, aesthetics, and linguistics.

Most north-German philologists, particularly those of an older generation, were deeply disturbed by Creuzer's challenge to the integrity of ancient Greece, even if they did not share Voss's zest for theological-political polemic. Wilhelm von Humboldt privately questioned the attempt to mix the Greek gods with deities from other religions, while the Königsberg philologist Christian August Lobeck delivered a scathing critique of the *Symbolik* on historical and methodological grounds.[30] Yet given the extensive evidence that Creuzer had uncovered testifying to a "dark side" of Greek antiquity, the attempts by Humboldt, Voss, Lobeck, and others to uphold the Winckelmannian image of Greece were doomed to failure.[31] The most effective reply to Creuzer came instead from the Göttingen scholar Karl Otfried Müller.[32] His work marks a transition from Enlightenment neohumanism to a moderate scholarly liberalism in German philology and, with it, to a much more self-conscious approach to issues of nationality and race.

Müller was not completely averse to the *Symbolik*. The son of a Silesian pastor and a student of August Boeckh (himself a former colleague of Creuzer), Müller was influenced early on by Romantic ideas of *Naturphilosophie* and of religion.[33] He rejected Voss's euhemeristic interpretation of Dionysus as a dead Greek hero and insisted on the antiquity and the orgiastic quality of his cult.[34] On the other hand, he traced the Dionysian mysteries not to the Orient but to a primitive stage of Greek religious history, which he associated with the agrarian Ionians. This early cult of Dionysus had been driven underground by the conquering Doric tribes, whom Müller viewed as the "authentic" Greeks and whose history he chronicled in *Die Dorier* (1824).[35] According to Müller, the Dorians had invaded ancient Hellas from the north and established a cult of Apollo that was both more ethical and more humanistic than the nature-religion of the Ionians. This invasion was commemorated subsequently in Hesiod's myth of the Olympians and the Titans. Based on this argument, Müller sharply rejected Creuzer's theory that the Greeks had received their gods from abroad.[36] While he acknowledged a limited influence from the Phoenicians and from Near Eastern cults on later Greek religion, he insisted that Greek development in its earliest phase was a result of the "genius" of the Greek "nation."[37]

The eventual triumph of Müller's theory of Greek autochthony against a theory of Egyptian or "Oriental" origins has been interpreted by Martin Bernal as the victory of a Romantic, racist, religious agenda against the tolerance of the Enlightenment.[38] Josine Blok, in her essays on this controversy, has sought to moderate the differences between Creuzer and Müller and to save Müller from the charge of being a racist and an anti-Semite. In the main, Blok succeeds in refuting Bernal's more spurious accusations, demonstrating his slight acquaintance with Müller's works and his indiscriminate translation of various German words as "race."[39] Yet Müller did not completely eschew the word "race" (*Race*), nor did he see Greek and Egyptian cultures as simply following two different, but equally valid paths of development. Rather, he viewed the Greeks as clearly superior to the Egyptians. "In every higher intellectual activity the weak and cowardly Egyptians stood far behind the young Hellenic nation, as a nobler race always prevails over a baser one," he wrote at one point.[40] Further, although Müller's theory was not driven by a biological notion of race, his conception of "nationality" acquired an almost deterministic force in his conception of ancient Greek history.[41]

What Bernal and many other historians have failed to see, however, is that this conception of nationality was consistent with early political liberalism as it had emerged in the immediate aftermath of the Napoleonic Wars.[42] In general, Müller favored an expansion of political freedoms in Germany, and he would offer moderate (if rather tepid) support for the protest of Jacob Grimm and the Göttingen Seven against the Hanoverian government in 1837.[43] While suspicious of the political demands of such left-leaning liberals as Rotteck and Welcker, Müller believed that a culture should develop in freedom and in autonomy, expressing the principles of its "nationality" through indigenous laws, practices, and institutions.[44] To this end, he rejected the "mixing" of nations promoted by Creuzer's *Symbolik* and praised Greece, India, and ancient Germany as nations that had followed paths of (relatively) autonomous development.[45] Müller's rhetoric of nationality contained an undeniable racial element, yet in the early nineteenth century it also served as a way to challenge the "foreign" Metternichian regime and to promote a moderate, nationalist, and deeply Protestant form of liberalism.

Karl Otfried Müller's understanding of ancient Greece did not go unchallenged by the south-German Romantic intellectuals, including Friedrich Schelling. Since first moving to Bavaria in 1804, Schelling had come to reject the identity-philosophy of his Jena period, as well as G. W. F. Hegel's increasingly influential form of idealism. Starting from the premises of a personalist monotheism, Schelling now argued that the freedom of God demanded that He remain above logical proof or demonstration. Thus, although a purely rationalist or "negative" philosophy (such as Hegel's) could deduce the necessary parameters of God's potential existence, it was the task of empirical or "positive" philosophy to describe God's actual revelation. Philosophy, in other words, could not start with a concept of God and prove His existence. Instead, God's existence had to be taken as a given and as the foundation of all subsequent thinking.[46]

Schelling's late philosophy reflected a fundamental shift in his views away from republicanism and in the direction of theological and political conservatism. The Christian religion, he had come to believe, provided the only adequate foundation for political life in modern Europe. In particular, he saw the personal relationship between God and the Christian believer as the model for the relationship between the monarch and his subjects.[47] Also, the former pantheist now insisted on the literal truth of such biblical stories as the Fall and the Tower of Babel, which he backed up with references to other Oriental mythologies, namely, those of Egypt, Persia, and Asia Minor.

This brought Schelling close to Creuzer's position. Indeed, during the *Symbolik* controversy he spoke favorably of Creuzer while criticizing Voss and Müller. Still, Schelling recognized the difficulties of Creuzer's claim that something so fundamental as mythology could be transmitted from one culture to the next by a roving band of priests. Such cultural diffusionism flew in the face of the diversity of national cultures and struck Schelling as a relic of eighteenth-century thought. In addition, the notion of a common *Symbolik* passed between Egypt and Greece had been rendered implausible by Jean-François Champollion's discovery in 1821 that the hieroglyphs encoded a phonetic, rather than a symbolic, language.[48] Finally, Schelling was suspicious of the Orientalists' claim that the ancient Indians (or any other people) had possessed the entirety of religious truth. Instead, he identified a clear progression from the earliest forms of religion to the full-blown polytheism of the Greeks, who—even more than the Jews—had anticipated the Christian revelation in the teachings of their mystery religions. In this way, Schelling hoped to reassert the primacy of Greece within a Christianizing narrative of history (at a time when the Bavarian King Ludwig I was promoting a cultural policy based on both Philhellenism and Romantic Christianity), while asserting the importance of his own philosophy for defining the "philosophical religion" of the future.

Schelling developed these arguments in his lectures on the philosophy of mythology, which he first delivered in 1821 and which he repeated in various versions over the next twenty-five years.[49] Here Schelling explained the course of world history as an interplay of three "potences," which together comprised the substance of God, the basis of the material world, and the content of human history. The exact configuration of potences shifted from one culture to the next, giving rise to a "theogonic process" that determined the different forms of mythology and hence the different forms of national life.[50]

But the interplay of the potences was expressed not only at the level of religion, social life, and government—it also was manifest in the physical appearance of a nation. Although Schelling's comments on this theme remained fragmentary, he clearly saw race as fundamental to the nature of civilization insofar as race expressed at the physiological level what was later expressed at the level of religion.[51] By treating race as an aspect of the theogonic process, Schelling was able to avoid the difficulties of Creuzer's diffusionism whilst suggesting a *telos* beyond nationality in the notion of a broader European Christendom.[52]

The theogonic process began with a catastrophe roughly equivalent to the biblical Fall, which had destroyed the original "golden age" and given rise to the different languages and nations of the Earth. The differences between peoples were first expressed at the level of race. "Still more than outward events, it is differences of physical development that emerge in the interior of mankind, which begin to express themselves in the human species according to a hidden law and through which as a consequence certain spiritual, moral, and psychological differences also emerge, that can be thought of as the factors through which humankind was determined to diverge into the nations."[53] Like his friend and disciple Henrich Steffens (and Immanuel Kant before him), Schelling saw the development of "race" as a purely negative event, a fall from ideal human form that had to be overcome by the subsequent theogonic process.[54] Those peoples most subject to "race" were the black Africans or the South American Indians, who lacked any real religion and thus could not be seen as nations (*Völker*) at all. In other cases, the development of mythology had made it possible to "overcome" race: thus, the ancient Egyptians had acquired a nobler countenance than the native black Africans, while the Indians' corporeal physiognomy reflected the orientation of Indian mythology toward the spiritual rather than the material realm.[55] The Europeans, as evidenced by their white skin and ideal physiques, had completely "overcome" race through the harmonious interplay of the three potences that formed the basis of the Christian religion.[56] Thus, whereas Karl Otfried Müller had viewed physical appearance as just one of numerous factors (along with language, law, and religion) that determined the character of the *Volk*, Schelling's search for an inner, unconscious principle of world history led him to a far more biological and deterministic concept of race, which expressed at the "real" level what mythology expressed at the level of the "ideal."

In Schelling's scheme, the theogonic process passed through a pre-mythological stage of "limited" monotheism before progressing to the properly polytheistic systems of Egypt, India, and Greece. Following his theory of the potences, he treated the bizarre, often orgiastic quality of the ancient religious liturgy as springing from inward psychological necessity rather than from a moral lapse. Likewise, half-animal or half-monstrous deities of Indian and

Egyptian mythologies reflected not so much animal-worship as the incomplete harmony of the potences in these religions. In general, Schelling lavished praise on the artistic and metaphysical achievements of Egyptian civilization, while criticizing ancient India and those contemporary "Indomaniacs" who treated that land as the source of human civilization.

Nonetheless, it was only with the Greeks that the theogonic process reached completion and self-consciousness. Hesiod's poem recapitulated the entire history of mythology, taking up the Egyptian and Indian gods into its genealogy of deities before bringing the Olympians onto the stage.[57] Meanwhile, the Attic mysteries anticipated the Christian revelation not only in the figure of the suffering Dionysus, but also in the birth of a *new* god to the virgin Demeter. Judaism, by contrast, remained at the level of a "limited" or "relative" monotheism that could not conceive the triune nature of "true" (i.e., Christian) monotheism.[58] In this respect, Schelling's philosophy of mythology made the Greeks (rather than the Jews) the true witnesses to the Christian revelation while placing Israel two steps away from the "genuine" religion of Christianity.

Schelling's philosophy of mythology offered a modern alternative to the biblical narrative, going beyond the traditional economy of Old and New Testaments in order to Christianize the entire history of world religion. With this scheme, he attempted to demonstrate the dependence of not only the free subject but also the white body of European liberalism on a broader theogonic process. As for the other races, Schelling foresaw that they would eventually disappear on repeated contact with the European nations.[59] In this respect, his mythography offered a legitimation for European colonialist expansion. Yet in the context of early nineteenth-century Germany its most immediate effect was to reappropriate the Philhellenist ideals of freedom and (white) beauty for an explicitly Christian philosophy and a deeply conservative politics.

Martin Bernal was correct to identify the problem of racism as crucial for the development of modern classical scholarship, including mythography. In his account of the early nineteenth century, however, he tends to link the growth of racism exclusively with the emergence of a Romantic, anti-Enlightenment, and anti-Egyptian Philhellenism.[60] In doing so, he overlooks the links between Philhellenism and the growing political and cultural aspirations of middle-class intellectuals in Germany, who saw in ancient Greece a model of political and religious freedom as well as of a healthy public life. By exposing the non-anthropomorphic, orgiastic, and yet pious underside of Greek mythology and by tracing its origins to Egypt and India, Friedrich Creuzer's Romantic mythography challenged not only the autochthony of ancient Greece, but also early liberal notions of republicanism and of religion. This conservative theological-political dimension of Romantic Orientalism drew the fire of Johann Heinrich Voss, who zeroed in on the non-anthropomorphic, multi-gendered beings that populated the *Symbolik.*

Karl Otfried Müller, while more conservative politically than Voss, sought nonetheless to emphasize the human and heroic dimensions of Greek mythology; unlike the early Philhellenists who focused on the situation of the individual artist, however, Müller traced these dimensions to the qualities inherent in the Doric tribes and, hence, in the Greek "nationality" or "race." Yet it was the older Schelling, an opponent of Müller and the advocate of a world-historical perspective on mythology, who raised race to the status of a near-metaphysical force. By tracing the evolution of religion from its beginnings in Babel to the onset of European Christianity, he justified a deeply conservative political and religious position while avoiding the "Catholic" Orientalisms of Schlegel, Görres, and Creuzer. In his scheme, race was not a permanent material condition but rather a religious stigma that only the Europeans had overcome—an argument that reinforced racial difference all the more effectively by ascribing it solely to non-whites. Through its world-historical conception and its close linkage of race and religion, Schelling's philosophy of mythology foreshadowed the anti-liberal racisms of Arthur de Gobineau, Richard Wagner, and Houston Stewart Chamberlain, as well as their twentieth-century disciples.

NOTES

1. *Hesiod: Theogony, Works and Days; Theognis: Elegies,* trans. Dorothea Wender (Harmondsworth: Penguin, 1973), 46.

2. Anthony Grafton, "Polyhistor into Philolog: Notes on the Transformation of German Classical Scholarship, 1780–1850," *History of Universities* 3 (1983): 159–192; Anthony La Vopa, "Specialists Against Specialization: Hellenism as Professional Ideology in German Classical Studies," in *German Professions, 1800–1950,* eds. Geoffrey Cocks and Konrad Jarausch (Oxford: Oxford University Press, 1990), 27–45; Suzanne Marchand, *Down from Olympus: Archaeology and Philhellenism in Germany, 1750–1970* (Princeton: Princeton University Press, 1996); on these themes, see also George S. Williamson, *The Longing for Myth in Germany: Religion and Aesthetic Culture from Romanticism to Nietzsche* (Chicago: University of Chicago Press, 2004).

3. Martin Bernal, *Black Athena: The Afroasiatic Roots of Classical Civilization,* vol. 1, *The Fabrication of Ancient Greece 1785–1985* (New Brunswick: Rutgers University Press, 1987); see the vehement replies against Bernal in Mary R. Lefkowitz and Guy MacLean Rogers, eds., *Black Athena Revisited* (Chapel Hill, NC: University of North Carolina Press, 1996); and Bernal's reply, *Black Athena Writes Back,* ed. David Chioni Moore (Durham: Duke University Press, 2001); see also the bemused discussion of the whole affair by Jacques Berlinerblau, *Heresy in the University: The Black Athena Controversy and the Responsibility of American Intellectuals* (New Brunswick, NJ: Rutgers University Press, 1999). While I consider *Black Athena* deeply

problematic at the level of both scholarly detail and historical argumentation, its emphasis on race and racism served to highlight a critical and long repressed issue in the historiography of classical scholarship.

4. This is the approach of Josine Blok, who offers a trenchant critique of Bernal's methodology but rarely addresses the broader issues arising from *Black Athena*. See Josine Blok, "Quest for a Scientific Mythology: F. Creuzer and K. O. Müller on History and Myth," in *Proof and Persuasion in History, History and Theory,* theme issue, eds. Anthony Grafton and Suzanne L. Marchand 33 (1994): 26–52; idem, " 'Romantische Poesie, Naturphilosophie, Construktion der Geschichte': K. O. Müller's Understanding of History and Myth," in *Zwischen Rationalismus und Romantik: Karl Otfried Müller und die antike Kultur,* eds. William Calder III and Renate Schlesier, with Susanne Gödde (Hildesheim: Weidmann, 1998), 55–97; also "Proof and Persuasion in *Black Athena*: The Case of K. O. Müller," *Journal of the History of Ideas* 57 (1996): 705–24; among other works, see esp. Evá Kocziszy, "Samothrake: Ein Streit um Creuzers Symbolik und das Wesen der Mythologie," in *Antike und Abendland* 43 (1997): 174–189, which offers a subtle reading of Creuzer's theory of the symbol but likewise does not deal with the historical context; Marchand, *Down from Olympus,* 43–48, takes a broader perspective, linking the affair to the development of art history, but does not address the specific theological-political context of the controversy; for this, see *Longing for Myth in Germany,* 121–150. For the main texts and an anti-Creuzerian introduction, see Ernst Howald, ed., *Der Kampf um Creuzers Symbolik: Eine Auswahl von Dokumenten* (Tübingen: Mohr, 1926); also the comments in Walter Burkert, "Griechische Mythologie und die Geistesgeschichte der Moderne," in *Les études classiques aux xixe et xxe siècles: leur place dans l'histoire des idées,* eds. Willem den Boer et al. (Geneva: Droz, 1979), 159–207; and Albert Baeumler, "Bachofen der Mythologe der Romantik," in Johann Jakob Bachofen, *Der Mythus von Occident und Orient,* edited by Manfred Schröter (Munich: Beck, 1926), xxii–xxcxiv; Raymond Schwab, *The Oriental Renaissance: Europe's Rediscovery of India and the East, 1680–1880,* trans. Gene Patterson-Black and Victor Reinking (New York: Columbia University Press, 1984), is particularly good at charting Creuzer's considerable influence in France.

5. F. W. J. Schelling, *Sämmtliche Werke,* ed. K. F. A. Schelling, 14 vols. (Stuttgart: Cotta, 1856–61) [cited hereafter as *SSW*], 11:226.

6. The history of conceptions of race in early-nineteenth-century Germany has yet to be written. In addition to the contributions in this volume, see Leon Poliakov, *The Aryan Myth: A History of Racist and Nationalist Ideas in Europe,* trans. Edmund Howard (New York: Basic Books, 1971); George Mosse, *Toward the Final Solution: A History of European Racism* (New York: Howard Fertig, 1978); Susanne Zantop, *Colonial Fantasies: Conquest, Family, and Nation in Precolonial Germany, 1770–1870* (Durham, NC: Duke University Press, 1997); idem, "The Beautiful, the Ugly, and the German: Race, Gender, and Nationality in Eighteenth-Century Anthropological Discourse," in *Gender and Germanness: Cultural Productions of Nation,* eds. Patricia Herminghouse and Magda Mueller (Providence, RI: Berghahn, 1997), 21–33; David Bindman, *Ape to Apollo: Aesthetics and the Idea of Race in the 18th Century* (London: Reaktion, 2002). See also the suggestive comments of Michel Foucault, *The History of Sexuality: An Introduction,* trans. Robert Hurley (New York: Vintage, 1978),

esp. 115–161, who links the valorization of the white body to the early nineteenth-century bourgeois project of modernity; and Ann Laura Stoler, *Race and the Education of Desire: Foucault's* History of Sexuality *and the Colonial Order of Things* (Durham, NC: Duke University Press, 1995), 55–94. For meditations on the meanings of the monstrous in Western thought, see (among many recent books) Richard Kearney, *Strangers, Gods, and Monsters: Interpreting Otherness* (London: Routledge, 2002).

7. On Winckelmann in this context, see esp. Alex Potts, *Flesh and the Ideal: Winckelmann and the Origins of Art History* (New Haven, CT: Yale University Press, 1994).

8. Winckelmann, *History of Ancient Art*, trans. G. Henry Lodge, 4 vols. (New York: Frederick Ungar, 1969), 1:181; see also 1:210–211.

9. On the political implications of the Winckelmannian ideal and its afterlife, see Potts, *Flesh and the Ideal*, esp. 182–253; also Josef Chytry, *The Aesthetic State: A Quest in Modern German Thought* (Berkeley: University of California Press, 1989).

10. Friedrich Schiller, "Letters on the Aesthetic Education of Man," trans. Elizabeth M. Wilkinson and L. A. Willoughby, in *Essays*, ed. Walter Hinderer and Daniel O. Dahlstrom (New York: Continuum, 1995), 163.

11. On Schiller's political frustrations and their implications for his aesthetics, see Jonathan M. Hess, *Reconstituting the Body Politic: Enlightenment, Public Culture and the Invention of Aesthetic Autonomy* (Detroit, MI: Wayne State University Press, 1999).

12. F. W. J. Schelling, *The Philosophy of Art*, trans., and ed. Douglas W. Stott (Minneapolis, MN: University of Minnesota Press, 1989), 35; ibid, 186.

13. Schelling, *Philosophy of Art*, 61.

14. See esp. Schwab, *The Oriental Renaissance*; and Kveta E. Benes, "German Linguistic Nationhood, 1806–1866: Philology, Cultural Translation, and Historical Identity in Pre-Unification Germany" (Ph.D. diss., University of Washington, 2001), ch. 2; also Poliakov, *Aryan Myth*, 183–214; Todd Kontje, *German Orientalisms* (Ann Arbor, MI: University of Michigan Press, 2004), 64–83.

15. Friedrich Creuzer, *Symbolik und Mythologie der alten Völker, besonders der Griechen*, 1st ed., 4 vols. (Leipzig: Leske; Darmstadt: Stahl, 1810–12); 2nd ed., 6 vols. (Leipzig and Darmstadt: Heyer and Leske, 1819–23); 3rd ed., 6 vols. (Leipzig and Darmstadt: Leske, 1837–42). Although Creuzer's work first appeared in 1810, the controversy gathered force only following the publication of the second, more complete edition of the *Symbolik*. On Creuzer, see Koczisky, "Samothrake," also Marc-Mathieu Münch, *La "Symbolique" de Friedrich Creuzer* (Paris: Ophrys, 1976).

16. Koczisky, "Samothrake," 181, attempts to refute the charge that the *Symbolik* overly emphasized the role of priests in the formation of Greek mythology. In her view, Creuzer saw the priests primarily as exegetes of an already given symbol. Still, it seems clear that Creuzer wanted to stress the role of an esoteric, divine wisdom in his theory of myth. Moreover, his account of this wisdom often stands closer to enlightened notions of an original *Naturphilosophie* than to the more ineffable, unconscious realm of the "symbolic."

17. Creuzer, *Symbolik*, 2nd ed., 1:xviii–xix. These passages anticipate Bernal's later complaints about the neglect of Herodotus. See Bernal, *Black Athena*, esp. 98–101.

18. Creuzer, *Symbolik*, 2nd ed., 1:55.

19. Creuzer, *Symbolik*, 2nd. ed., 4:552.

20. Among the most important works in this controversy were Gottfried Hermann and Friedrich Creuzer, *Briefe über Homer und Hesiodus, vorzüglich über die Theogonie* (Heidelberg: August Oswald, 1818); Gottfried Hermann, *Ueber das Wesen und die Behandlung der Mythologie* (Leipzig: G. Fleischer, 1819); Johann Heinrich Voss, *Antisymbolik*, 2 vols. (Stuttgart: Metzler, 1824–26); Wolfgang Menzel, *Voß und die Symbolik* (Stuttgart: F. Franck, 1825); Christian August Lobeck, *Aglaophamus; sive, De Theologiae mysticae Graecorum causis libri III* (Königsberg: Borntraeger, 1829); and the works of K. O. Müller cited below.

21. On Voss, see esp. Frank Baudach and Günter Häntzschel, eds., *Johann Heinrich Voss (1751–1826)* (Eutin: Struve, 1997); also the long biography by Wilhelm Herbst, *Johann Heinrich Voss*, 2 vols. in 3 (repr. Bern: Herbert Lang, 1970).

22. Hegel to Voss (main draft, August, 1805), in *Hegel: The Letters*, trans. Clark Butler and Christiane Seiler, with commentary by Clark Butler (Bloomington, IN: Indiana University Press, 1984), 107.

23. Heinrich Heine, "Die Romantische Schule," *Werke und Briefe*, ed. Hans Kaufmann, 10 vols. (Berlin: Aufbau, 1961), 5:39.

24. Voss, *Antisymbolik*, 1:44.

25. On the "symbolic geography" of the Orient, see Kontje, *German Orientalisms*, 1.

26. On Voss's politics in the post–1815 period, see esp. Herbst, *Johann Heinrich Voss*, vol. 2, pt. 2:175–80.

27. See, e.g., Joseph Görres, *Mythengeschichte der asiatischen Welt* (Heidelberg: Mohr und Zimmer, 1810); Friedrich Schlegel, *Ueber die Sprache und Weisheit der Indiener: Ein Beitrag zur Begründung der Alterthumskunde* (Heidelberg: Mohr und Zimmer, 1808).

28. See Schwab, *Oriental Renaissance*, 175–6, 235, and esp. Owen Bradley, *A Modern Maistre: The Social and Political Thought of Joseph de Maistre* (Lincoln: University of Nebraska Press, 1999), 50–58, 151–159, 193–4. Bradley provides an illuminating discussion of de Maistre's "penchant for ancient Oriental wisdom" (193), showing that this paragon of Catholic traditionalism was actually rather heterodox in his theological views. Indeed, de Maistre's theology parallels Creuzer's in terms of both content and ideological orientation.

29. On the mood of religious exaltation that seemed to grip Voss during his confrontation with the Catholic convert Friedrich Stolberg, see Herbst, *Johann Heinrich Voss*, 2: 190.

30. Rudolf Haym, ed., *Wilhelm von Humboldt's Briefe an F. G. Welcker* (Berlin: Gaertner, 1859); Lobeck, *Aglaophamus*. Lobeck had already written a critical review of the *Symbolik* in 1811 for the *Jenaische Allgemeine Literatur-Zeitung* (excerpted in Howald, *Kampf*, 77–81).

31. For the notion of a "dark side of antiquity" and its role in later nineteenth-century German-speaking culture, see Lionel Gossman, *Basel in the Age of Burckhardt: A Study in Unseasonable Ideas* (Chicago: University of Chicago Press, 2000), esp. 149–70.

32. On Müller, see the works by Josine Blok cited above, as well as the essays in Calder and Schlesier, eds., *Zwischen Rationalismus und Romantik*; also G. P. Gooch, *History and Historians in the Nineteenth Century*, 2nd ed. (Boston: Beacon, 1959),

33–38; Günther Pflug, "Methodik und Hermeneutik bei Karl Otfried Müller," in Hellmut Flashar, Karlfried Gründer, and Axel Horstmann, eds., *Philologie und Hermeneutik im 19. Jahrhundert: Zur Geschichte und Methodologie der Geisteswissenschaften* (Göttingen: Vandenhoeck und Ruprecht, 1979), 122–140; A. D. Momigliano, "K. O. Müller's *Prolegomena zu einer wissenschaftlichen Mythologie* and the Meaning of Myth," in *Annali della Scuola Normale Superiore de Pisa*, ser. 3, 13 (1983): 671–89; Klaus Nickau, "Karl Otfried Müller, Professor der Klassischen Philologie 1819–1840," in *Die Klassische Altertumswissenschaft an der Georg-August-Universität Göttingen: Eine Ringvorlesung zu ihrer Geschichte*, ed. Carl Joachim Classen (Göttingen: Vandenhoeck und Ruprecht, 1989).

33. On this, see esp. Blok, "'Romantische Poesie,'" 57–60, 80–83.

34. Review of Johann Heinrich Voss, *Antisymbolik*, in *Kleine Deutsche Schriften*, ed. Eduard Müller, 2 vols. (Breslau: Josef Max, 1847–8) [cited hereafter as *KDS*], 2:25–30; see also the similarly critical review of Lobeck's *Aglaophamus*, in *KDS*, 2:54–69.

35. Karl Otfried Müller, *Geschichten Hellenischer Stämme und Städte*, pt. 2, *Die Dorier*, 2 vols. (Breslau: Josef Max, 1824).

36. Review of *Symbolik und Mythologie*, 2nd ed., vols. 1–2, in *KDS*, 2:3–20; review of vols. 3–4, *KDS*, 2:21–5; also the introduction to *Geschichten Hellenischer Stämme und Städte*, pt. 1, *Orchomenos und die Minyer* (Breslau: Josef Max, 1820), and *Prolegomena zu einer wissenschaftlichen Mythologie* (Göttingen: Vandenhoeck und Ruprecht, 1825).

37. Review of *Symbolik*, *KDS*, 2:5, 10–11; see also "Ueber den angeblich ägyptischen Ursprung der griechischen Kunst" [1820], *KDS*, 2:523–37; review of Heinrich Meyers, *Geschichte der bildenden Künste bei den Griechen*, and Friedrich Thiersch, *Ueber die Epochen der bildenden Kunst unter den Griechen*, *KDS*, 2:315–98, and the review of Klenze and Schorn, *Beschreibung der Glyptothek*, *KDS*, 2:447–54, esp. 450–1.

38. Bernal, *Black Athena*, 308–16.

39. See esp. Blok, "Proof and Persuasion," 712–7 (on Müller as "Anti-semite"), and 720–23 (on Bernal's use of the term "race"). Also important in this context is Brian E. Vick, "Greek Origins and Organic Metaphors: Ideals of Cultural Autonomy in Neohumanist Germany from Winckelmann to Curtius," *Journal of the History of Ideas* 63 (2002): 483–500. Vick challenges the claim that early nineteenth-century historians were interested simply in promoting cultural purity. He shows instead that Romantic historicism rested not just on a metaphor of organic autonomy for the individual nation but also, and equally, on a metaphor of organic continuity *between* cultures. After all, neohumanism assumed the possibility of a fruitful exchange between cultures: the key was that the foreign influences be received actively rather than passively. Yet Vick, to my mind, underplays what I take to be the anticolonial moment in German thought in the postrevolutionary period. Moreover, his line of analysis does not account for the bitter disputes among various types of Philhellenists, including those discussed in this essay.

40. "Ueber den angeblich ägyptischen Ursprung," *KDS*, 2:536. For Blok's commentary on this article, "Proof and Persuasion," 718. Bernal, as Blok notes, was apparently unfamiliar with this essay.

41. cf. Müller, *Die Dorier*, 2nd ed. (Breslau: Josef Max, 1844), 1:5: "In this way the [Thessalonians] are sufficiently different from the naturally noble [durch die Natur

edelgeschaffnen] tribe of the Greeks." At times, Müller's theory does rely on the evidence of race (e.g., "Ueber den angeblich ägyptischen Ursprung," *KDS*, 2:531–2), yet he attributes little explanatory power to skin color and physiognomy in themselves.

42. On the relevance of these issues for *Vormärz* liberalism, see esp. Brian E. Vick, *Defining Germany: The 1848 Frankfurt Parliamentarians and National Identity* (Cambridge: Harvard University Press, 2002).

43. Nickau, Karl Otfried Müller, 47–8.

44. For evidence of Müller's moderate liberal nationalism (emphasizing freedom of nations vs. freedom of individuals), see also the preface to *Die Dorier*, 1:v–xvi.

45. *KDS*, 2:318–9.

46. On the foundations of Schelling's later philosophy, see esp. Manfred Frank, *Der unendliche Mangel am Sein: Schellings Hegelkritik und die Anfänge der Marxschen Dialektik*, 2nd ed. (Munich: W. Fink, 1992); Joseph Lawrence, *Schellings Philosophie des ewigen Anfangs: Die Natur als Quelle der Geschichte* (Würzburg: Könighausen & Neumann, 1989).

47. For a brilliant study of the rejection of this theology by Ludwig Feuerbach, Arnold Ruge, and August von Cieszkowski, see Warren Breckman, *The Young Hegelians, Marx, and the Origins of Radical Social Theory: Dethroning the Self* (Cambridge: Cambridge University Press, 1999).

48. The key work was Jean-François Champollion, *Précis du système hiéroglyphique des anciens Egyptiens* (Paris: Treuttel et Würtz, 1824). On this, see Erik Iversen, *The Myth of Egypt and its Hieroglyphs in European Tradition* (Princeton: Princeton University Press, 1961), 124–145.

49. On Schelling's philosophy of mythology, see Edward Allen Beach, *The Potencies of God(s): Schelling's Philosophy of Mythology* (Albany: State University of New York Press, 1994); also Xavier Tilliette, *La mythologie comprise: L'interprétation schellingienne du paganisme* (Naples: Institute Italiano per gli Studi Filosofici, 1984); J. E. Wilson, *Schellings Mythologie: Zur Auslegung der Philosophie der Mythologie und Offenbarung* (Stuttgart: Frommann-Holzboog, 1993). The comments here are based on the 1842 version of the lectures presented in the *Sämmtliche Werke*, vol. 12.

50. cf. *SSW*, 12:425: "In mythology nothing is taken from nature. Instead, the natural process repeats itself as a theogonic process in consciousness."

51. The role of race in Schelling's latter philosophy of mythology has been largely ignored by previous commentators. For several telling excerpts, however, see Poliakov, *Aryan Myth*, 239–40.

52. Schelling's emphasis on race as the marker of an unconscious theogonic process challenged the philologists who emphasized the primacy of language for human culture, as well as those comparative philologists who sought to establish a linguistic and cultural connection between the ancient Greeks and the Aryans of India. On K. O. Müller's later reception of comparative linguistics, see esp. Benes, "German Linguistic Nationhood," ch. 4.

53. *SSW*, 11:95–6.

54. Steffens had published *Anthropologie*, 2 vols. (Breslau: Josef Max, 1822). On Kant and Steffens' theories of race, see the essay in this volume by Mark Larrimore.

55. *SSW*, 11:99; 12:572–3.

56. *SSW*, 11:98.

57. See *SSW*, 12:587–8.

58. See, e.g., *SSW*, 12:315–21; also Schelling, *Philosophie der Offenbarung 1841/ 42*, ed. Manfred Frank (Frankfurt a.M.: Suhrkamp, 1977), 278–285.

59. *SSW*, 11:97: "[It] may be . . . rather spiritual and moral differences that can lead to a physical incompatibility of certain human races [*Menschengeschlechter*]. This includes the quick dying off of all natives that come into contact with Europeans, before whom all nations that are not defended by innumerable hordes, like the Indians or Chinese, or by climate, like the Negroes, appear destined to disappear. In Van Diemen's Land the entire native population has died off since the settlement of the English. Similarly in New South Wales. It is as if the higher and freer development of the European nations becomes deadly to all others."

60. Bernal, *Black Athena*, 189–223.

9

From Indo-Germans to Aryans

Philology and the Racialization of Salvationalist National Rhetoric, 1806–30

Tuska Benes

As part of the post–WWII reaction against German Romanticism, a number of scholars, including Léon Poliakov and Raymond Schwab, attributed the origins of the "Aryan myth" to early-nineteenth-century Indologists, drawing a fairly direct connection between Germany's "Oriental Renaissance" and the violent anti-Semitism of the Third Reich.[1] These critiques rightly note that National Socialists claimed descent from a master race originating in India; that they adopted Indian symbols such as the swastika; and that they created a cult of the "Aryan." In the critiques' view, German nationalism fatefully departed from the "humane" ideals of the French Enlightenment, espousing deep cultural authenticity at the expense of reason, universalism, and progress. But this sort of argument is often dissatisfying given its reliance on an essentialist view of the German national character, as well as its tendency to project a biological understanding of the terms "Aryan" and "Semite" onto earlier periods and to conflate important historical distinctions, such as the changing political aspirations of the German nationalist movement.[2]

167

The question of historical continuity and of the role of Indology in a possible German *Sonderweg* may be approached more critically by asking whether the early-nineteenth-century Orientalist definition of German nationhood set a precedent for the Nazis' exclusionary and racialist notion of national community. More recent scholars have ascribed a xenophobic, expansionist drive to the emphasis German nationalists placed on culture and ethnicity. During the Napoleonic occupation and the Wars of Liberation, the German nation was conceived primarily as a cultural entity existing independently of the state in the collective consciousness of German-speakers. A political definition of Germanness based on participation in a shared institutional or legal framework was untenable because the German-speaking population of central Europe was dispersed across numerous multiethnic states and principalities. Language, history, and culture were the principal bonds believed to unite the German nation and the chief pillars around which a collective German self was defined.[3]

Early-nineteenth-century German nationalists put particular value on the inheritance of German as a mother tongue because it was thought to testify to native speakers' shared historical descent from a common cultural origin. This paper examines the implications this concern for origins had for German notions of community. It suggests that glorifying shared historical descent from a single point in antiquity reinforced an ethnic and racial definition of nationhood. As will be seen, German Orientalists introduced a racial understanding of physical difference to the categories of language and of culture as they searched for the primordial homeland (*Urheimat*) of German-speakers in Asia. German national narrative was racialized within that philological discourse on early German migration from India and Central Asia which evolved in response to the publication of Friedrich Schlegel's *On the Language and Wisdom of the Indians* in 1808.

THE SALVATIONIST RHETORIC OF ORIENTALIST NATIONAL NARRATIVE

Friedrich Schlegel's narrative of German descent from India followed traditional biblical notions of the emergence of cultural difference by which German-speakers and related linguistic groups originated from a sacred homeland in the East that had also been the site of the "first revelation" (*ursprüngliche Offenbarung*).[4] As his well-known letter to Ludwig Tieck proclaimed, Schlegel (1772–1829) believed ancient Indic to be "the source of all languages, all thought, and all poetry of the human spirit; *everything*, everything stems from India without exception."[5] Humankind had experienced its first religious awakening and been introduced to the Idea of the true God in a terrestrial Indian paradise. At the same time, Schlegel drew on affinities in language, in mythology, in law, and in architecture to conclude that "the greatest empires and most noble nations" of antiquity, including those of the Egyptians and Hebrews, were "colonies" founded by Indian priests. He distinguished the first Germans as one of several "descended nations" or emigrant groups, including the Persians, who had left Asia during a period of religious strife and civil war that followed disagreement over the meaning of God's word.[6]

This view of prehistory relied on the model of Genesis. The first five books of the Old Testament suggest that all people descended from a primordial Garden of Eden, which late-eighteenth-century scholars often located in the East near Kashmir and Tibet.[7] The world's nations had supposedly parted ways and been dispersed across the globe only after Noah's Ark landed on Mt. Ararat and after attempts at Babel to build a tower to heaven failed. Schlegel assumed Sanskrit to be the "oldest descendent," the most proximate historical language of the lost *"Ursprache"* or divine first language.[8] The religious qualities of ancient Indic interested Schlegel more than any evidence the language might hold of early German culture; and Schlegel's work had a mixed reception in German-speaking lands due to his converting to Catholicism and accepting employment at the Austrian imperial court, the symbol of reactionary politics.[9]

Schlegel, however, altered the Christian narrative of the emergence of cultural difference by claiming only one people to have been witness to the first revelation. In 1808 he opposed to those populations whose languages pointed to a "common descent" from Sanskrit, those for whom "no original kinship" could be determined.[10] In his view, Latin, Greek, Persian, and German could be "derived from Indic and understood based on her composition."[11] Offering proof of their lexical similarity but also of affinities in their "comparative grammar,"[12] Schlegel asserted that the above idioms displayed a

> shared principle by which all relationships and subtleties of meaning
> are signified not by appended particles or helping verbs, but rather
> by inflection, that is by modification to the root.[13]

The inflection of a verb determines its grammatical function in a sentence by assigning number, tense, voice, and mood to the root. In the English verb "to eat," for example, the past tense "ate" is formed or inflected by a change in the initial vowel of the stem.[14] Schlegel held that those languages related to Sanskrit were united by the similar way the roots of verbs ("living seeds") took form in a sentence.[15]

The conglomeration of languages to which Schlegel attributed Indian origins was set apart from a more varied second group, including Chinese, Hebrew, Arabic, and American-Indian languages, all of which shared, by comparison to languages of Indian origin, a "diametrically opposed grammar."[16] He characterized these lesser tongues as "mechanical" rather than "organic,"[17] because they made use "only of *affixa* rather than inflection"[18] and because they expressed grammatical relationships with the help of an "added word."[19] This second group supposedly evolved from the languages of primitive "natives" (*Urbewohner*) who lived in areas outside of India and who, since they had not been privileged to the word of God, developed their speech instead from simple cries and sounds found in nature.[20] These "wilder peoples," in Schlegel's view, tended to be "isolated" and "uncultivated"[21] and had contributed little to the "moral development"[22] of humanity.

In his *Lectures on Universal History* (1805/6), Schlegel based this hierarchical distinction on a polygenetic view of human origins; only the "honorable" and "cultured" nations of Asia and Europe were said to have their roots in India.[23] Having resolved to convert to Catholicism while writing his 1808 essay on India, Schlegel later associated this division of humanity with the biblical story of Cain and Abel.[24] Explaining human "degeneration" through the metaphor of a fallen brother enabled the author to reconcile, with a monogenetic Christian philosophy of history, his distinction between cultured and barbaric peoples.[25] It also allowed Schlegel to privilege German-speakers as a chosen people destined to recreate the lost religious knowledge of divine revelation following an enlightened return to the paradise from which they had been expelled. Significantly, he believed the first Germans had left India in search of the holy mountain Meru and had headed towards Scandinavia, drawn by "a wonderful notion of the great dignity and splendor of the north."[26]

With a tantalizing reference that further research into Indian antiquity was "very important for our fatherland," Schlegel invited those scholars with more directly nationalist concerns to turn eastward.[27] His work found a host of welcome readers among Bavarians, including Othmar Frank (1770–1840), Franz Bopp (1791–1867), and the poet-Orientalist Friedrich Rückert (1788–1866). Rückert, in particular, followed Schlegel in associating India jointly with the origins of the German nation and with a Golden Age before Babel in which the divine had been revealed in language. The celebrated author of the patriotic *Fiery Sonnets* (1814) reworked Schlegel's expectations of finding religious revival in the East into Salvationist national narratives that promised the resurrection of spiritual harmony as the basis of German national unity. In Rückert's view, ancient Indian texts gave testimony to a divine first revelation, as well as to a period of intense communal integration among German-speakers.[28] By translating Sanskrit literature into German, Rückert hoped to reacquaint modern speakers with a more authentic version of the national self that would strengthen their national consciousness and would draw them together as a cultural community, as it rejuvenated them spiritually.[29] This fusion of Christian and national narratives resulted in an enduring conception of German national culture that anticipated a kind of millenarian fulfillment in which German speakers resurrected Babel and emerged as a people chosen by God.

Moreover, Orientalist histories of German national culture made use of the Christian rhetorical structure that M. H. Abrams has described as the "Romantic spiral." Metaphors of life as a circular journey, of prodigal return, of sin and redemption were superimposed onto the collective history of the German nation—with one slight alteration. Romantic writers added an extra twist to the Christian philosophy of history by concluding with a sudden resolution of a higher order, that is with an "*Aufhebung*" of the dissonances that resulted from expulsion from paradise.[30] During the Napoleonic period, the notion of the Fall enabled direct criticism of those forces thought to be obstructing unification, while it also held out hope that greater national cohesion was imminent. Friedrich Rückert, for example, lamented the apparent collapse of the compelling collective identities of antiquity, describing the events of the occupation and early Restoration as the culmination of an extended process of cultural degeneration. At the same time, he took advantage of the redemptive promise of this Salvationist rhetoric to construct millenarian narratives of national rebirth.[31]

More stringent philological techniques gradually rendered the Romantic search for divine inspiration in the East, as well as Schlegel's very focus on India, obsolete. Schlegel had borrowed heavily from the Third Discourse of William Jones, but ignored the latter's admonition that ancient Indic was not the mother tongue of humanity. The Berlin Indologist Franz Bopp (1791–1867) was the first in Germany to historicize Sanskrit as one of several natural tongues that had descended from an unknown, more ancient mother. His claim that Sanskrit was not the universal first language helped to secularize earlier narratives of German descent from the East by challenging Christian notions of the monogenetic origins of humanity. The metaphor of Babel ceased to serve as an adequate conceptual framework for early linguistic history, and Bopp encouraged German Orientalists to enlist language-study in a more precise form of ethnology not based on Old Testament notions of the emergence of cultural difference. As will be seen, however, the Salvationist rhetorical structure and millenarian expectations introduced by Friedrich Schlegel continued to shape notions of German descent from Asia even as those notions were enshrined in scientific rhetoric.

"Indo-Germanic" Migration from Central Asia

Bopp's invention of the Indo-European language-family in 1816 invalidated the search for a terrestrial paradise and for a universal first language. His study of verb-conjugation patterns in Greek, Latin, German, and Persian proved empirically that these languages "descend[ed] from Sanskrit or with it from a common mother." In each of the above tongues, Bopp showed, "no grammatical relationship" was "expressed through an inflection not shared with this original language."[32] His ability to convince contemporaries of the basic structural identity of Indo-European tongues was partly a result of his not following the Indic grammatical tradition in his treatment of Sanskrit.[33] He disassociated what he saw as the structure of the language from the system presented in native and missionary grammars, transferring the apparatus of Greek grammar to Sanskrit.[34] According to Bopp, one could construct a genealogy of languages by identifying and comparing certain affinities in the "linguistic organism" (*Sprachorganismus*) of each language, which he believed was an internal mechanism of growth evolving over time and space.[35] His numerous empirical studies aimed to group the world's tongues into families by isolating their dominant linguistic principles and by tracing them back to a few distinct points of origin.[36]

The "truly organic way" in which Indo-European verbs took shape in a sentence was not, according to Bopp, replicated in other families such as Semitic or Chinese.[37] Incongruence in their grammatical structures suggested that there had been neither a time before Babel when humanity had lived together in mutual understanding, nor an Eastern paradise from which all of the world's nations had emerged. Philologists after Bopp postulated an original diversity of languages and nations and began to replace biblical notions of the emergence of cultural difference with secular linguistic genealogies. At the same time, preconceptions of the universal language's grammatical perfection, intellectual dexterity, and universal cultural significance were transferred to the inflectional forms typical of the Indo-European language family. Those characteristics that had been associated with the divine *Ursprache* continued to be linked to Sanskrit and to archaic forms of related languages such as Gothic.[38]

Bopp's work likewise sparked a search for the exact geographical location of the Indo-European homeland in Asia by denying that any one of the presumed *Ursprachen* (Sanskrit, Avestan, ancient Greek, or Hebrew) was actually the truly most ancient mother tongue. India was still considered by some to be the likely German homeland as late as the mid–1850s.[39] But Bopp speculated that an even older prehistoric language, now known as Proto-Indo-European, had been spoken to the north and west of the subcontinent. Starting in the 1820s, German Orientalists began searching outside of India for a new Asian homeland where the common ancestors of all Indo-European speakers had presumably resided. These Orientalists spatialized and territorialized Schlegel's narrative of expulsion from paradise, mapping out the likely location of this *Urheimat* and identifying the migration routes the first Germanic tribes reputedly took from central Asia into Europe.

The first scholar to situate the German homeland outside of India and to map out the early diffusion of linguistic groups in central Asia, Julius Klaproth (1783–1835), did so in the service of the Russian imperial state. In the early nineteenth century, Russia was progressively pushing its southern-most border through the Caucasus, annexing territory from Persia and from the Ottoman Empire, and exploring the steppes of Kazakhstan and Turkmenistan. Language scholars, such as Klaproth, were invaluable aids in this process. The development of Oriental Studies in the reign of Czar Alexander I (1801– 25) was part of a larger project of the Europeanization of Russia and generally relied on foreign scholars[40]; several German Orientalists, including Christian Martin Frähn, Isaac Jacob Schmidt, Bernhard Dorn, and A. Richter, built their careers in Russia. Klaproth himself helped author an influential 1810 plea by the future Minister of Education, Sergei Uvarov, calling for the establishment of an Asian Academy.[41] Klaproth's research into the German *Urheimat* was enabled by two extended trips through Kazakhstan, Kyrgyztan, and Mongolia (1805–7) and the Caucasus mountains (1808–9), trips which he undertook as an emissary of the Russian Academy of Sciences charged with completing linguistic and geographic surveys of the expanding Empire's borderlands. For his services the German scholar was made a member of the Russian Academy of Sciences and knighted into the order of Vladimir.[42]

In *Asia Polyglotta* (1823), Klaproth laid out a comprehensive "system of Asian peoples and languages" based on his travels, summarizing his scheme in an appended "linguistic atlas."[43] The spread of distinct national tribes and language-families across the globe, he claimed, was antediluvian. When high waters covered the Earth, certain individuals had found refuge on the mountain peaks of India and America, as well as on Mt. Ararat, and had independently preserved elements of their unique languages. These survivors formed the core of the "main tribes" (*Stammvölker*); their language was the basis of the "core languages" (*Stammsprachen*) from which Klaproth derived thirteen separate language-families simultaneously, named for the mountain peaks whence various earliest speakers likely descended. According to Klaproth's scheme, early speakers of Indo-Germanic had migrated into the plains of Europe and into southern Asia from two separate mountain chains, the Himalayas and the Caucasus, which explained the physical differences among the family's speakers. Ancient Indians, he believed, had traveled south from the Himalayas and quickly mixed with "brown or Negro-like natives" who themselves had retreated to the hills of Malabar. The Goths, on the other hand, left the Himalayas for the north and entered Europe through Scandinavia. The other Germanic tribes (Medo-Germans) had wandered from the Caucasus to the shores of the Caspian Sea, through Persia and into Europe from the south.[44]

Klaproth's findings relocated the geographical origins of the German nation from the Ganges, as specified by Schlegel and Rückert, to the northern

Himalayas and the Caucasus. Klaproth identified the mountainous region to the north and west of India as the German *Urheimat*; it lay at the source of the Amu-Darya and Syrdarya rivers in present-day Tajikistan, Kyrgyzstan, and Uzbekistan. He found it "absurd" to derive "the German people (*das deutsche Volk*) from the Hindu" since the first speakers of German and of Sanskrit had evolved independently from an even older mother tongue.[45] At the latest, these two peoples had lost contact "on the meridional slopes of the Himalayas," a conclusion he based on the fact that the birch was the only tree whose name was found in all Indo-European languages. Sanskrit names for trees that grew south of the mountain range had been borrowed from unrelated languages native to the Indian subcontinent.[46]

During the 1820s, the Salvationist rhetoric of Schlegel's account of German speakers' cultural origins was reworked into a celebration of the successful territorial expansion of the western-most branch of the Indo-European language-family. Whereas Schlegel believed German speakers to be a chosen people destined to bring about the spiritual rejuvenation of humankind, subsequent Orientalists celebrated the Germanic tribes as the carriers from Orient to Occident of a higher civilization. As introduced by Klaproth in 1823, the designation "Indo-Germanic" (*indogermanisch*) was intended to emphasize the supposed inclination of the western members of the group to expand territorially, referencing as it did the outermost limits of the family.[47] Before this, various terms, including Sanskritic and Japhetic, had been used to describe that conglomeration of nations and of peoples which was identified by Bopp. "Indo-European" was an earlier (1816) invention of the Englishman Thomas Young, and despite Bopp's approval it never gained currency in German-speaking Europe.[48]

Orientalists explained the apparent success of Indo-Germanic migration as a function of member tribes' inherent cultural and intellectual superiority. The source of Indo-Germanic mobility was thought to lie in the tribe's use of inflection, or internal modification of the root, to signify grammatical relationships in a sentence. In other languages, the root form of the verb was thought to remain constant and to rely on additional appended endings to express tense, mood, or number. The unique ability to inflect verb roots supposedly preconditioned the Indo-Germanic mind for activity, exploration, creation, and the spread of its culture and traditions.[49]

The use of Oriental philology as ethnology also invited speculation on the physical attributes of linguistic groups. As Klaproth classified the inhabitants of central Asia as Turkish or Indo-Germanic, he made ready reference to their "physiognomy." In one instance, for example, his memoirs recall encountering speakers of the Ossetian language in the northern Caucasus. Klaproth was intrigued by the "European" appearance of this Medo-German people and by their "blue eyes, blond or red hair" which, in his mind, distinguished them from other tribes in the area.[50] In *Asia Polyglotta*, Klaproth likewise referred to "physical uniformity" and the "shape of the skull" as criteria determining the proximity of linguistic relations, the "characteristic physical qualities" of Indo-Germans being those of the "white... races (*Geschlechter*)."[51]

THE RACIALIZATION OF "ARYAN" GERMANS

With the substitution of the term "Aryan" in 1830 to describe the Indo-European tongues and the peoples that spoke them, the association between language, territorial expansion, and cultural superiority was broadened to include a more prominent racial dimension. Concerned that conventional designations were "unhistorical," the Bonn Indologist Christian Lassen (1800–1876) urged scholars to use the label "Aryan" (*arisch*) instead of "Indo-Germanic" because the former gave a better sense of the shared historical descent and subsequent geographical expansion of the people. In a footnote to an article published in the *Indian Library*, Lassen recommended "Aryan" as the "common name" for the family of Indo-European languages, as well as for the people (*Volk*) that spoke them.[52] The German word *Arier* was a creation of the 1770s and a translation of Abraham Hyacinthe Anquetil-Duperron's French term, *Ariens*, which he had derived from ancient Indic and Persian sources. The bards in the *Rigveda*, a collection of sacred Hindu verses, apparently described their gods and themselves with the root form "Ary·." In the *Zend-Avesta*, the founding religious text of the Zoroastrians, the same root is applied to the legendary, primordial homeland of early migrants into Iran and northern India; to these tribes themselves; and to the regions they came to inhabit.[53]

Friedrich Schlegel's use of the term suggests that the Christian narrative of expulsion from paradise was superimposed onto historical accounts of the migration into Germanic Europe of an expansionist Aryan people from an idealized, primordial Asian homeland. In 1819, Schlegel had introduced the word "Aryan" into the vocabulary of German philologists while trying to reconcile Old Testament notions of divine revelation with that secular history of human origins which J. G. Rhode had constructed from passages in the *Zend-Avesta*. Schlegel suggested that the word of God had been imparted in an "Aryan language"[54] that was closely related to Avestan (Zend) and to Sanskrit; this "primordial, mother tongue" was "multi-syllabic and organic."[55] The ancient people (*Stammvolk*) chosen to receive it were likewise called "Aryans," and they lived in the mountainous heights between Persia and India.[56] Schlegel believed the ancient Germanic tribes to be the direct descendents of this people. "Our German ancestors," Schlegel wrote, had been known by the "name of the Aryans" while still in Asia and they had been a "warlike, heroic people." He interpreted the Sanskrit root "*Ari*" as meaning "splendid and excellent, famous" and related it to the German word for honor, "*Ehre*." The frequency with which it appeared in archaic German names for heroes pointed, in his mind, to the close historical ties between modern German-speakers and the chosen people of revelation.[57]

The philological discourse on the Indo-European language family was racialized, more specifically, through studies of Indian prehistory that tried to reconcile the presence of dark-skinned Indians on the continent with notions of Aryan cultural superiority. During the 1830s and 1840s, two leading German Indologists at the University of Bonn, Christian Lassen and August Wilhelm Schlegel (1767–1845), wrestled with this question and in so doing made race a defining aspect of German nationhood. In an influential 1834 article "On the Origin of the Hindous," August Wilhelm Schlegel, who had received the first professorship of Sanskrit in 1819, argued that the Indian "nation" was a fusion of two distinct peoples that descended from two separate races (*races différentes*) with different linguistic traditions. Indigenous Indians, in his analysis, were "savages" and "black" in color; they were badly armed and lived "in vast primitive forests."[58] Migrants from the Indo-European homeland had entered India through the Punjab region and had continued their migration towards the southeast, occupying the basins of the Ganges and its tributaries and intermixing with the native population. Schlegel described the Sanskrit-speaking immigrants as belonging to "the white race"[59] and as having introduced the natives to the "first rudiments of civilization."[60]

In the first volume of his encyclopedic work on *Indian Antiquities* (1846), Christian Lassen, who had studied with August Wilhelm Schlegel in Bonn, expanded his mentor's racial interpretation of German prehistory. In Lassen's analysis, it was impossible that India had been the original German homeland: an Aryan people would never have let itself be conquered by a tribe of darker skin color. Ancient Aryans, he wrote, always proved to be "the dominant, victorious race (*Geschlecht*)," successfully driving away (*verdrängen*) the "weaker, yielding" natives who lacked equivalent "power." According to Lassen, the original "black natives" of India were "defeated races" just like "the Australian Negroes . . . and the red men of America." The Aryans distinguished themselves as "white people" and represented, to Lassen, "the more perfectly organized, entrepreneurial and creative nation." In India this unequal relationship had, he believed, been consolidated politically in the caste system. The Sanskrit word for caste, Lassen noted, originally meant "color," and while the three dominant Aryan castes, including the Brahmins, had "the whitest color," the indigenous underclasses had "the darkest."[61]

German philologists of the first half of the nineteenth century did not equate the consolidation of national unity with the recovery of the racial purity thought to have existed in a primordial Aryan homeland. Neither Lassen nor the Schlegel brothers directly contrasted the "tarnished" identity of those Sanskrit-speaking Indians who had mixed among a darker native people, with a Germanic ideal of racial integrity. German Orientalists ceased to apply the designation Aryan to the western branch of the Indo-European language family around midcentury, and the designation was eventually restricted to a limited number of ancient Indo-Persian languages.[62] In the face of physical anthropology and evolutionary biology, language scholars began to question the correspondence of racial and linguistic categories, ultimately rejecting the use of philology as ethnology.[63]

However, already by the mid–1830s, several major components of "Aryan theory" as it was adopted by later racial theorists had been articulated. German-speakers were imagined to be the descendents of a culturally dominant white race of Aryans that hailed from a primordial homeland in the East. The conceptual categories introduced by German Indologists gained a life of their own within a broadly European racial discourse, influencing among others Ernest Renan, Friedrich Max Müller, and Joseph Arthur Comte de Gobineau.[64] Within the German states, the same Orientalists set a pattern of defining nationhood as based on ethnicity and on the propensity of Indo-Germans to expand territorially. Most troubling, they introduced a Salvationist national rhetoric that reworked the importance of historical descent: namely, from a common cultural starting point into a millenarian expectation of returning to an idealized moment of homogeneity and purity.

NOTES

1. See Lèon Poliakov, *The Aryan Myth: A History of Racist and Nationalist Ideas in Europe*, trans. E. Howard (London: Chatto & Heinemann, 1974), 183ff; Raymond Schwab, *The Oriental Renaissance: Europe's Rediscovery of India and the East, 1680–1880*, trans. Gene Patterson-Black and Victor Reinking (New York: Columbia University Press, 1984), 184ff. Peter Viereck was the first to link German Romanticism with National Socialism in *Metapolitics: From the Romantics to Hitler* (New York: Alfred A. Knopf, 1941). More recently, Sheldon Pollack has argued that from the early nineteenth century on German Orientalism was directed "inward" to the "colonization" of European Jews. See his article "Deep Orientalism? Notes on Sanskrit and Power beyond the Raj" in *Orientalism and the Postcolonial Predicament: Perspectives on South Asia*, eds. Carol A. Breckenridge and Peter van der Veer (Philadelphia: University of Pennsylvania Press, 1993).

2. Raymond Schwab, for example, readily drew on the metaphor of "language as a weapon of war," generalizing that the "confusion of linguistic facts and ethnic theories perpetuated . . . more ravages than . . . the wars of faith." (Schwab, *The Oriental Renaissance*, 184–7). Both he and René Gérard believed to have identified a particular German affinity for the "irrational," the "unconscious," and the "mystic,"

virtues supposedly extolled in Indian texts. Schwab, *The Oriental Renaissance,* 482–4; René Gérard, *L'Orient et la pensée romantique allemande* (Paris: M. Didier, 1963), 1–2, 257. Lèon Poliakov made an "emphasis on biology" a basic element of Aryan theory as it was formulated by Friedrich Schlegel and assumed that a conflation of the concepts of language and race had already taken place in the first German empire. (Poliakov, *Aryan Myth,* 197 and 74f). He likewise justified "short-circuiting fifteen centuries of history" with the claim that the roots of Nazi racism could be found in pre-Christian Germanic myths of origin. (*Aryan Myth,* 4–5).

3. On the linguistic and cultural definition of early-nineteenth-century German nationhood see Rogers Brubaker, *Citizenship and Nationhood in France and Germany* (Cambridge, Harvard University Press, 1992), esp. ch 3; Michael Townson, *Mother-tongue and Fatherland: Language and Politics in Germany* (New York: Manchester University Press, 1992); and B. Giesen and K. Junge, "Vom Patriotismus zum Nationalismus. Zur Evolution der 'Deutschen Kulturnation'" in *Nationale und kulturelle Identität. Studien zur Entwicklung des kollektiven Bewußtseins in der Neuzeit,* ed. B. Giesen (Frankfurt am Main: Suhrkamp, 1991).

4. Friedrich Schlegel, *Über die Sprache und Weisheit der Indier. Ein Beitrag zur Begründung der Alterthumskunde* (Heidelberg: Mohr und Zimmer, 1808), 105.

5. *Ludwig Tieck und die Brüder Schlegel: Briefe,* ed. Edgar Lohner (Munich: Winkler Verlag, 1972), 135–6.

6. Schlegel, *Über die Sprache und Weisheit der Indier,* 175.

7. In 1806, for example, the language scholar Johann Christian Adelung (1732–1806) located the cradle of humanity and the Germanic homeland in eastern Kashmir, near Tibet. See his *Mithridates oder allgemeine Sprachkunde mit dem Vater Unser als Sprachprobe in bey nahe fünfhundert Sprachen und Mundarten,* vol. 1 (Berlin: Voss, reprt. New York: Georg Olms Verlag, 1970), 11.

8. Schlegel, *Über die Sprache und Weisheit der Indier,* 66.

9. Konrad Koerner, "Friedrich Schlegel and the Emergence of Historical-Comparative Grammar," in *Practicing Linguistic Historiography* (Amsterdam: John Benjamins Publishing Company, 1989), 285.

10. Schlegel, *Über die Sprache und Weisheit der Indier,* 3–4.

11. Ibid., 16.

12. Ibid., 28.

13. Ibid., 35.

14. *International Encyclopedia of Linguistics,* ed. William Bright, vol. 2 (New York: Oxford University Press, 1992), 213–15.

15. Schlegel, *Über die Sprache und Weisheit der Indier,* 44.

16. Ibid., 44.

17. Ibid., 41.

18. Ibid., 50–1.

19. Ibid., 45.

20. Friedrich Schlegel, "Vorlesungen über Universalgeschichte," in *Kritische Ausgabe seiner Werke,* ed. Ernest Behler, vol. 9 (Munich: Verlag Ferdinand Schöningh, 1960), 17.

21. Ibid., 17–8.

22. Ibid., 3.

23. Ibid., 12, 17, 19.

24. Schlegel, *Sprache und Weisheit der Indier*, 180f and 197f. See also Manfred Petri, *Die Urvolkhypothese: Ein Beitrag zum Geschichtsdenken der Spätaufklärung und des deutschen Idealismus* (Berlin: Duncker & Humblot, 1990), 194–95.

25. Schlegel, "Philosophie der Geschichte," 31–49.

26. Schlegel, *Über die Sprache und Weisheit der Indier*, 194.

27. Ibid., 195.

28. He also imagined a reconstructed, German version of the divine *Ursprache* emerging as the foundation of German nationhood. See Friedrich Rückert's 1811 dissertation "Dissertatio Philologico-Philosophica de Idea Philologiae" translated in an appendix to Viktor Suchy, *Friedrich Rückert's 'Idee der Philologie' im Lichte der romantischen Sprachphilosophie: Grundlagen zu Rückert's Sprachanschauung* (Vienna: n. p., 1945).

29. See Friedrich Rückert, "Selbstschau," in *Friedrich Rückert's gesammelte poetische Werke in zwölf Bänden*, ed. Heinrich Rückert, vol. 7 (Frankfurt am Main: J. D. Sauerländer's Verlag, 1882), 74f.

30. See M H. Abrams, *Natural Supernaturalism: Tradition and Revolution in Romantic Literature* (New York: W. W. Norton & Company, 1971).

31. For example, he believed that the "sleeping" German emperors of the thirteenth century would reawaken and come to the aid of the nation. See Friedrich Rückert, "Barbarossa" in *Gesammelte poetische Werke*, 108. Schlegel similarly believed that a period of "degeneration" and "destruction" following the expulsion from paradise would be resolved in a "higher order" marked by the onset of the empire of God. Schlegel, "Vorlesungen über Universalgeschichte," 249–252.

32. Franz Bopp, *Über das Conjugationssystem der Sanskritsprache in Vergleichung mit jenem der griechischen, lateinischen, persischen und germanischen Sprache. Nebst Episoden des Ramajan und Mahabharat in genauen metrischen Uebersetzungen aus dem Originaltexte und einigen Abschnitten aus den Vedas herausgegeben und mit Vorerinnerungen begleitet von K.J. Windischmann* (Frankfurt am Main: Andreäische Buchhandlung, 1816), 8–9.

33. *Encyclopedia of Language and Literature*, vol. 5, 2580–81.

34. See Vivian Law, "Processes of Assimilation: European Grammars of Sanskrit in the Early Decades of the Nineteenth Century," in *La linguistique entre mythe et histoire: Actes de journèes d'ètude organisèe les 4 et 5 juin 1991 à la Sorbonne en l'honneur de Hans Aarsleff*, ed. Daniel Droixhe and Chantal Grell (Münster: Nodus Publikationen, 1993), 254–57.

35. Bopp, *Über das Conjugationssystem*, 11.

36. See, for example, Franz Bopp, *Vergleichende Grammatik des Sanskrit, Zend, Griechischen, Lateinischen, Littauschen, Gothischen, und Deutschen* (Berlin, n. p., 1833–52).

37. Bopp, *Über das Conjugationssystem*, 7.

38. See, for example, Jacob Grimm, "Über den Ursprung der Sprache," *Kleinere Schriften*, vol. 1 (Berlin: n. p., Ferdinand Dümmlers Verlagsbuchhandlung, 1879).

39. O. Schrader, *Sprachvergleichung und Urgeschichte. Linguistisch-historische Beiträge zu Erforschung des indogermanischen Altertums* (Jena: Hermann Costenoble, 1906), 9.

40. Susan Layton, *Russian Literature and Empire: Conquest of the Caucasus from Pushkin to Tolstoy* (Cambridge: Cambridge University Press, 1994), 75–77.

41. Sergei Ouvaroff, "Projet d'une Acadèmie Asiatique," in his *Études de philologie et de critique* (Paris: Didot Frères, 1845), 1–48.

42. Klaproth published accounts of these travels in *Die russische Gesandtschaft nach China im Jahre 1805* (Leipzig: in Comm. Bruder und Hoffmann, 1809) and "Bemerkungen über die chinesisch-russische Grenze, gesammelt auf einer Reise an derselben, im Jahre 1806," in *Archiv für asiatische Litteratur* (1810). In 1810 Klaproth fled to Berlin under suspicion of having stolen valuable manuscripts from the St. Petersburg library. He was also accused of being a Prussian spy while in Paris. On the scandals associated with Klaproth see his entry in the *Encyclopaedia Britannica*, 8th edition, vol. VIII (1857), 105.

43. Julius Klaproth, *Asia Polyglotta* (Paris: J. M. Eberhart, 1823), 42.

44. Ibid., 42–44.

45. Ibid., 43.

46. Julius Klaproth, "Observations sur la critique faite par M. Sam. Lee," in *Nouveau Journal Asiatique* 5 (1830): 112–3.

47. August Friedrich Pott, "Indogermanischer Sprachstamm," in *Allgemeine Encyklopädie der Wissenscahften und Künste von J. S. Ersch und J. G. Gruber II* 18 (1840): 79.

48. See the introduction to Bopp's *Vergleichende Grammatik*.

49. See Pott, "Indogermanischer Sprachstamm," 26.

50. Julius Klaproth, *Tableau historique, gèographique et politique du Caucase et des provinces limitrophes entre la Russie et la Persie* (Paris: Ponthieu et C., 1827), 70.

51. Klaproth, *Asia Polyglotta*, 35, 40–43.

52. Christian Lassen, "Über Herrn Professor Bopps grammatisches System der Sanskrit-Sprache," *Indische Bibliothek III*, ed. August Wilhelm Schlegel (Bonn: Weber, 1830), 70.

53. Hans Siegert, "Zur Geschichte der Begriffe 'Arier' und 'arisch,'" *Wörter und Sachen. Zeitschrift für Indogermanische Sprachwissenscahft, Volksforschung und Kulturgeschichte*, ed. Walther Wüst (Heidelberg: Carl Winter, Universitätsverlag. Neue Folge IV, 1941–42), 84.

54. Friedrich Schlegel, "Über den Anfang unserer Geschichte und die letzte Revolution der Erde, als wahrscheinliche Wirkung eines Kometen. Von J.G. Rhode," *Jahrbücher der Literatur*, ed. Matthäus von Collin (Vienna: Carl Gerold, 8.1819), 459.

55. Schlegel, "Über den Anfang unserer Geschichte," 454, 452.

56. Ibid., 458–59.

57. Ibid., 459–60.

58. August Wilhelm Schlegel, "De l'Origine des Hindous," in his *Essais littéraires et historiques* (Bonn: Edouard Weber, 1842), 474–75.

59. Ibid., 469.

60. Ibid., 473.

61. Christian Lassen, *Indische Altertumskunde*, vol. 1 (Bonn: H. B. König, 1847), 513–14.

62. See August Friedrich Pott's discussion in "Indogermanischer Sprachstamm," 1.

63. See August Friedrich Pott's review *Die Ungleichheit menschlicher Rassen hauptsächlich vom sprachwissenschaftlichen Standpunkte, unter besonderer Berücksichtigung von des Grafen von Gobineau gleichnamigen Werke. Mit einem Überblicke über die Sprachverhältnisse der Völker. Ein ethnologischer Versuch* (Lemgo: Meyer'sche Hofbuchhandlung, 1856), which argues against the correspondence of language and race.

64. On J. A. Gobineau's use of "Aryan" terminology see Schwab, *Oriental Renaissance,* 215ff.

IV

Race in the Political Sphere

10

Policing the *Menschen=Racen*

Sara Eigen

"The police must ensure that the human races are refreshed from time to time with foreign blood."

—Johann Peter Frank,
System for a Complete Medical Police, 1779

In the German language of the eighteenth century, a race as we now understand it could be labeled variously a *Rasse, Art, Unterart, Varietät, Stamm, Volk,* or *Nation.* On the other hand, the word *Rasse* itself could refer to far more than a genetically derived, geographically localized subset of the species: indeed, it was used commonly to designate a family line; a regionally or politically defined collective of any size; any group identified by some particular characteristic (a race of giants); or the entire species, that is the human race. This imprecision made race a productive generic referent of imputed kinship or origin: it was a catchall term that could be applied whenever a speaker wished to signal a natural binding principle (most often visibly manifest in shared physical traits) that constructed the identity of a particular group.[1] The use of the term race—a floating signifier used to identify the individual procreating family at one extreme and the entire human species at

185

the other—simultaneously draws on and reinforces ideas of a familial stamp, of a national character, and of an inclusive human kind.

I propose in this essay to linger with these multiple meanings of race—in short, to dwell on one particular writer who makes very productive use of race's imprecision. In examining one highly influential text that circulated throughout German-speaking lands at the turn of the nineteenth century, I propose not to rush the meanings of race or to look for ways in which those meanings do or do not participate in the contemporary scientific and philosophical refinement of a particular concept. I hope instead to gain a richer understanding of the cultural meanings of race that were possible so long as the systematizing process could be ignored, and to suggest that in certain cases those meanings were antithetical to scientifically authorized racism. In the work of Johann Peter Frank, racial difference is a symptom and product of the human tendency to construct social boundaries between self and other, between home and foreign; indeed, within Frank's work racial difference signals a social desire for the perpetuation of sameness (coupled with a desire for conflict with the different)—a sameness that leads to patterns of inbreeding ultimately devastating for the species.

Johann Peter Frank (1745–1821) was one of the most influential physicians and medical professors of the late eighteenth century, with a career that included positions of authority in Göttingen, Pavia, St. Petersburg, and Vienna. Frank was a pioneer of and advocate for the "medical police," a branch of eighteenth-century *Policeywissenschaften* charged, among other things, with developing policy to improve the all-around health of populations, including their physical well-being, strength, beauty, moral sensibility, and civic discipline.[2] His great publication in the field is the six-volume *System for a Complete Medical Police*, which began appearing in 1779.[3] During ensuing decades this work was read, translated, adapted, and adopted piecemeal throughout German-speaking lands and beyond.[4]

Frank's work had an unprecedented scope: it provided scientific explanations, social analysis, and policy recommendations for a range of issues including prenatal and infant care, the structure of schools and of charitable institutions, the regulation of food, drink and housing, the containment and prevention of illness, the prevention of accidents, and the education of the poor in basic hygiene. (Also treated were such varied issues as gambling, noise pollution, superstition, theater censorship, the regulation of dancing, military conscription, and proper clothing.) Frank synthesizes an extraordinary range of medical, scientific, legal, philosophical, and anthropological sources to support, and often to complicate, his proposals. His arguments reflect an eighteenth-century attention to statistics, to new ways of assessing population and productivity; they reflect broader goals that include the promotion of a stronger tax base, increased yields in domestic productivity, a reduction in crime, and a reduction in the number of destitute requiring public support.

With regard to our local purposes, a focus on the two initial volumes is of primary importance; it is therein that Frank repeatedly employs the term *Rasse* (or *Race,* reflecting its appropriation from the French language) in ways that are both inconsistent and extremely effective. Within Frank's text, "race" is used as an equivalent term for a range of genealogically produced groups which include families, inbred villages and classes of people, regional and ethnic groups, and the species itself. His object in so identifying these groupings of people is not to challenge or expand an idea of race; rather, he uses the term of race to mark the fundamental similarity of these groups.

The idea that all so-called races are extended kinship groups—and that all kinship groups can be identified under the loose category of race—is an unstated but necessary premise of Frank's work, which advances a radical, proto-eugenic, state-sponsored program of restricted breeding practices. Frank proposes the regulation of marriage and the production of offspring to improve the race(s): specifically, he proposes to eliminate heritable diseases; to mitigate individual suffering; to lessen the public burden of caring for the orphaned and infirm; and to proactively generate a healthier, more productive population. There are, he insists, no issues more central to political interest than the study of heredity and the translation of knowledge thereof into practical legislation.

IMPROVING THE RACE(S)

While the possible benefits of regulated reproduction were contemplated by many during the eighteenth century, Frank knew that he was writing the first comprehensive book on the subject, and that he would have to create an appropriately persuasive tone for what would amount to a new discourse.[5] Any treatment of the mechanics and consequences of regulated reproductive sex was both novel and bold; it was also open to charges of immorality and of heresy. In order to preempt any protest over the sexual subject matter, Frank opens his book with an admission of his own fear of the controversies that might be aroused by his treatment. Convinced, however, of the book's potential social value, he describes how he silenced his fears in favor of his sense of responsibility, determining to deliver to the public the first-ever systematic and explicit presentation of human reproduction (*menschliche Fortpflanzung*).[6]

Sexual reproduction and transmission were, Frank notes, increasingly the subject of scientific inquiry; and while scientists had not yet identified all the patterns of heritability that contributed to human propagation, it was nevertheless certain that with each new generation, nature worked from the model of the parents to fashion the child.[7] The potential social rewards for controlling this pattern of production were tantalizing:

> Would it not be wonderful if only a portion of the care devoted to the development of good animal breeds—which involves identifying precisely which animals one will use for reproduction and excluding badly formed or poorly developed fathers or mothers—would be applied to humans, thus prohibiting marriage among those who are entirely degenerate, dwarfish, crippled, and misshapen; if, on the contrary, we saw to it that beautiful people blessed with a strong, well formed and healthy body, even if they were robbed of all other resources, were supported in marriage with their equals in health and bodily perfection, and further supported in the raising of large families just like themselves, so that the number of strong, well-endowed citizens would eventually be increased?[8]

All human suffering, Frank maintains, should be understood "as damage wrought by the degeneration that is linked to civilization, which itself, however, is the product of the existing social order."[9] This seems at first to resemble an anticivilization rhetoric, common enough at the end of the eighteenth century and used particularly in the wake of Jean-Jacques Rousseau to bemoan the physical and moral weaknesses which characterized city dwellers and the overly refined. Frank, however, limits his attack: the degeneracy he identifies is not attributed to civilization as such, but to specific elements of the social order that can be changed. Among these elements is unregulated individual procreation, responsible for the negative consequences of illness and weakness spread among entire lines and peoples—peoples for whose plight the remedy is to be found in the authority of medical police.[10] As the book tirelessly attempts to demonstrate, the harms that the human race and its various races have suffered are not simply part of a monodirectional, teleological force; rather, these harms are the product of social determinants that can be controlled. Hence, just as racial traits per se are identified by the science of the day as manifestations of degeneration, so too should diseases injurious to humankind be understood as marks of *Entartung*, comparable to (and subsets of) racial traits; simply put, heritable disease should be understood as the manifestation of a gradual process of falling away from the integral *Art* or species of human being. Frank is not alone in elevating illness to a category within human taxonomy: when Johann Karl Illiger, in his *Attempt at a Systematic and Complete Terminology for the Animal and Plant Worlds* (1800), delineates the variously identified types of *Abartungen*, or lines of degeneration from species, he discusses not only "race," but also the catchall category of "varieties," which include heritable diseases.[11]

Placing disease within a classificatory schema has several advantages. First, since disease must according to Frank be regarded as more than the uncertain subject of an oft-idiosyncratic medical practice, it instead accrues the prestige granted to those subjects of theoretical and experimental scientific inquiry which have their own ontological status, and are identified as fundamental forces or entities shaping natural history[12]; the study of heritable disease, when configured in this way, is transferred out of the uncertain realm of medicine and into the increasingly prestigious domain of science. Second, by placing disease within the taxonomic order of the genealogical species and of its subsets, Frank (along with Illiger and others) identifies disease as something singular, that is, he ensures that disease (rather than many different and sketchily understood ailments) is collectively understood to be a producer, as well as a product, of variation. Thus, instead of Frank's being compelled to justify claims regarding the heritable nature of and control for each particular heritable malady that he believes threatening to the human race, he can advocate for a broad policy overseeing the process of a singular, degenerative (and effectively racializing) phenomenon. And so he is able to maintain that, with a policy of controlled breeding developed by the medical police—one that combines medical and scientific expertise with political authority and resources—certain *Abartungen* can be expunged from the body and blood of the populace so as to allow a healthier, more beautiful race its birth.

(RACES OF) FARMERS AND SOLDIERS

As soon as Frank raises the issue of breeding, he links it immediately and inextricably to socially regulated marriage, which he in turn identifies as "the first condition of human reproduction."[13] This is a predictable gesture given the mores of his readership and his era; it is also an important component of his larger endeavor to identify individual procreation as a political project. As Frank presents it, breeding is never unconnected to some kind of socially recognized (and regulated) family. Thus, he makes breeding's place in the formation of larger families, for example, of the national family or race, appear natural rather than conceptual and rhetorical.

There is no question that the bulk of Frank's work belongs unambiguously to the era of enlightened absolutism for which he wrote it. The program of his *System* is paternalistic: his mechanisms for state-regulated prosperity require the significant curtailment, and in some cases the outright elimination, of individual freedoms. Frank himself manifests ambivalence with regard to the elimination of the right to reproduce; he cannot resolve the dilemma, and so he urges individuals afflicted with heritable diseases (or otherwise "unfit" to produce healthy offspring) to voluntarily forego their natural inclination to reproduce. Such individuals can thus serve the greater good; further, Frank argues (in a maneuver worthy of Schiller), these individuals may through self-discipline free themselves from suffering the oppressive force of legislation.

Over the course of his *System*, Frank in various ways stresses the higher claim of the "Fatherland" on an individual's life choices. In order to prevent the betrayal of the "Fatherland in its expectations," for example, Frank suggests all young betrothed couples swear an oath that they are not, to their knowledge, carrying any severe, contagious, or hereditary diseases; further, he suggests these couples be required to swear explicitly that they will bear children "of use to the Fatherland, not only Christian but also healthy."[14] By so pairing health with Christian piety in maintaining the well-being of the state, and by so linking the two elements as he does ("not only Christian but also healthy"), Frank gives health a moral cast. Certainly, religion must not be denied a role; but ultimately health, understood in its fullest bodily and spiritual sense, serves to guarantee a physically and morally thriving generation.

Religion, though, is not the only entrenched category of social organization over which health ascends: differences based upon geographical, political, and economic factors are also subordinated by Frank to the newly identified, overriding criterion of identity—that is, to biological ancestry. In order to smooth the transfer of social value from caste or estate to physiology, Frank selects "race" as his signifier of choice. Instead of speaking of sickly subsets of "the poor" or "indentured farmers," he speaks about a "sickly race of men"; and he so reconfigures the healthy poor, whose possibilities for marriage are currently hindered by economic prohibitions, as to render them a "healthy race" who should be provided the material resources necessary to establish families. On the other hand, he describes the ill health and poverty characteristic of the farming class in essentially "racial" terms: their misery, he claims, is the manifestation of gradual degeneration (*Abartung*) caused by lack of good breeding stock. As strong young men are conscripted, the reproductive work in the countryside is left to a remaining "small and ill formed race of men"—a selection of men who, upon being deemed unfit for military service, find their health further compromised by early, strenuous labor and by poverty. Frank identifies this social problem—namely, the loss of the strongest sons of the farming class to the military—not only as the "origin of human degeneration among the peasantry," but also as that which has catalyzed (as the origin or *Ursprung*) a subsequent natural, historical, genealogical process (*Abartung*) resulting in the physical and social character of an entire estate (the *Bauernstand*).[15]

Such problems are, however, correctable; degeneration, affecting the peasant "race," for example, can be remedied by making at the level of state administration such changes as would require, rather than prevent, the marriage of soldiers (particularly fit specimens).[16] Frank's system, by instituting this policy and others—all of which take seriously the supply and quality of potential fathers—cannot help but gradually redress the problem of degeneration among peasants. Yet, these policies would necessitate changes to the myriad legal prohibitions restricting marriage among the lowest classes. Hence, to challenge such prohibitions, and to pave the way for healthy pairings without regard to social or economic position, Frank again casts his argument in racial terminology. In the case of healthy young people too poor to qualify by law for marriage, he proposes that the state financially support their union, and that the state then consider as its property the union's offspring, who will be relocated to areas where "human perfection appears to have suffered the most."[17] This policy would guarantee a necessary infusion of better blood into degenerate communities; without such intervention, Frank warns, the "good race of human beings" (*die gute Race der Menschen*) itself is threatened with extinction.[18]

Frank does not limit his proposed restrictions to the less privileged; he argues repeatedly that, if "rights" have anything to do with the social good, then members of the decadent aristocracy should have far less right to propagate than do the healthy poor. His health-based meritocracy requires that the diseased members of bourgeois or aristocratic classes be legally excluded from corrupting future generations and from contributing to the deterioration of the body politic's health. The civil status of an individual is still, under Frank's program, to a great extent determined by birth; but instead of "birth" being assessed according to the social determinates of one's lineage, it is infused with meaning gleaned from one's medicalized, and indeed racialized, ancestry. Along similar lines, Frank appeals to a general concern for the well-being of the "race" in order to promote "mixed marriages" between classes or estates, and to urge intermarriage with "foreigners" from other villages, cities, and even ethnic groups and nationalities. He states unambiguously that the well-being of the political order relies upon its integrity as a genealogically healthy state; thus, "the police must ensure that the human races (*Menschenracen*) be refreshed periodically with foreign blood, whereby the tendencies to heritable diseases (*Familienkrankheiten*) will be eliminated and the fullest potential of the races (*Geschlechter*) might be served."[19] Here, Frank's use of language conveys a many-hued concern for not merely the state, but also necessarily the family, the species, and indeterminately scaled groups—in particular, the *Geschlechter*, synonymous with races—in between the two. To prevent decay and restore their vitality, these races require the infusion of a "foreign blood" which is not simultaneously foreign to all races (thus challenging the species boundary), but which rather marks the boundaries of the "human races" mentioned. These boundaries, signaling racial distinction and foreignness (both transmitted by blood), should be overcome— all under the auspices and in the interest of the state—by mixing that racially foreign blood. Therefore, while both the administrative state-structure and some sense of humanity's division into "human races" survive Frank's revitalization (at least according to the grammar of the statement itself), the specific distinctions between races and foreign others are constantly reconfigured, constantly in biological and geographical flux. Insistence upon the necessary infusion of blood that is foreign or *fremd* underscores the transregional, transracial, and certainly transnational scope of his program.

MIXING THE "MENSCHEN-RACEN"

We have seen that the different *Menschenracen* or *Geschlechter* for whom Frank is concerned might be groups of varying scales, organized any number of ways. One might, then, fairly ask how he identifies and discusses groups that conform to narrower notions of racial identity. Just as individuals pass traits from parent to child that eventually become identifiable within certain family lines, Frank observes that entire peoples often bear physical characteristics that are intensified when transmitted over generations, particularly among peoples who avoid intermarriage with others:

> We know that entire peoples, as long as they infrequently or never mixed with foreign nations, carried particular identifying characteristics upon their faces which, like a personal legacy from father to son, always and in a predictable manner were transmitted. The lovely blue eyes and the golden hair of the German made him recognizable among all peoples, as long as the blood of German fathers exclusively engendered children of German mothers.[20]

It is tempting to identify via Frank's use of value-laden adjectives (the blue eye that is beautiful) and of the potentially nostalgic tone that colors his final comment a cultural prejudice, and to suspect him of advocating that peoples—and particularly the Germans—maintain (or attempt to reclaim) their racial purity through the proper alliance of (German) *Vaterblut* with (German) mothers. If we read on, however, noting Frank's comparison of the German appreciation of (its own) golden hair with the Chinese preference for (its own) small feet,[21] we might grant that Frank acknowledges the cultural relativity of the beauty attributed by a people to their own peculiarities.[22] We might be tempted to conclude that Frank believed, along with Johann Gottfried von Herder, that all peoples should be respected equally for their various and unique characteristics, but that it was at the same time advisable to preserve the boundaries between those peoples; thus Herder admonished against the "wild intermixing" of peoples and races, urging: "Wheresoever and whosoever you were born to be, oh Man, that is where and who you ought to be;

do not let go of the chain, nor place yourself outside of it, but rather fasten yourself to it!"[23]

However, while Frank might describe as "beautiful" the blue eyes of the genealogically pure German (located in an indistinct past), such an example functions merely as evidence for the heritability of traits over time. Significant is that the example functions as part of a larger argument against, and not for, sexual insularity. In fact, Frank ventures further than most of his contemporaries in his thinking about the consequences and the benefits of racial mixing. And while we cannot overlook the evidence of his personal belief in a European cultural superiority, Frank devotes a significant amount of text to his advocacy, on biological grounds, for intermarriage among all cultures and races.

Frank issues an authoritative declaration that the perfection of the various "human races" clearly suffers when they don't mix with others (*Fremden*), but instead always marry amongst themselves "and continue to sow the same fruit upon the same acre."[24] Pointing out that the law against incest is regarded by "us" (his European readership) as a law of God, he argues that it should be understood more expansively as a law of nature, designed to protect all creatures from degeneracy.[25] One need merely heed the example of numerous animal species: the members of many strong groups, when they are ready to breed, leave their established habitat and "emigrate from their fatherland." It is this migration alone, claims Frank, that allows their flourishing over time.[26] A contrary example presents itself in the condition of many domesticated animals, and even more so in the condition of those found in zoos: such animals that are not free to wander and to mix with "foreign races" inevitably weaken and gradually die off.

The terms "fatherland," "emigrate," "migration," and even "foreign races" anchor the reader's attention to the fundamental concern motivating Frank's argument "that is," the identification of optimal behaviors for a flourishing humanity. These behaviors, Frank is well aware, run counter to the inclination of many. His word choice is provocative, even inserted as it is within a discussion of animal breeds: we read "fatherland," a term signaling familial roots, belonging, and insularity; we read "foreign races," words announcing a confrontation with alien bodies and with cultures. Frank's animal analogy translates into an order: "emigrate, leave your fatherland, wander into the regions of foreign races and there select your mate—for the good of the human race." He employs culturally fraught terms in such a way that he reverses the negative/positive valuations placed upon them; while fatherland becomes something no doubt desired but nonetheless debilitating, foreign races are understood to be initially daunting but ultimately the source of positive partnership in propagating one's own healthy race (family) and so reshaping, indeed strengthening the human race.

Frank does not try to soften his program with circumlocutions, with softer language (he might have written about "neighbors" rather than about "foreign races," for example), or with admonitions against insularity left unchallengingly vague. On the contrary, his argument demands that the reader first confront entrenched binary values of home and foreign, same and other, and then choose consciously what he (or possibly she) has hitherto been socially conditioned to reject. Frank does not propose or even imply that such a mixing of the races might ultimately eradicate these crude and difficult binaries. One has the sense that, though his program would certainly eradicate all fixed biological boundaries between groups, human social behavior would still produce self-understandings that include simultaneously an inclusive human race and potentially divisive, separate human races. This is not a problem, however, that Frank has set out to solve. Important for him is not those fictional identity-boundaries between groups which appear to be a human cognitive necessity; he simply seeks the elimination of the static physiological and genealogically produced identities separating the same groups.

Stressing that human races have suffered whenever they have failed to intermarry, Frank cites as results of inbreeding arguments ubiquitous in contemporary anthropological literature, including references to both the constitutional weakness of the Native American and the particular physiognomy of the Jews.[27] While praising Jews for their migratory practices—for the fact that they as a people were detached from any particular *Acker* or geographical area—he observes that they nevertheless suffered physiologically as a result of vigilant, religiously regulated inbreeding. In the case of Native Americans, Frank observes that tribal insularity has resulted in the transmission of debilitating diseases through generations until the seed of each disease is spread throughout an entire community. There is no end to the misery, writes Frank, "when the evil is not defeated through the influx of pure sources and through certain reciprocal effects."[28] "Reciprocal effects" are in all probability a tacit answer to the challenge that, by mixing good and bad blood, the strong lines might be corrupted by the sickly foreign influence; and this argument is more along the lines of Frank's advocacy for the exclusion of sickly individuals from the social-breeding program. Frank, though distinguishes importantly between individuals and populations: individuals who carry particular diseases must not reproduce; a population that exhibits weakness or degeneration, meanwhile, must aggressively pursue remedy through intermarriage with vigorous individuals from outside its self-identified boundaries.

According to Frank, any static link between a group of people, as well as any static notion of either blood or soil, is dangerous for the flourishing of humankind since both the failure to migrate and the decision to intermarry lead to inbreeding, which results in progressive degeneration. All creatures must move, and they must marry outside their own lines; this form of racial deterritorialization is a kind of ideal for the production of the "good race of human kind." By advocating the state-supported mixing of *Menschenracen* (be it on a local or ultimately on an international scale), Frank directly challenges a legal status quo that carefully restricted the movement of people and that defined citizens as "native born"; in other words, he challenges a status quo that, by virtue of *ius sanguinus*, reinforced geographic conceptions of race, emphasizing the restricted kinship nature of political affiliation and a hostility to any foreign element. Frank's advocacy of intermarriage for the good of the "race" or "races" could, therefore, be understood to deploy the notion of race and of its reproductive mechanism so as to counter what he identified as a human inclination to cling to—and perpetuate—small, exclusive, and incestuous (racial) units.

The Aesthetics of Racial Blending

As a sign of the positive effects of mixing the human races—specifically, as a sign that intermarriage between ethnic groups is blessed by nature—Frank claims that such unions produce offspring with more ideally regular features. That is, it is within these unions that the more extreme signs of physical difference—the signs of degeneration that determine the existence of racial boundaries—are blended and thus made more beautiful. Frank observes:

> The half-Tartar Persian mitigates his natural ugliness through mixing his blood with the blood of a beautiful slave from Tiflis; among the Calmuck, [certain tribes] distinguish themselves through their height and through the better formation of their faces, "which they possess thanks to the strong influx of Tartar blood via captive women"; and we daily see the influence that the natural difference of parents expresses upon the formation of their children, as when a white blonde woman, through the mixing of her fluids with those of a coal black Negro, so re-forms the fruit that she receives from him, that only half of the paternal ugliness is retained.[29]

Writing in greater detail of another racial combination, that between Europeans and Mongols, Frank writes that "such marriages produce a race of mulattos who are somewhat Mongolian in appearance, have black or very dark hair, and generally have extremely regular and appealing features."[30]

Frank's unqualified attributions of ugliness to those features most different from northern European norms do provide evidence of a connection between racial prejudice and European aesthetics. However, his suggestion that beauty should be characterized by "regularity" (a classic European requirement) is a

bit complicated, since he believes regularity is produced by the gradual elimination of extreme racial traits—including those of northern Europeans. It is as
unusual as it is significant that, when discussing marriages between people of
different races and their typical offspring, Frank identifies as a positive gain for
the species the eradication of what amounts to all race-determining traits.
Certainly, the traits he is happiest to see go are those characterizing non-
Europeans. But he never expresses concern that the characteristic traits of the
"white blonde woman" who marries a black man will be lost to subsequent
generations as a result; he never suggests that certain races or peoples—even
those with particularly robust health or beauty—should isolate themselves to
protect their better blood from contamination or compromise. On the contrary,
he advocates a mixing of all types. We might therefore ask whether, if taken
to an extreme, his position leads to an eradication of racial difference altogether. While such questions were pursued to their logical end by some thinkers
(including the anxious Kant, who wanted as a result to protect the white race
from further degeneration), Frank himself was far too practically minded to
lose sleep over such a thought experiment. As far as his text is concerned, the
human "race" and its "races" (the indeterminacy of and between which is
crucial) will flourish if and only if breeding is attended to along those principles
derived from nature, confirmed by science, and promoted by the state.

SEXUAL SELECTION

Frank seems to suggest repeatedly that male desire, following its natural
course, would probably take care of the physical perfection of the species if
two conditions could be met: first, if male desire for (and competition for)
mates who are foreign (visibly other, racially different) were unimpeded by
counterproductive social regulations curtailing mobility and intermarriage;
and second, if the potentially disruptive force of male sexual aggression that
accompanies this desire were properly channeled.

Elaborating on mixed marriages between Europeans and Mongols, Frank
notes, first, that Mongol men are happy to baptize their daughters that they
might marry Europeans (for the girls, a step up a ladder which is simultaneously and indistinguishably social and racial); and second, that European
men want to marry Mongol girls because they are "hot-blooded." Rich Mongol men, for their part, often marry Russian (Caucasian, European) young
women who are, by implication, not of wealthy families and glad to acquire
a rich husband.

The role that gender plays throughout these and other examples is critical. In each case, women are identified as the object of male sexual desire,
whereas men offer women a boost in social, racial, or financial status. In most

of Frank's examples (culled from other travel and anthropological sources), the women are of lighter races; by virtue of their racial beauty, they dilute by half the "ugliness" passed from mates to their offspring. On the other hand, white European men are drawn to the exotic and hot-blooded darker women, producing children with ideally regular features. In every instance of beneficial mixing of the *Menschenracen*, women are the crucial factors in the process of physical improvement. Never does Frank write about the mitigating influence of a racially beautiful man upon the progeny of an ugly woman; and the beneficial role he imputes to racially attractive women in improving all the races exists in fascinating parallel to the idea that women, by virtue of their natural spiritual beauty and virtue, act as civilizing agents upon their mates so as to transform the latter into milder, better citizens.

In the example of European men marrying Mongol women, Frank identifies a "natural" desire for the racially exotic other that he will also describe in his discussion of village rivalries and relations. A natural attraction between different ethnic peoples, which results in marriages yielding strong and particularly beautiful progeny (as in the case of the European/Mongol mix), is, Frank contends, evidence of nature's guiding the species. One might conclude by extending the logic of this argument that natural perfection should be brought about by unfettered sexual selection;[31] however, Frank implies that the reality of human social interaction is sufficiently complicated to require that the state take active measures to promote and to restrict breeding when most beneficial. More specifically, Frank seems to distinguish conflicting natural tendencies—ones which pit groups against each other, not only through the pattern of individual sexual attraction that he identifies, but also through a drive to wage war.

Let us return to the more local concerns Frank had about the mixing of *Menschenracen* (in this case, those races which identified themselves with particular village communities or *Dorfgemeinschaften*). One distinct social problem he identifies as threatening the flourishing of a "good race" is the murderous animosity felt between neighboring villages, where hatred and fear toward the respective other are expressed in part through violent attempts to prevent intermarriage. He states as a truism that men who come courting from a "foreign" village often place their lives at risk,[32] and that the results are predictable and disastrous: in some cases, healthy young women remain unmarried because there are not enough men within their own village to go around; and those who do marry within the community only contribute to the gradual weakening of the population because of their inbreeding.

Identifying this as a significant problem across all of Europe, Frank cites with approval a French ordinance from 1718 that severely penalizes anyone causing disruption and violence when a village youth brings in a "foreign" girl as his bride.[33] Frank attributes adoption of this law both to the wise recognition of the benefits of intermarriage and to the need to combat what is a destructive product of xenophobic tendencies throughout the lands. (In fact, the actual document seems more concerned with public order and the potential disruption of local business than with the hereditary health of the villages, but Frank is clearly eager to use it for the advantage of his argument.) Extending the argument, he discusses at length the necessity of reducing "the universal jealousy among the young of various communities," and he speculates that irrationally intense sexual rivalry between adolescent boys is the root cause and continuing fuel for such conflict.[34] Hence, if villages could somehow be brought together and sexual energy rechanneled (which ought to be easy, since the erotic excitement that is dulled at home by "daily exposure" to local girls would be ignited by exposure to those from another village), not only would public order gain, but everyone in a given village would—in what amounts to equal or greater benefit—also be prevented from eventually being related to each other.

There is at work in Frank's various examples and in his arguments an insinuation of universal male sexual desire—that for a beauty in women which specifically balances a man's racial traits during subsequent production of progeny. In short, men desire different women (while wanting to compete with different men); to that desire Frank attributes a natural, unconscious impetus, which, because it seeks to produce children approaching some ideal of "balance" in their color, stature, and features, might prevent genetic weaknesses that result from inbreeding. Nature, evidently, works through male desire. Meanwhile beauty, it seems—and we speak here of physical female beauty—functions as the driver of successful sexual selection: this beauty is, by Frank's account, crucially associated with a physical difference that he identifies as hereditary, as historical, and as "racial." At the same time, a more general and nongender-specific human beauty marked by "regularity" is the legible result of the natural eradication (that is, the correction) of degeneracy-related (that is, racial) differences. According to Frank's program, an effective medical police can restrain the psychological and social behaviors that prevent the flourishing of such beauty; and it is under this program that controlled breeding potentially becomes a global technology.

CONCLUSIONS

The concept of *Volk* that emerged at the end of the eighteenth century carries at least the implication of shared kinship-origins of community—origins that served as a basis for regional, national, and racial self-understanding. To combat such *völkisch* thinking, Frank offered a striking critique of xenophobia insofar as he linked ideas about the nature of human sexuality to the cultural and physiological phenomenon of biological community. Contrary to the goals of eugenics research that were identified and pursued during the late nineteenth and early twentieth centuries, Frank theorized a program of state-controlled breeding, not to defend and to preserve racial difference with its entrenched hierarchies of better and worse, but ultimately to eliminate altogether precisely those physically generated and physically manifested patterns of sameness and of difference that were fueling the scientific invention of race. If a group of people could be identified as a race of some sort (be it a family or a country), then by definition that group was the product of potentially detrimental inbreeding. For the good of the human race, urged Frank, such a group's racial identity (distinguished from its familial or national identity) should be sexually blended out of existence.

Frank exhibits an almost postmodern sensibility in his resistance to stasis, in his understanding of thriving peoples as constantly shape-shifting, and in his advancing the freedom of the individual to move through and integrate with limitless geographic regions, social strata, and racial or ethnic communities. Frank does not imagine that human society will forego delineations of sameness and of difference; he does not advocate the end of a community. He does, however, insist upon its constant variation through sexual migration. And if, in the end, communities *are* always reformed; if there are no populations (smaller than the species) consisting predominantly of people genetically related to one another, then—among other profound implications—there can be no tenable claim for race as anything but a floating signifier used to mark the various efforts of human beings at configuring their communities—more or less literally—as families.

NOTES

1. The word "race" (along with its synonyms) is multivalent and often confusing during the eighteenth century. For an introduction to the adoption of the term, see Nicholas Hudson, "From 'Nation' to 'Race': The Origin of Racial Classification in Eighteenth-Century Thought," *18th-Century Studies* 29 (3): 247–64.

2. Roy Porter maintains that, while the "*médecin-philosoph*, doctor of a sick society"—an image propagated in particular by Frank—appealed to French thinkers attracted to enlightened absolutism, the practice of medical police remained for the most part confined to German-speaking territories. Roy Porter, "Medical Science and Human Science in the Enlightenment," in *Inventing Human Science. Eighteenth-Century Domains*, eds. Christopher Fox, Roy Porter, and Robert Wokler (Berkeley and Los Angeles: University of California, 1995), 53–87.

3. Johann Peter Frank, *System einer vollständigen medicinischen Polizey* (Mannhein: C. F. Schwan, 1779–1827). All citations are from the "second, improved edition" of 1784; translations are my own.

4. In describing the move by eighteenth-century physicians to proclaim "a new vision of medicine that stressed its utility to society and state," Thomas Broman writes: "These activities received a tremendous boost in 1779 with the publication of the first volume of Johann Peter Frank's epochal *System einer vollständigen medicinischen Polizey*. . . . At the universities, *medicinische Polizey* became the basis for new courses and textbooks with a more applied orientation. During the last two decades of the century, a rising flood of treatises, articles, and periodicals on *medizinische Polizey* appeared, each following the trail that Frank had marked." Thomas Broman, "University Reform in Medical Thought at the End of the Eighteenth Century," *Osiris* 5 (1989): 38. For a more extended history of the work's reception, see Harald Breyer, *Johann Peter Frank* (Leipzig: S. Hirzel Verlag, 1983); also see Anke Pieper, *Medizin in aufgeklärten Absolutismus. Das Programm einer 'vollständigen medicinischen Polizey' und die Reformtätigkeit Johann Peter Franks in Pavia 1785– 1795.* (Master's thesis, Kiel, 1994). Pieper points out that "medicinal Polizey" was taught by the Vienna medical faculty until 1875, and a steady production of new books (that she calls "epigonale Nachahmungen") appeared until then in various European lands (158).

5. For an overview of European and American writing on regulated breeding, see Victor Hilts, "Enlightenment views on the genetic perfectibility of man," in *Transformation and Tradition in the Sciences. Essays in Honor of I. Bernard Cohen,* ed. E. Mendelsohn (Cambridge: Cambridge University Press, 1984), 255–271. Acknowledging the increasing interest in the topic, Frank points out that, "nevertheless there remain numerous important ideas about which an unbroken silence has been maintained; it shall become clear in the following that such topics deserve our fullest attention" (*System,* vii).

6. Frank, *System,* x.

7. Ibid., 353.

8. Ibid., 353–354.

9. Ibid. Frank cites other "experts" writing about the ills produced by civilization, 67: for a discussion of hypochondria and an increasing frequency of *Nervenkrankheiten,* he cites [Johann Georg] Zimmermann's *Von der Erfahrung [in der Arzneykunst (1763–64)]* and [Samuel Auguste André] Tissot's *Abhandlung über die Nerven [und deren Krankheiten]* (1781–). These problems result from an "increasing delicacy of our bodies" and the "excessive excitement of our mental and emotional powers" (*System,* 67). Frank also cites [Thomas] Withers *Bemerkungen über die Fehler, die bey dem Gebrauch der Arzneymittel begangen werden* (1776) on the problems that arise as urban populations get less and less exercise (*System,* 68).

10. Works that picked up on this theme, generally citing Frank, include: G. H. Berg's *Handbuch des Teutschen Policeyrechts* (Hannover: Verlag der Gebrüder Hahn, 1804), esp. 737ff; E. G. Baldinger's *Neues Magazin für Aerzte,* Zweyter Band (Leipzig: Friedrich Gotthold Jacobäer und Sohn, 1780); Johann Daniel Metzger's *Kurzgefaßtes System der gerichtlichen Arzneiwissenschaft* (Königsberg und Leipzig: Verlag der Hartungschen Buchhandlung, 1793), esp. 370 ff.; W. H. S. Bucholtz's *Beyträge zur gerichtlichen Arzneygelahrheit und zur medicinischen Polizey* (Weimar: Carl Ludolf Hoffmanns see. Witwe und Erben, 1782); and J. Bernt's *Systematisches Handbuch der*

Staats—Arzneykunde zum Gebrauche für Aerzte, Rechtsgelehrte, Polizeybeamte und zum Leitfaden bey öffentlichen Vorlesungen, Erster Theil (Wien: Kupffer und Wimmer, 1816).

11. Johann Karl Illiger, *Versuch einer Systematischen Vollständigen Terminologie Für das Thierreich und Pflanzenreich* (Helmstädt: C. G. Fleckeifen, 1800), 7, sec. 15.3.

12. On the attempts to make eighteenth-century medicine more "scientific" (including various attempts at mapping disease onto a taxonomic framework), see Porter, "Medical Science and Human Science in the Enlightenment."

13. Frank, *System,* x.

14. Ibid., 380.

15. Ibid., 355.

16. J. M. R. Lenz made several similar points in his essay, "Über die Soldatenehen," written in 1776, copies of which he intended both for the Weimar court and the French Ministry of War. See volume 2, 787–827 in Jakob Michael Reinhold Lenz, *Werke und Briefe in drei Bänden,* edited by Sigrid Damm (Frankfurt/M: Insel, 1992).

17. Frank, *System,* 354–55.

18. Ibid., 357.

19. Ibid., 321–322.

20. Ibid., 352.

21. Ibid. He notes that the Chinese have small feet, which he claims began with a custom of binding and then became an inherited trait. Frank maintains that many traits distinguishing populations begin with some kind of cultural modification, and then they "take root and thereafter transmit themselves, thereby distinguishing this Volk from others." He also refers to the disputed belief that, as a result of such modification, Jewish boys are often born circumcised.

22. This is not an unusual position. Charles Vandermonde discusses different cultural standards of beauty and its association with moral good and evil; he uses as an example the European appreciation of white skin and the African appreciation of dark skin, so that "their" devils are painted white and "ours" are painted black. He suggests that tolerance is the best approach to these opinions since all are imaginary beauties. Charles Augustin Vandermonde, *Essai sur la Manière de Perfectionner l'Espece Humaine,* 2 vols. (Paris: Vincent, 1756), 11–12.

23. Herder also writes about the negative consequences of migration upon peoples who have evolved to live in particular climates. See Johann Gottfried Herder, *Ideen zur Philosophie der Geschichte der Menschheit* (Bodenheim: Syndikat, 1995), 194–96.

24. Frank, *System,* 452.

25. Ibid., 453. Here he follows Georges-Louis Leclerc Comte de Buffon.

26. Ibid., 452.

27. Ibid., 454. Both are commonplace observations in travel accounts and anthropological writings. Vandermond writes similarly that the Jews marry only within their faith, with the (degenerative) result that "they maintain their promise to God upon their faces." Vandermonde, *Essai sur la Manière,* 112–113.

28. Frank, *System,* 456.

29. Frank, *System,* 457. The quotation is from Peter Simon Pallas, *Physikalische Reise durch verschiedene Provinzen des russischen Reichs im 1768 und 1769sten Jahre* (St. Petersburg: Kayserliche Akademic der Willenschaften, 1771).

30. Ibid., 458–59.

31. Charles Darwin explains his identification of "sexual selection" (and distinguishes it from "natural selection") in *The Descent of Man*, 1871. My anachronistic use does not presume that Frank's theories connect directly to Darwin's zoological theory of competition and selection; however, I do think it might productively be included among the intellectual and conceptual antecedents that filter into subsequent discourse.

32. Frank, *System,* 450–51.

33. Ibid., 459–62.

34. Ibid., 463.

11

Jewish Emancipation and the Politics of Race

Jonathan M. Hess

Blumenbach has proven with certainty that the cause of degeneration among human beings is the receptivity toward stimuli affecting the external body and the activity of the animal mechanism in responding to these stimuli. . . . All anatomists are agreed that the color of human beings is caused by the color of the Malipighian layer of the skin, and Meckel found when dissecting a Negro that the brain itself was black. It is a universal assumption that the various colors of human beings derive from bile and the liver affecting the blood. There is not a physician or natural scientist who will contradict these statements, and this is the ground on which I base my claim that the Jews are the sole cause of the human beings' degeneration from the beautiful Caucasian race, . . . the sole cause of the dark color of all colored human beings.

—*Indisputable Proof that the World, Humanity, Christendom and all the States Will Have to Perish Unless Jewish Men are Promptly Slaughtered and Jewish Women Sold Into Slavery*, a parodic work published in 1804.

At a key juncture in his 1799 treatise *Moses and Christ*, the theologian Gottlob Benjamin Gerlach noted the role discourses on race were playing in

203

the debates over Jewish emancipation inaugurated some eighteen years earlier by Christian Wilhelm Dohm's 1781 book *On the Civic Improvement of the Jews*. Unlike the scores of other works that had come out in favor of or against Dohm's proposals to transform Jews into productive, useful citizens, Gerlach's book argued from the perspective of human rights, casting certain novel visions of "race" as the ultimate threat to any plans to grant Jews political equality:

> Up until now we have believed—and philosophers have argued this as well—that all human beings on the globe descend from a single pair of parents and are all members of the great human family. . . . But the keen perception of the philosophers, particularly Meiners in Göttingen, has made discoveries that have robbed this beautiful and pleasant thought of its truth claim and consigned it to the realm of metaphysical fantasies. For according to the confessions and parables of these men, the various human races are further apart according to their physical and intellectual predisposition than the English mastiff and the Bolognese. If it were true that bodily dexterity and strength, that wit, keen perception and judgment were simply found mostly in the Celtic tribe, less so in the descendents of the Scythes and the Slavs, even less so among the Hindostans, to which Jews and Gypsies belong, and least of all among Indians and Negroes—if this were true, then one could still claim for all these peoples the rights and privileges which every simpleton among us enjoys, however limited he may be. But these philosophers go so far as to claim that moral character—that noble proclivity that first makes all humans human—is lacking in the poor creatures of these peoples, who could only gain it by mixing with the blood of the noble Celts. . . . These people, like animals, are not capable of feeling moral duty and have thus no rights . . . , an argument that comes up in England to justify the slave trade and in Germany the oppression of the Jews.[1]

I open with this passage not because I wish to rehabilitate this minor theologian as an important race theorist. Indeed, an early reviewer of *Moses and Christ* already took Gerlach to task for categorizing the Jews as Hindostans—a fateful blunder considering the opposition between the "Semite" and the "Aryan" already on the rise among philologists and biblical critics at the time.[2] However sloppy his summary of Enlightenment racial typologies may be, Gerlach here nevertheless offers an important insight into the political function of race in eighteenth-century Germany. Explicitly grounding secular, modern political universalism in the Judeo-Christian narrative of human origins, he holds up the emancipatory impulses of *all* monogenic race think-

ing, stressing the qualitative distinction between the hierarchies of value involved in these views on race and the insistence on radical difference found
among polygenic theorists such as Christoph Meiners. In his 1790 essay, *On
the Nature of the African Negro*, Meiners equated the permanently degenerate
nature of Blacks with that of Jews in such a way as to argue, in one fell swoop,
against both the liberation of slaves and Jewish emancipation.[3] For Gerlach,
Jews may, like Blacks, indeed be inferior in terms of their current physical and
mental predisposition; but monogenic race theory makes it possible to think
their *regeneration*, to envision a scenario in which Jews might be able to hold
the same rights and privileges as anyone else. It should not be surprising, in this
context, that Gerlach's goal in *Moses and Christ* was not to argue for the
emancipation of Jews as Jews but to facilitate their conversion to Christianity;
as an antiquated and stagnant "Oriental" religion, Judaism ultimately poses for
Gerlach as much a stumbling block to realizing the emancipatory potential of
Christian universalism as do philosophers such as Meiners.[4] Realizing the full
political promise of the Judeo-Christian account of monogenesis apparently
requires that Judaism be removed from the playing field.

It is precisely this political alliance between race thinking and Christian
universalism in its relation to Jews and Judaism that I would like to explore,
focusing on the way this alliance was negotiated in the debates over Jewish
emancipation that dominated much political discourse from 1781 on. Here
my concern is less with race discourse proper than with the functioning of
"race" outside Enlightenment anthropological theory. That is, my concern is
less with the eighteenth century's reflections on what race *was* than with its
experiments regarding what the novel category of race could *do*. This distinction is important because Jews themselves tended to be peripheral to much
eighteenth-century racial theory, concerned as it was with racial varieties that
would coincide with continental land masses.[5] From the beginning, however,
discussions over the "civic improvement" of the Jews unfolded in close proximity to contemporary racial theory's concern with the category of "regeneration." When Dohm first proposed emancipating the Jews in the early 1780s,
he did so with explicit reference to popular appropriations of racial thinking,
claiming, in opposition to Göttingen professors Michael Hißmann and Johann
David Michaelis, that an "unimproveable race of humans" was simply an
unthinkable proposition.[6] The issue that political writers, theologians, philosophers, and lay intellectuals alike ruminated over in recurring waves of
heated debates, accordingly, was not the question of Jews' rights to citizenship but that of the causes of their "degenerate" nature and the possibilities
of their moral, political and physical "regeneration"—an issue that enacts a
political analogue to those theoretical musings over the "degeneration" and
"regeneration" of human varieties which one finds in the work of monogenic
theorists such as Johann Friedrich Blumenbach. My goal, therefore, will not

be to reconstruct a distinct vision of a "Jewish race." Indeed, this sort of unanimity is prominently lacking in the literature of the period, although there were certainly individuals, such as the anti-Semitic pamphleteer Karl Wilhelm Friedrich Grattenauer, who characterized the Jews in 1803 as an "Oriental foreign people" whom historians and anthropologists alike agreed were a distinct "race."[7] The issue I wish to explore is a more general one: namely, the tensions that the issue of Jewish emancipation exposed in the alliance between the universalism of monogenic race thinking and visions of universalism that took their cue from the Judeo-Christian tradition.

Let me begin here within race discourse proper, considering the ambivalent position Jews already occupy in Blumenbach's theories of degeneration. In his treatise *On the Natural Varieties of Mankind* (1775, 1781, 1795), Blumenbach presented "degeneration" as a tool one might use both to salvage the monogenic theory of human origins and to dispute the notion—put forth, say, by Immanuel Kant in his 1775 essay "On the Various Races of Human Beings"—that human beings could indeed be classified into distinct races. Blumenbach stresses the spectrum of imperceptible transitions between his four, and later five "varieties" of human beings, casting the "Caucasian" (his neologism) as the original variety of human beings from which all others have degenerated. All other human "varieties"—from the "extremes" of the Mongolian and the Ethiopian to the intermediary varieties of the American and Malay—clearly lack the proper sense of proportion Blumenbach claims for his white Caucasians. Nevertheless, given the proper environmental conditions, each would have the potential to retrieve, in a series of generations, the "mean and primeval" beauty of the Caucasian type. In situating the origins of the human race on the slopes of Mount Caucasus, Blumenbach both salvages and transposes biblical accounts of monogenesis. In this context, he classifies Jews, like Arabs, as Caucasians; yet he also grants the people most closely linked to biblical monogenesis a unique status within his system. The 1775 edition of *On the Natural Varieties of Mankind* speaks of Jews as having a particular physiognomy: "the Jewish race . . . can easily be recognized everywhere by their eyes alone, which breathe of the East."[8] The 1795 edition makes an even stronger case for Jewish racial peculiarity: "[T]he nation of the Jews . . . , under every climate, remain the same as far as the fundamental configuration of the face goes, [they are] remarkable for a racial character almost universal, which can be distinguished at first glance even by those little skilled in physiognomy, although it is difficult to limit and express by words."[9] As a particular variety of Caucasians, Blumenbach's Jews continue to bear the marks of the racial character inherited from their ancient, Near Eastern climate of origin. They do so despite the various climates and conditions they have lived in since the onset of Diaspora, manifesting a racial character that is "almost universal" and thus distinct from all other human varieties. Unlike the "Ethiopians," who under the proper conditions might be able to retrieve the beauty of the Caucasian type, Jews have somehow become impervious to environmental influences—a degenerate variety of Caucasian with no possibility of regeneration, members of the original human family with no purchase on the vitality of their origins. The passages cited above, moreover, explicitly reflect on the disruption Jews cause to Blumenbach's system. The permanent racial character of the Jews, though immediately legible in their eyes and face, still eludes the anthropologist: unlike everything else he describes and categorizes, the Jewish racial character "is difficult to limit and express by words."

Blumenbach, to be sure, never explicitly links this vision of Jewish difference to the debates over emancipation, but his doubts over the possibility of regeneration where Jews are concerned clearly qualify Gerlach's enthusiastic equation of monogenesis with political universalism. For Blumenbach, unlike Gerlach, it is not Judaism that is the problem; Jews themselves disrupt the link between monogenesis and a universalist politics, making what Gerlach sees as the emancipatory potential of monogenic race discourse contingent on the exclusion of that "nation" traditionally linked, symbolically and genetically, to the origin of humanity. This gesture of exclusion, moreover, is hardly peculiar to Blumenbach: it finds its way directly into the debates over emancipation, in polemics against Dohm published by Blumenbach's Göttingen colleauge, the pioneering Orientalist Johann David Michaelis. Perhaps German Protestantism's foremost authority on ancient Judaism, Michaelis published in 1782 an influential critique of Dohm in his *Oriental and Exegetical Library*, one of the major organs of biblical scholarship at the time.[10] Echoing arguments formulated in his six-volume historical treatment of *Mosaic Law* (1770–75), Michaelis insisted that Jewish law, designed as it was to promote separatism, would stand in the way of integrating Jews into a modern, secular state. He asked:

> Do the laws of Moses contain anything that would make it impossible or difficult for the Jews to be completely naturalized and melt together with other peoples? One should nearly think so! Their intention is to preserve the Jews as a people separated from all other peoples, . . . and as long as the Jews retain the laws of Moses, as long as they, for example, do not dine with us . . . they will never melt together with us—like the Catholic and Lutheran, the German, Wend and Frenchman, who all live in a single state."[11]

In his work on ancient Judaism, Michaelis followed Montesquieu in emphasizing the role of "climate" in shaping law and legal institutions. In his polemics against Dohm, he went further, claiming that modern Jews were themselves products of the southern climate of ancient Israel and as such unable to be assimilated into a German state. Mosaic law, however, is only part of the problem as Michaelis sees it. Writing as a biblical critic, he never questions biblical accounts of monogenesis—or, for that matter, any other fundamental truths transmitted by Scripture. Michaelis does argue quite explicitly, though, that the Jews constitute an "unmixed race of a more southern people" who "even in ten generations" will never have the proper bodily strength to perform military service.[12] Like Blumenbach, he defines the Jews as an alien race defying the logic of regeneration, and he makes this claim with reference to familiar discourses of climatology.

Let us consider, for instance, his hypothetical solution to the problem posed by the political status of the Jews:

> Such a people can perhaps become useful to us in agriculture and manufacturing, if one manages them in the proper manner. They would become even more useful if we had sugar islands which from time to time could depopulate the European fatherland, sugar islands which, with the wealth they produce, nevertheless have an unhealthy climate."[13]

The ideal—if not the most practical—solution to the Jewish question, Michaelis suggests, lies thus in colonial expansion, in relocating the "southern" Jewish race to a climate that would enable Jews to become economically productive, namely, to "colonies . . . where one might send malefactors and degenerates."[14] As a "southern race" descended from the ancient Israelites, the Jewish diaspora apparently needs to be displaced once again, this time to a Caribbean climate analogous to the Jewish place of origin and in which Jews might become colonial subjects promoting the wealth of the European fatherland.

The link that emerges here between this Protestant biblical critic's intellectual hegemony over Judaism on the hand, and visions of political domination over Jews on the other, clearly exemplifies the power-knowledge configurations the last two decades of postcolonial criticism have been so eager to unmask. But Michaelis's Orientalist fantasy of colonial power over the "southern" Jewish race is also important because it serves to legitimate political universalism on the domestic front. Clearly, Michaelis sets the Jews, as a more southern race, in explicit opposition to Europeans, speaking frequently, as Moses Mendelssohn complained, of "Jews" and "Germans" rather than of "Jews" and "Christians."[15] But Germans for Michaelis includes a variety of northern Europeans—the Catholic and Lutheran, the German, Wend and Frenchman—all of whom, unlike the "southern" Jews, can gain the bodily stature necessary for military service. Michaelis supports a multiconfessional, multinational state that would "naturalize" and "melt together" its subjects, and he defines this political order in opposition to a Jewish race that resists naturalization and amalgamation. Jews here do not merely cause a disruption in the alliance between monogenesis and a universalist politics; colonial utilization of Jews on German sugar islands would clearly enable the realization of political universalism at home.

In this context, of course, it is certainly possible to link thinkers like Michaelis to the rise of racial anti-Semism. My interest here, however, is less in looking to the eighteenth century for "origins" than in exploring the multifaceted functioning of the race concept in debates over Jewish emancipation. The power dynamic Michaelis exposes is important because it often emerges in writers who explicitly *support* the civic improvement of the Jews. To illustrate this point, I will cite one final example, a text from 1799 that echoes Gerlach's *Moses and Christ* insofar as it advocates baptism as a means of regeneration. Like Michaelis's critique of Dohm, this text, the "Political-Theological Exercise on the Treatment of Jewish Converts," also provided a frequent reference point in the emancipation debates.[16] The main concern of this "political-theological exercise" was not whether Jews could be regenerated, but rather the ways in which the state might best monitor just how the "external" act of baptism would reshape the Jews' inner character. As the anonymous author emphasized, this was clearly a political rather than a theological issue; and it was a problem best approached from an anthropological angle. Indeed, the only rational explanation why Jews have hitherto been excluded from the rights and privileges of citizenship, he asserts, is a "certain disharmony, wrongness and uselessness of their bodily and intellectual capabilities."[17] The problem with the Jews is not their religion but that

> an inherited mixture of fluids has lamed or slackened their bodily powers; that the forms of education and learning propagated by their ancestors have mutilated the higher faculties of their soul and given them an adverse direction; that both inherited opinions, maxims sucked in with their mother's milk, and intercourse with each other have altered and corrupted their inclinations and feelings, particularly their social ones, and made them detrimental to society as a whole. . . . [18]

Here Jews emerge as an anthropological aberration: a people whose minds and bodies have been deformed, disfigured and mutilated both by the process of racial degeneration and by their own dubious intellectual culture. Clearly, the mere act of baptism cannot produce the physiological and cultural transformation necessary to make these people worthy of citizenship; and it is for this reason, the text's author contends, that the state would do well to treat Jewish converts as "convalescents" in need of "medical care" before granting them equal rights.[19] Countering Michaelis's and Blumenbach's vision of the permanence of Jewish character with what seems almost a parody of Blumenbach's belief in the possibility of racial regeneration, the essay suggests that just six years—rather than a series of generations—will suffice to make converts ready for citizenship.

This essay does more than propose a quick fix for Jewish degeneracy. It exposes the power dynamic of the anthropological discourse that casts the Jews as a people in need of regeneration. In hypothesizing that a "certain disharmony, wrongness and uselessness of their bodily and intellectual capabilities" is the only rational explanation why Jews have hitherto been excluded from the rights and privileges of citizenship, the author clearly seeks to legitimate the political power Christians have historically held over Jews. Moreover, he does so self-consciously, claiming that without this hypothesis one would have to regard Christians' treatment of Jews as an outrageous "presumption on the part of the powerful party, or . . . as the result of a passionate maliciousness lacking all jurisprudence"—something simply unthinkable when dealing with the "wise rulers and peoples" of Europe.[20] The only way to legitimate Christian persecution of Jews in the past—and, by extension, the proposals to regenerate Jews in the present—is to assume that the postulate of Jewish degeneracy is not the product of power relations but simply a rational insight into the order of the world. As the text's author stresses: "it would be inconsistent for us to withhold the duties and rights of citizenship from hundred thousands if not for the reason that their entire internal being makes them incapable of these."[21] In this way, the "political-theological exercise" legitimates both the political power of Christians over Jews and Christianity's particular claims to universalism—all by using a monogenic theory of degeneration to authorize the restoration of the Jewish mind and Jewish body, whose assimilation to ideals will be dictated by the wise rulers and peoples of Christian Europe.

In all the cases we have been examining, the civic improvement of the Jews does not merely pose a *political analogue* to anthropological ruminations on de- and re-generation. The exclusion of Jews and/or Judaism from monogenesis's support for a universalist politics is not something that *happens* to race discourse when it enters the political arena. It is arguably a constitutive element of eighteenth-century race thinking itself, a problem inscribed into the very heart of the attempt to salvage and modernize via anthropology the Judeo-Christian narrative of human origins. My point here is not to stress the Christian biases of Enlightenment race thinking. Nor is it to foreground the way monogenic race theory secularizes earlier Christian traditions of anti-Judaism—although both of these problems are clearly worthy of discussion. For, given the debates over Jewish emancipation unleashed in the 1780s, Jews' ability to be incorporated into the universal community of humankind was first and foremost a political issue, not a theological problem.

On some level, of course, the vision of the Jews as "degenerate," shared by nearly all participants in the debates over "civic improvement," was clearly indebted to earlier theological traditions. In accounting for the Jews' current state of degeneration, however, Enlightenment ideologues rarely drew on theological modes of explanation; Jewish degeneracy was a complicated phenomenon, best understood as the hybrid product of environment, persecution, climate, and inbreeding as well as of religion. In its extreme formulation, Michaelis's vision of the Jews as degenerate colonial subjects only makes explicit the power dynamic of so many discussions on how to manage this population of undesirables. Dohm himself, after all, avowedly framed his project of emancipation with reference to visions of internal colonization, presenting the regeneration of the Jews as a substitute for Prussia's practices of subsidizing foreign "colonists" to promote internal expansion.[22] Clearly, as Susanne Zantop has argued, eighteenth-century race theory may have had the function of securing northern Europeans an imagined position of physical and moral superiority over the rest of the world.[23] But in its direct instrumentalization in Enlightenment political discourse, race was much more than an abstract, colonial fantasy. It was a practical tool for discussing the possible regeneration of a subject people: a people, endowed with an obvious genetic link to the biblical account of human origins, who posed the ultimate test case for monogenesis's claim to political universalism.

NOTES

Unumstößlicher Beweis, daß ohne die schleunige Niedermetzlung aller Juden, und den Verkauf aller Jüdinnen zur Sclaverei, die Welt, die Menschheit, das Christenthum und alle Staaten nothwendig untergehen müssen, von Dominikus Hamann Epiphanes, dem Judenfeinde. Ein Sendschreiben an Herrn Justiz-Commissarius Grattenauer (Königsberg: n. p., 1804), 24–27.

1. Gottlob Benjamin Gerlach, *Moses und Christus, Oder über den innern Werth und die wahrscheinlichen Folgen des Sendschreibens einiger Hausväter jüdischer Religion an Herrn Probst Teller und dessen darauf ertheilte Antwort* (Berlin: Maurer, 1799), 11–13.

2. Review in *Allgemeine Literatur-Zeitung* 1800, vol. 2: 101–04. See Maurice Olender, *The Languages of Paradise: Race, Religion, and Philology in the Nineteenth Century,* trans. Arthur Goldhammer (Cambridge: Harvard University Press, 1992).

3. Christoph Meiners, "Ueber die Natur der Afrikanischen Neger," *Göttingisches Historisches Magazin* 6 (1790): 385–456.

4. Gerlach, *Moses und Christus,* 54–70.

5. See Nicholas Hudson, "From 'Nation' to 'Race': The Origins of Racial Classification in Eighteenth-Century Thought," *Eighteenth-Century Studies* 29 (1996): 247–64; also Susanne Zantop, *Colonial Fantasies: Conquest, Family, and Nation in Precolonial Germany, 1770–1870* (Durham: Duke University Press, 1997), 66–80.

6. Christian Wilhelm Dohm, *Ueber die bürgerliche Verbesserung der Juden* (Berlin, n. p., 1781–83), 2: 23. On Dohm, Michaelis and Hissmann, see Jonathan M. Hess, *Germans, Jews and the Claims of Modernity* (New Haven: Yale University Press, 2002), 25–90.

7. See Karl Wilhelm F. Grattenauer, *Wider die Juden* (Berlin: Schmidt, 1803), Grattenauer, *Erklärung an das Publikum über meine Schrift: Wider die Juden* (Berlin: Schmidt, 1803), 36–37, and Grattenauer, *Erster Nachtrag zu seiner Erklärung über seine Schrift: Wider die Juden* (Berlin: Schmidt, 1803), 29–30.

8. Johann Friedrich Blumenbach, *De generis humani varietate nativa*, 1775 and 1795 editions, *On the Natural Varieties of Mankind* (1865; New York: Bergman, 1969), here 122.

9. Blumenbach, *Degeneris humane*, 234.

10. Johann David Michaelis, *Orientalische und exegetische Bibliothek* 19 (1782): 1–40. Michaelis's essay, reprinted by Dohm in volume II of *Ueber die bürgerliche Verbesserung der Juden* in 1783, was frequently cited in subsequent years of debate.

11. Dohm, 2: 40–41. Compare Michaelis, *Mosaisches Recht*, third edition (Frankfurt/M, 1793), 1: 229–34, also vol. 4 (1778, second edition), 185ff.

12. Dohm, 2: 51, 63.

13. Dohm, 2: 40–41.

14. Dohm, 2: 56.

15. Mendelssohn, "Anmerkungen über diese Beurtheilung von Hrn. Moses Mendelssohn," printed in Dohm 2, here 76.

16. [Anonymous], "Politisch-theologische Aufgabe über die Behandlung der jüdischen Täuflinge," *Berlinisches Archiv der Zeit und ihres Geschmacks* 1 (1799): 228–39, reprinted in pamphlet form as well (Berlin: Maurer, 1799). The "Politisch-theologische Aufgabe" helped, along with David Friedländer's open letter to Wilhelm Abraham Teller, to unleash two years of heated debates in Berlin and elsewhere about the pros and cons of Jewish baptism; this is, I should note, the debate Gerlach was participating in as well. See Hess, *Germans, Jews and the Claims of Modernity*, 169–204.

17. [Anonymous], "Politisch-theologische Aufgabe," 230.

18. Ibid., 239, 230–31.

19. Ibid., 238.

20. Ibid., 231.

21. Ibid., 239.

22. See on this point, Hess, *Germans, Jews and the Claims of Modernity*, 25–49.

23. Zantop, *Colonial Fantasies*.

Contributors

Tuska Benes is Assistant Professor of History at The College of William and Mary.

Robert Bernasconi is the Lillian and Morrie Moss Professor of Philosophy at The University of Memphis.

Michel Chaouli is Assistant Professor of German at Indiana University, Bloomington, Indiana.

Sara Eigen is Assistant Professor of German at Vanderbilt University.

Peter Fenves is the Joan and Sarepta Harrison Professor of Literature at Northwestern University.

Jonathan M. Hess is Professor of German and Director of the Carolina Center for Jewish Studies at University of North Carolina at Chapel Hill, North Carolina.

Mark Larrimore is Assistant Professor of Religious Studies and Philosophy at Eugene Lang College and the New School for Social Research.

Susan M. Shell is Professor of Political Science at Boston College.

Han F. Vermeulen is a cultural anthropologist and historian of anthropology at the University of Leiden.

George S. Williamson is Associate Professor of History at the University of Alabama.

John H. Zammito is the John Antony Weir Professor of History and Chair of the Department of German and Slavic Studies at Rice University.

Index

Abrams, M. H., 171
Adam, 17, 19, 100–2. *See also* Eden
Adickes, Erich, 36, 39, 40, 42–43
aesthetics, 2, 3, 29, 39, 154, 195
Africa, Africans, 14, 15, 46, 63, 69, 95, 96, 108, 113, 138, 157, 205
Alexander I, 173
Americans (Native), Amerindians, 42, 48, 56, 57, 63, 66, 82, 84, 89n19, 94, 96, 105, 107–8, 138, 194, 204
animals, 16, 40, 55–56, 62, 65, 70n8, 76, 78, 80–81, 94, 99, 101, 103, 116n15, 133, 158, 188, 193, 203–4; Animal Kingdom, 12, 91, 120; half-animal, 14, 148–49, 157; rational animal, 18–20, 22
Anquetil-Duperron, Abraham Hyacinthe, 175
anthropology, 12, 24, 38, 43, 45, 123–45, 210; Kant's, 36–37, 38–39, 42, 57, 65–66, 75, 82, 101–2, 104, 109–14, 119n,40 136–38; philosophical, 124, 140; physical, 4, 5, 115, 123–24, 136, 138, 177; Steffens', 6, 91–96, 108–9, 111, 114. *See also* ethnology
anti-Semitism, 155, 167, 206, 209
Aquinas, Thomas, 20
Ararat, 169, 173
Argus, 29
Aristotle, 25, 59, 60, 93
Aryan, Aryan myth, 5, 153, 164n52, 167–81, 204

Asia, Asians, 5, 47, 63, 94–95,123, 125, 131, 138–39, 168, 170–71; Central, 42, 168, 171–75; Northern, 126, 128
Australians, 138, 176; imaginary, 18–20, 22n

Babel, Tower of, 156, 159, 169–72
Bacon, Francis, 59
barbarism, 14, 48, 170
Baumgarten, Alexander, 120n53
Beattie, James, 39
beauty, 24–25, 27–28, 60, 63, 147–48, 151, 158, 186, 192, 195–97, 201n22, 206–7
Belaj, Vitomir, 133
Benes, Tuska, 5, 173–81
Bering, Vitus, 126
Berlin, 171, 212n16; Berlin Academy of Sciences, 11, 37; Berlin Wall, 124, 130
Bernal, Martin, 5, 148, 153, 155, 158
Bernasconi, Robert, 3, 4, 35, 50n19, 51n34, 73–90
Bernier, François, 17
Bildungstrieb, 74–82, 84–86
black, blackness, 24–26, 29, 42, 44–45, 47, 49, 52, 53n55, 56–57, 59, 66, 76, 83–85, 105, 107–8, 138, 157, 176, 195–96, 202, 205–6. *See also* Africa, Africans; Negro
blonde, 42, 107, 173, 195–96